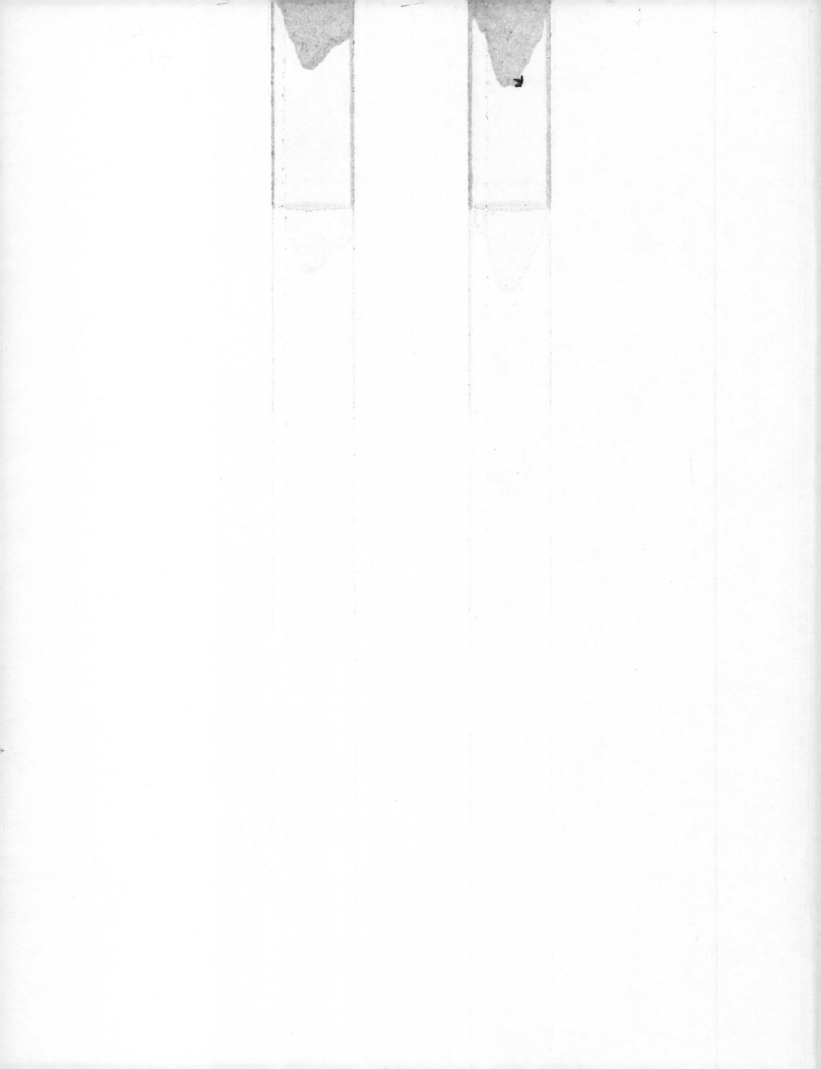

The Illustrated Encyclopedia of

EQUESTRIAN SPORTS

The Illustrated Encyclopedia of

EQUESTRIAN SPORTS

Contributing editors
Sally Gordon · Peter Roberts · Elwyn Hartley Edwards

**CHARTWELL
BOOKS, INC.**

Published by
Chartwell Books Inc.
A Division of Booksales Inc.
110 Enterprise Avenue,
Secaucus, New Jersey 07094
1982

ISBN 0 89009 522 1

Art Editor: Nick Clark
Art Assistant: Helen Kirby
Editor: Patricia Mackinnon
Special Photography: Bob Langrish
Art Director: Bob Morley
Editorial Director: Jeremy Harwood

Typeset in Great Britain by SX Composing Ltd., Essex
Origination by Rainbow Graphic Arts, Hong Kong, Rodney Howe Ltd.,
London, Speedlith Photolitho Ltd., Manchester
Printed in Hong Kong by Lee Fung Asco Printers Ltd.

This book was designed and produced by Quarto Publishing Ltd,
32 Kingly Court, London W1

Illustrations: Edwina Keene, Dave Weeks, John Woodcock,
QED Publishing

Special thanks to Christine Bell, Belmont Equestrian Centre,
Hugo Bevan, The British Horse Society, Moira Clinch, P. de Coti Marsh,
Betty Day, George Goring, Claire Graham, Sheila Inderwick,
Carmen Janes, Pam Jones, John Line, Linda Lydig, Robert Oliver,
Norman Patrick, Lynda Poley, Minette Rice-Edwards, Sally Stainer,
Margaret Seaward, Stroud Pony Club, Talland School of Equitation,
Hugh Thomas, Graham Thomas, Richard Thorpe.

CONTENTS

FOREWORD

TODAY, RIDING IS A PASTIME without barriers. People from all walks of life and from all nations enjoy the thrill – and the rough and tumble – of equestrian sports, whatever their ages and whatever their levels of competence.

This encyclopedia is a comprehensive practical handbook to all the varied forms of organized equestrian activity. It takes as its starting point the eight major horse sports, from the informal bustle of mounted games through the challenge and thrill of the hunting field to the quiet concentration of dressage and the stamina required for long distance trail riding. It analyzes the programmes and routines that both horses and riders should follow in order to acquit themselves to the best of their ability in competitions. In addition to the detailed description in the main text, training information is also encapsulated in a calendar feature for each chapter, which shows in easy reference form the annual routine that the horse and rider should follow in order to give of their best.

Every aspect of the various sports is described in detail. In dressage, for instance, the topics covered include how dressage is organized, the rules, scoring, judging, what type of horse is best suited to the sport, and the purpose of the various tests and how they should be executed. The training programme ranges from the basics of lungeing to teaching the aids and practising the movements from elementary to advanced stages. Turnout for horse and rider and the layout of the dressage arena are among the many special features, extensively captioned and illustrated. Similarly, the chapter on long distance trail riding offers a definition of the various types of ride, a description of the sport's attractions and dangers, what sort of horse is needed and how to tell if it is suitable for the demands of the sport, the full training programme for a horse – with special emphasis on such factors as pulse and respiration rates and general health – the fitness of the rider, suitable tack, stable management and feeding, plus all you need to know about competing in the ride itself. In addition, and perhaps most importantly, the chapter includes details of the care you should give your horse after the ride.

Nor is the historical side ignored. Riding, after all, has its roots thousands of years in the past and many of the equestrian sports of today have their origins in somewhat surprising areas, or in more serious activities. Eventing, for instance, was closely linked in origin with the demands of war; fox hunting emerged as a response to the agricultural revolution of the 18th century, which created open areas over which to gallop and fences to jump.

But above all, the keynote to *The Encyclopedia of Equestrian Sports* is enjoyment. The aim has been to combine the mass of information this book contains – both in text and illustrations – with an informal, enjoyable style, fitting the nature of riding itself.

CHAPTER ONE

MOUNTED GAMES

MORE THAN WITH any other sport included in this book, a mention of mounted games conjures up widely differing views of equestrian activity to varying groups of people. To cavalry or mounted police, they are likely to mean skill-at-arms. This is a term that encompasses a number of 'games', often ridden competitively, but principally designed to perfect the riders' use of weapons when mounted, at the same time as training their horses in obedience and combat tactics. The cowboys and girls who spend their days in the saddle, riding the range and working with cattle, will think of the competitive games that form part of the day's events at a rodeo. Members of riding clubs and similar organisations will associate the words with various non-competitive, activity rides, such as 'mock hunts' in which riders take the place of the fox and hounds, while others act the parts of the hunt staff and members of the field. The words could just as easily refer to the various informal permutations of the game of polo – such as cushion polo or paddock polo; to a type of mounted lacrosse known as *tshenkburti* in some countries and polocrosse in others; to mounted paper-chases and treasure hunts, or to any number of the hundreds of horseback games that have been devised throughout the centuries all over the world as tests of skill and obedience or as pleasurable relaxation.

International gymkhana

For many young riders, mounted games mean the competitive games that make up a major part of the schedule at gymkhanas or local horse shows. In Britain, the best-known version of these is the Pony Club Mounted Games Championship, known widely as the Prince Philip Cup Games. This is a keenly contested team event that takes place throughout the country between Pony Club branches during the Easter and summer holidays, culminating in the exciting finals that take place annually at the Horse of the Year Show, London. They were first staged there in 1957, when 45 branches of the Pony Club competed. From these beginnings, the idea spread to Europe. British Pony Club teams have demonstrated these mounted games in Holland, Germany and France and youngsters from Belgium have

Left: A winning combination! Both pony and rider are obviously experienced in the skills of mounted games. The rider is showing great precision as she takes a flag from the container and the pony has anticipated the next move as he has already begun to turn tightly round the obstacle. **Above:** An old print showing a mounted officer in India indulging in the one-time popular sport of pig-sticking. Rather more gruesome than the mounted games of today, the skills needed for success are nonetheless much the same.

begun to compete in mounted games internationally by sending a team to participate in an international event held at the Windsor Horse Show.

Pony Clubs in Canada and the USA also run a mounted games competition, known in Canada as the Prince Philip Cup Games, but in the USA as the Mounted Games of the United States. Just as the British have zone and regional rounds to qualify for the national finals at Wembley, teams in the USA and Canada compete in various qualifying rounds in the hope of getting to their national finals. These tend to be a whole day affair, and though competition is fierce, the principal emphasis is on fun. At about the same time each year there is also an event known as an 'international visit' in which teams from Canada, the USA and Britain compete against one another. The venue is rotated among the three countries and the competition is open to children who are under 16 years old on May 1st of that year. (Competitors in the Prince Philip Cup Games competition in the UK must be under 15 years old on May 1st.) Australia and New Zealand, too, have their own versions.

Origins and value

Whatever the interpretation of the words – whether the game is a tent-pegging competition at the British Royal Tournament, a barrel race at a Texan rodeo, a bending race at a gymkhana or a furious game of *buzkashi* played in the blazing deserts of Turkistan, the origins of all mounted games are the same. In their myriad forms of today, each one has evolved from the 'games' and exercises practised by mounted soldiers throughout the ages to prepare them for the skills and disciplines they would need to fight their enemy from horseback. The great Greek horsemaster, Xenophon, who lived in the fifth century BC, is known to have included such games as part of the training of his soldiers and every cavalryman since has been similarly trained.

One of the great values of mounted games lies in the precision and accuracy they demand from both horse and rider. A horse must be instantly obedient – stopping, starting and turning at a moment's notice. Because the rider is involved so often in some additional activity – such as spearing some object with a lance, putting a flag in a bucket or passing a baton to a team member – the horse also must be both unperturbed by what his rider is doing and yet ready to respond to a command the instant it is given. For young riders, mounted games are particularly valuable, since they serve as an introduction to more serious competitive equestrian riding, teaching competition tactics, behaviour and etiquette.

Few mounted games, however, have the professionalism and thus the seriousness of competition associated with such sports as eventing or show jumping. This could be attributed to the fact that they have traditionally been played for relaxation and enjoyment – as light-hearted competition among friendly rivals and a way of promoting team spirit.

The mounted games horse

Because of the nature of mounted games – that is their somewhat light-hearted competitive element or their general use as part of more complex overall training – few riders seek to buy a horse or pony solely to take part in them. A cavalry horse, for example, would not be purchased just for its prowess in mock battles or a tent-pegging competition; nor would a cowboy buy a pony simply because it showed remarkable aptitude in the rodeo mounted games. In both cases the suitability of the animal for its daily work is more important. In addition, almost any horse or pony can be trained to participate in some form of mounted games, providing its rider is sympathetic, rides well and knows what he or she is trying to achieve. The chairman of the organizing committee of the British Prince Philip Mounted Games, Norman Patrick, says, for instance, that even given the highly competitive nature of these games today success is within range of

Below: It is not only young riders who enjoy mounted games! Here polo players compete against each other in a light-hearted costume race.
Below right: Tent-pegging is one of the mounted games practised by mounted police and soldiers. This picture dates from the end of the nineteenth century, showing that such games are not new.

Left: Barrel racing is the rodeo equivalent of a gymkhana bending race. Note the angle of the pony's legs to the ground; he is well prepared to make a very tight turn round the barrel. **Top:** Jousting competitions could be described as the medieval knight's answer to mounted games. Competitions were held in front of a large crowd and were usually conducted in a spirit of friendly rivalry. **Above:** A modern-day 'knight' prepares to joust with an opponent. Considerable practice is needed in order to handle the unwieldy lance.

any pony and child, *providing they train hard enough*. Having said this, however, there are some valid points to look for if choosing a pony.

Selecting your mount

The size of horse depends on the rider. Never be tempted to buy a pony that is too small for you because you happen to know he is a good gymkhana pony. It is not fair on the pony and in another year's time the chances are you will be too big to ride him at all. There is also now a rule in the Prince Philip Mounted Games which states that no child who weighs more than 54 kg (8½ stone) when dressed in riding kit may ride a pony of 12.2hh or under.

Points to bear in mind about size are that smaller ponies are useful for games that involve, for example, bending down and dropping

something into a bucket – it is not so far to reach, so the margin for error is less – or when vaulting on and off your mount quickly is involved. On the other hand, such ponies will often have a short stride, which means that they cannot move as fast as their longer-striding, taller rivals, and speed is undoubtedly an important factor in some games. It is sensible, therefore, simply to look for a pony that is the right size for you to ride on an everyday basis.

The age of the pony is another factor. No pony under four years old is allowed to compete in Prince Philip Games; indeed if you buy a pony of this age, you will need to be a good enough rider to train him completely in the art of mounted games. Undue excitement – which is certainly part of any competition, can easily cause him to 'blow-up' – that is, become excitable and uncontrollable – whereas an older

Above: Competitors and helpers gather for an event at a gymkhana. You can see from this picture that ponies of all shapes and sizes can take part in the world of mounted games.

pony of six years or more is likely to be more settled and to act more maturely and sensibly. Many Pony Club mounted games trainers consider the ideal age for a Prince Philip pony is 10 to 12, by which time such animals have considerable experience, are thoroughly used to life and are less likely to be upset by the noises and distractions of a mounted games event.

Conformation is important. A horse or pony that is 'well put-together' will always perform better than one with poor conformation. The ideal animal will be short rather than long in the back, as this makes for greater agility of movement. The neck should be slender rather than thick, and the head small but well-proportioned to the rest of the body. A horse uses his head and neck to balance himself, particularly when moving at speed, and a large head and thick neck tends to lead to clumsier movement. The legs are important, as they have to take considerable strain when, for example, a horse is asked to turn and stop at a moment's notice. They should be clean, strong and unblemished, but not excessively fine or slender. Make sure the pastern slopes forward correctly; an upright pastern has a less efficient shock-absorbing action.

Smoothness and evenness of paces are things to look for and you should check these by watching the horse or pony moving towards you, past you and away from you, as well as by the feel of the movement when you are on his back. Check the three major paces – walk, trot and canter. They should look and feel evenly-balanced and rhythmic. Similarly, the animal should feel well-balanced as you ride him round corners and in a circle. It is extremely important for a mounted games pony to answer his rider's leg commands instantly. If you feel he does not do so as you are trying him, consider whether he is sufficiently young or amenable to respond to training.

The temperament is of paramount importance. A nappy or bad-tempered animal – one that lays his ears back as you approach him or looks generally bad-tempered – is best avoided. He will be a menace to you and others. The ideal temperament is one that lies midway between being very high-spirited and hot-blooded and very docile and too easy-going. An excessively high-spirited horse or pony could prove too excitable for competition, but a very docile one might just be too lazy when it matters. Look for an animal, therefore, with a certain amount of spirit and certainly one which takes an interest in what he is doing and what is going on around him.

There is nothing particularly remarkable or

exceptional in the horse or pony that has just been described. Indeed it is because millions conform to such a specification, that the field of mounted games is wide open to so many riders and their mounts. It is fair to say, however, that the higher up the scale you go in competition, the better the horse or pony you will need. Speed, combined with agility, willingness and obedience are the principal constituents of a good mounted games horse or pony.

Training – the first steps

The early training of a horse or pony for mounted games competition mainly revolves around the proper care and conditioning of the animal in order to get it to the required level of fitness. A certain amount of schooling may be necessary later within this programme in order to ensure the animal is obedient and responsive to his rider.

Most mounted games competitions begin in the early spring and continue through the summer into the autumn. Some 'friendly' competitions are held even earlier than this. When you begin your conditioning programme in order to take part in such events will depend on a number of factors, principal among them

being the time you have available. As far as a child is concerned, school work must be taken into account, since this may reduce leisure time considerably. Another consideration will be how hard, or in how many events you want to compete. Even if you only want to enter a gymkhana occasionally, however, it is still important that your pony has had some preparation. No pony can be expected to come up from a protracted period at grass, when he has had little or no exercise and certainly no training, and produce anything approaching his best in a competitive game.

If your pony has had a busy summer, you should begin a conditioning programme for the next season only after he has had a period of rest, during which he will have been turned out in the field. If he has really worked hard at gymkhana games, he will need a couple of months or so of complete rest, during which his shoes are taken off and he is not ridden at all. The first thing to do, therefore, when you decide to begin riding again (in the late autumn/ early winter), is to have him shod and to inspect him very thoroughly for any injuries. You should, of course, have checked him over each day during his rest period, too – all horses and ponies turned out to grass *must* be visited and inspected every day in case they become ill or are injured in some way.

As the principal contenders in mounted games are generally small, rather tough horses and ponies, whose riders will be involved with school work, it is likely that the animals will be kept permanently at grass, rather than stabled. By and large, this is preferable anyway; most small ponies or cross-bred horses keep healthier when living out-of-doors than they do when kept in a stable, particularly if their riders do not really have enough time to devote to their daily welfare. The training programme given here is designed for ponies kept under such conditions, although it can be adapted easily to suit horses or ponies that are stabled for part of the time.

Exercise and horse management

The conditioning of any horse or pony begins with slow exercise. If the animal has been rested for a while, only small amounts should be given at first. Ideally the horse or pony should be walked for half an hour or so each day for a week, increasing to an hour a day during the second week, plus a small amount of trotting.

However, it is not always possible to ride a pony every day during term time, especially during winter evenings, so you must adapt this programme to suit your particular circumstances. Ride whenever you can, but do not try to compensate for five days of no riding by riding for twice as long, twice as fast at the weekend. Racing around the countryside will never get a pony fit; instead it will ruin him. You must stick to slow work until the animal

Top: Leading a pony along the road is an alternative to riding him and can be useful in the early part of a conditioning programme. It is always advisable to lead a pony wearing a bridle rather than a headcollar, even if the road carries very little traffic; you will have more control should something cause him to jump or shy suddenly.
Above: Hacking out with friends is an important aspect of preparing a pony for mounted games. Besides helping to get him fit, it teaches him how to behave with other ponies and riders.

has lost some of his grass belly and begins to puff and blow less readily after any exertion. If a friend or a member of the family, who has some experience with horses and a little more time than you, is able either to lead your pony round the roads for half an hour a day, or exercise it for 20 minutes on a lunge rein, this would be extremely useful.

Horse management includes such varied aspects as feeding, grooming and the overall care of a horse's welfare, all vital factors in most conditioning programmes, particularly when getting a horse fit for top-level competition. However, again, these have to be tempered to fit the circumstances. For example, the feeding routine required for gymkhana ponies is not as exacting an art as the one required for a hunter. Most ponies need no extra feeding in the summer and nothing more than a few handfuls of bran mixed with some pony cubes in the winter. This, plus a haynet of good hay in the morning and evening, is perfectly adequate for most ponies; if you notice that yours is losing a little weight, increase the ration of nuts. Note that it is rarely wise to feed a pony oats; they tend to go straight to his head and usually make him over-excited and extremely hard to control.

If your pony has a large grass belly, you must reduce it, for he has no hope of becoming fit until this has been removed. If you are able to bring him in by day and turn him out only by night during the spring or the summer this will help considerably. Exercise and sensible feeding in the winter will soon reduce his waistline.

As far as grooming is concerned, a pony at grass in the winter needs very little grooming. Indeed, he should not have his coat brushed excessively or the essential oils that help to protect him against wet and cold will be removed. All that is necessary is to remove any mud once it has dried, using a dandy brush or a rubber curry comb, and to pick his feet out each day. In the summer, you can groom more thoroughly. The pony will benefit from this, as grooming helps to stimulate the muscles and blood circulation, as well as improving the animal's appearance.

If you are riding your pony after a period of rest, keep an eye on him to make sure he does not develop any saddle sores. This should not happen if you have kept your tack clean and supple and it fits well. The latter point is extremely important for the pony's comfort and performance; if a saddle is pinching or bridle straps rubbing and causing pain, a pony cannot be expected to give of his best. Similarly, make sure the new shoes are causing no discomfort; if there are any signs of unsoundness, get the farrier back.

The best bit to use on a gymkhana pony is a plain, smooth snaffle – either a straight bar type, or one, such as an egg-butt, that is jointed in the centre. If you are aiming at the Prince Philip Mounted Games or their equivalents, these bits are the only ones that can be employed. Martingales and any type of noseband may be used, but try your pony in the simplest combination of tack first. You should resort to more sophisticated and complicated combinations only if it proves necessary.

As soon as your pony can trot some way along the road without puffing too hard or sweating excessively, you can begin gentle schooling work in the paddock. Mark out a rectangular area about 40m x 20m (130ft x 65ft) – or less if you have not got that much room to spare – and practise riding around this on either rein at a walk, trot and a well-balanced, controlled canter. Make sure you really ride the corners correctly, taking them at almost a ninety degree angle rather than cutting across them. Include some circling work on either rein and at all paces. Remember

Above: Check over your pony every day to make sure he has not injured himself. The legs are the part most prone to injury; run your hands down each one carefully, looking for any cuts, bumps or signs of heat and tenderness. **Below:** Most ponies keep healthy and live happily out at grass the year round. They will be even more content if they have the company of other ponies in the field.

Above: Removing the droppings from a pony's field each day helps to conserve the grass and is a part of good management.

that the aim is to make both you and your pony work, so concentrate on what you are doing. The pony should be willing and ready to move forward freely when you ask him to do so. His hocks should be tucked well beneath him, so that his paces are well-balanced and springy. Never let him drift along at his own pace during these schooling sessions, or they will be of no value at all.

A good gymkhana pony should be responsive when ridden on a light rein. Your contact with the mouth should be just sufficient to be able to steer effectively, but the pony should stop when you take up the rein and sit back. Your pony should become so used to this light contact that the slightest feel on the reins from you will warn him that you are about to ask something of him. Thus he is thoroughly responsive. This aim should be born in mind during your schooling sessions.

Concentrate on your riding, too, making sure that you are sitting correctly at all times, giving clear and precise aids, using your legs

firmly, but discreetly, and keeping your hands down on the pony's neck. A criticism often levelled at gymkhana riders is that the minute they start a race, enthusiasm takes over and correct riding is forgotten. Their legs flap against their pony's sides and their arms flail about wildly, their hands jerking up in the air. The accompanying criticism is that many a good pony is spoilt in the pursuit of gymkhana games. Proper training for and sensible competing in mounted games should produce exactly the opposite result; a rider should become more proficient and more sensitive and a pony more responsive and obedient as a result.

When you are satisfied that your pony is moving forward freely on a light rein, is responsive to your aids and is now reasonably fit – that is, he is able to go for a good hack or go through a fairly hard schooling session without hotting up unduly – you can begin to think about some more specialist training. But first, you should give a thought to the second member of the team and consider your own physical fitness.

Top: The excitement of the race has caused this enthusiastic competitor to forget the importance of correct riding! **Above left:** Compare this to the picture above. Although the race is on, the rider is sitting quietly in the saddle, leaning slightly forward to encourage her pony. Her legs are closed against his sides and she is maintaining a light contact with the bit, keeping her hands forward on the pony's neck so as not to interfere with his movement. **Above centre:** Riding without stirrups is extremely good practice for the mounted games competitor. It helps to develop an independent seat that is not reliant on the stirrups for balance and security. Cross the leathers in front of the saddle. **Above:** Riding bareback is also good practice, for the same reasons as above. Some mounted games are conducted bareback, so it is as well to be experienced.

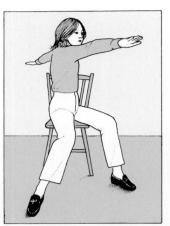

Right: The sack race is a perennial favourite, nearly always present on mounted games schedules at gymkhanas. **Above:** It is important that the rider should be as fit as the pony.
Opposite: Racing close together, side-by-side, is a feature of some mounted games. Practise doing this with a friend; it can be a little unnerving for a pony until he gets used to it.

Getting yourself fit

If you mean to compete seriously, or at least frequently, in mounted games, it is just as important for you to be as fit as your pony should be. The sheer excitement and anticipation of a competition can take a great deal out of a rider, while, besides the energy used in actual riding, competitors often have to run – or even hop – part of the race on their feet. Their speed on the ground could win or lose the race. Many people would say, too, that the secret of success in mounted games lies in the rider's ability to vault on to his mount. This can require great agility, particularly when it is called for while the pony is cantering.

It is therefore important to work a fitness programme for yourself, too. An hour or so's work-out in a gymnasium once a week is a good idea. Failing this, you could swim, cycle or do two or three jogging sessions weekly.

Vaulting on to your pony is discussed fully on p. 19. But before you start this, you should practise mounting and dismounting quickly, without jerking the pony in the mouth or digging him in the sides. Keep these actions smooth; do not jerk your right leg across the horse's back and settle into the saddle with a bump in your anxiety to mount in the shortest possible time. Remember to control the horse by the reins held in your left hand as you mount; if he moves away you will find it harder to produce a good spring.

Specialist training

Training a pony to compete in gymkhana-type mounted games will be both more fun and more effective if you can collaborate with some friends. This not only introduces the important element of competition, but also means you can help and correct each other as you progress. If a riding club runs selection sessions, go along to these. Even if you do not ultimately get picked for the team, participation in the sessions will give you a basic idea of how to train yourself and your pony.

There are two important rules connected with the training of a pony for mounted games. Firstly, a rider does not need a whip or stick. A pony should never be punished by hitting it, nor should a stick be used as a means to encourage him to go faster. Most competitive events ban the use of whips and spurs. Secondly, never jerk your pony in the mouth. In the excitement of the moment, when trying to turn sharply or stop quickly, an enthusiastic rider is quite capable of forgetting the proper use of the hands, so remember this warning and make sure this never happens.

BASIC SKILLS FOR MOUNTED GAMES

The following are the principal skills that horse and rider must acquire if they are to be successful in mounted games.

The Horse
To lead readily in hand.
Instant obedience to rider's commands.
Compatibility with other horses (for pairs and team races).
Ability to stand perfectly still when required, *whatever the circumstances.*

The Rider
Fitness and agility.
Ability to vault onto horse from any position.
Perfect control of horse at all times.
Skill with cane or sword.
Skill 'in hand' and accurate eye (for races involving passing objects to other team mates, dropping objects in buckets, etc.)

Among the most important things for a gymkhana pony to be taught are to lead readily, either alongside another pony and rider or while you run beside him, and to stand still while you mount or when another pony is coming full tilt towards you. This will be necessary in team relay races or some pairs competitions, in which you must receive a baton from a fellow-rider before moving off.

Most ponies will lead readily in hand, but you should practise this at a walk and a trot while you walk or run beside the pony. Put him in a halter the first few times; if you haul on the reins in an attempt to lead him, he will naturally shy backwards to try and get away from the bit banging on his teeth. If the pony does hang back, get a friend to stand behind him and urge him forward. The persuasion should be calm and gentle; a pat on the hindquarters and an encouraging click with the tongue – not a heavy slap, waving of arms and shouting.

It is basic good manners that a pony should stand still while you mount; and even top competition ponies, who know that they have to move off at a gallop a moment later, should stand still until their riders are in the saddle and give the signal to move. If your pony develops the habit of moving as you mount, get off and stand by his side, controlling him with the reins. Make him stand still until you are in the saddle, and then keep him still for a minute or two. Make sure that the aids you give when you ask him to move off are clear and definite. He must learn that sometimes he has to stand still for the start of the race and at other times you will want him to move off immediately.

Keeping a pony still while another is galloping flat out towards him may take a little patience on your part. The first few times they encounter this most ponies will jump to one side or whip round. Initially, therefore, ask someone to hold your pony's head in order to keep him still, while you pat his neck and talk to him. He will soon learn to stand still. This is important in a relay, for instance; you will be concentrating on receiving the baton and want the pony to stand still without having to think about it.

It is also a good idea to try to train your pony to understand and respond to your voice. If you can calm him at the start of a race by talking to him quietly or slow him down when you want to with the command 'steady' or 'whoa', you will find this an immense help. Get into the habit, therefore, of using such commands each time you slow down or come to a halt – making sure your voice is always slow, even and gentle. It is the tone and pitch of your voice he will come to recognize – 'whoa' screamed harshly will have the opposite effect to the one intended.

Turning and halting

Good gymkhana ponies must be able to turn sharply and to stop instantly. The ability of a pony to turn sharply – around a post, for example – depends not only on his flexibility and agility, but also on the rider's ability to use his legs correctly. Practise doing tight turns around a post at a walk and then a trot; the aids are the same for any turn – slight pressure on the rein in the direction you want the pony to turn, pressure with the outside leg – the leg on the opposite side to the turn – behind the girth and pressure with the inside leg slightly further forward. Make sure your hand does not move; it is a common sight to see a rider, when asking for a tight turn, with his hand pulled back into his stomach. Turning sharply back on your own tracks differs only from turning a 90 degree bend in that you keep on using your legs and keep on exerting slight pressure on the rein through almost 180 degrees. When you are making smooth, sharp turns at a walk and trot, you can begin practising a canter.

Stopping quickly should be practised carefully, for it is very important to stop correctly as well as quickly – that is, with the pony's legs well beneath him and his head properly positioned. Another common sight is a rider hauling sharply on the reins in such a way that the poor pony does indeed stop quickly, but with his legs askew and his head flung into the air in an attempt to avoid the pressure on his mouth. Ask your pony to stop from a trot by closing your legs against his sides – this will bring his hind legs under him – and resisting with your hands as he moves forward. When he is stopping smoothly, ask for the same thing from a canter. If anything, this will be easier; you are likely to be leaning forward slightly in the saddle as you have been urging him forward, so, when you want to stop, sit back in the saddle, apply the same closing action with your legs and once more resist with your hands. If you have been riding correctly on a loose rein, the shift of your weight in the saddle will already indicate that you want to slow down.

Rehearsing the game

Undoubtedly the best way to train for individual games is to ride through the actual procedure for them. Initially, it is best to do this quietly on your own at a walk, progressing slowly to a trot and finally to a canter. Do not start even friendly competition with others until both you and your pony are proficient.

Always work through the movements of a game from start to finish, and then go through them again until you get them right. You must ensure that your pony is performing correctly; that he is bending his body properly (if this is called for); that his head is properly positioned; that he is moving forward in a well-balanced fashion and that he is listening to you all the time. Be patient, since no horse or pony can be expected to know what he must do in a game until he has been taught, and it

Above: When teaching your pony to make tight turns round a post, begin by making the turn smooth and wide. **Right:** You can gradually decrease the arc of a turn until you stay close to the post throughout. Try to keep your hands in the proper position, not letting them stray downwards as this rider has done.

HOW TO VAULT

Being able to vault on to a pony without using the stirrup iron is an essential mounted games technique. You should learn to vault on to your pony both when he is standing still and when he is moving, and you should also be able to vault up behind another rider. In the picture on the **left**, the riders at the back have vaulted on to the ponies by running up behind them, putting both hands on the hindquarters and springing up with a scissor action of their legs as they slide onto the ponies' backs.

In the small pictures **below** the rider is showing how to vault on to a moving pony. He runs alongside the pony facing in the same direction, holding the reins at the pommel. Then he jumps up off both legs, pushing on his arms and throwing his right leg up over the saddle.

To vault on to a stationary pony, stand facing his shoulder, with your left hand (holding the reins) on the pony's back and your right hand on the pommel. Bend your knees and spring upwards, throwing your right leg over the saddle.

An alternative method which is useful if you are vaulting up behind another rider, is to stand facing towards the pony's tail, holding the reins in your left hand and the pommel in your right. Take one step forward and throw yourself up into the air, twisting as you leave the ground so as to land in the saddle.

may take him a little while to understand what exactly is required, particularly if you are asking him to learn all sorts of different games. If you are experiencing difficulty in some particular aspect of a game, do not go over and over it until both you and your pony are thoroughly frustrated. Leave it and come back to it, preferably after you have asked advice.

You cannot expect your pony to be brilliant at all gymkhana games. In some the emphasis is on speed; in others it is very much on the 'game' element. Few ponies are good at both, and also there are some games that individual animals simply do not like. If, however, your pony appears not to perform well in a particular race for no apparent reason, look at what you are doing or not doing, rather than instantly blaming him. Are you riding correctly, giving clear leg aids and using your hands sympathetically? Particularly if you were racing against others, think how you used your voice. The excitement of the race may have made you alter the tone or pitch and ponies are extremely sensitive to changes.

Intersperse gymkhana training sessions with other types of riding such as hacking or jumping. Ponies well versed in games get to know them so well that practising the same games over and over again will make them bored, stale and ultimately uninterested. Once you have mastered the technique of a particular game, there really is not much point in running through it endlessly; turn to some other game instead.

Bear in mind, too, that it is a good idea to limber up a pony gently before embarking on a training session. Give him a quarter of an hour going through a few gentle school paces, or try some light interval training. In this, you walk your pony for three minutes, rest him for three minutes, trot for three minutes, rest for three minutes, trot again, rest again and then canter for three minutes. Do this on either rein and concentrate on what you are doing. As well as making him obedient it is a great help in getting a horse or pony fit. It will also settle him a little before practising the games and make him co-operative from the start.

Other pointers

There are some other pointers that may help you. Remember to keep your eye on what you are doing – this is why it is so important that your pony is obedient to your instant command. Focus on the container into which you must put the flag, the balloon you must burst or the baton you are about to receive from a team mate. If you take your eyes off it, you will miss it. Similarly, practise leaning right over your pony's side to drop objects into a container. The closer you are to it, the less likely

HOLDING REINS IN ONE HAND

In many races it will be necessary to control your pony when holding the reins in one hand only. The rider on the **right** shows how to hold the reins correctly, and you will often find it helps to knot them so they do not slip through your hand. Beware of giving confusing aids. **Below: left:** The rider has just asked his pony to turn to the right by moving his hand sharply to the right. He has thus shortened the left rein in such a way that the pony has moved his head to the left to escape the pressure on the bit. The diagram **below right** shows the correct aid; the rider has just flexed his wrist to exert slight pressure on the right rein.

you are to miss; in most games, you have to dismount, pick up the object and start again if this happens. Leaning right down over your pony's neck as he is cantering forward is just a matter of gaining confidence in yourself and him – and the only way to do this is to practise.

By and large you will find that your pony gets used to the strange things asked of him – to trot along quietly while his rider is hopping alongside in a sack or to act as if there is nothing unusual in his rider carrying some strange object on his back, for instance – as you prac-

tise. If he is frightened by something, take him through that manoeuvre quietly on your own. If you have to drag something along the ground and this upsets him, begin merely by dragging a rope while asking him to walk. Then do this while he is trotting and cantering, gradually increasing the size of the object. If he does not want to go near the balloons in a balloon-bursting race, place a cavaletti parallel to the balloons so that he must go closer to them. You will find incidentally that a pony seldom seems to be frightened of the noise of a balloon popping, particularly if you are going fast enough to burst it at a fast canter.

If a pony shows reluctance in going near a bucket, barrel, or something else that is an integral part of the race, try leading him to it, talking to him gently all the time. Touch the object and show it to the pony, coaxing him to investigate. Do not persist with this in one session, but repeat it each time you are training until he gets used to it. Some ponies, however, simply never get used to an object that frightens them and however much you try they seem never to conquer their fear. In such cases, it is far better to forget about that particular race and concentrate on the others.

Another useful exercise is riding bareback – something else that may well be called for in races. Riding bareback is very helpful in teaching you to ride in balance with your horse. When riding with your feet in the stirrup irons – and again in the thrill of a race – it is extremely easy to find you are exerting more pressure on one iron than the other. This means your weight is not distributed evenly over the pony, which makes it much harder for him to perform as required. Riding bareback can help to cure this, as can riding without stirrups, but remember it when you are riding with your feet in the irons as well. Resist the temptation to lean with your horse as he weaves in and out of bending poles. If you sit quite straight in the saddle he can bend with the maximum efficiency and speed.

Finally include a few friendly races with the friends at your practice sessions – the operative word here being few. The whole session should

Right: Mounted games often include the use of strange or unusual objects. If your pony displays any fear of these, show them to him first and let him become thoroughly acquainted with them before racing. **Far right:** It may not be possible to become familiar with all the strange objects you might encounter!

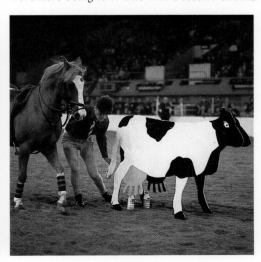

not be given over to racing, or the ponies will probably become over-excited and exhausted. If they associate this with the actual games, it may understandably make them reluctant and less willing to co-operate or instantly excitable whenever they sense competition. Instead, use the competitive part of your session wisely – to practise the start of a race for example. For this you want your pony to go straight into a canter from a standstill. Do not ask for this by waving your arms and flapping your legs frantically against his side. Instead, hold him at the start line on quite a tight rein, agitating your legs very slightly against his sides, so that he knows you are about to ask more of him. Then when you want him to move, sit well down into the saddle, kick his sides sharply and lengthen your reins, without moving your hands forward.

Preparing for competition

Practising mounted games in a paddock with a few friends and competing in a gymkhana against other keen contestants can be two very different things, unless you are well prepared.

If your pony is not already a seasoned competitor, you should consider the effect that going to even a small competition could have on him. He is going to be taken to a strange place (probably in a box or trailer) alive with noise and bustle. There will be numbers of cars and horse-boxes, and endless horses, ponies and people milling around. There will be tents and marquees, roped-off competition rings and very likely a voice booming over a public address system. This will naturally be quite a shock to a pony or horse who has not experienced it before. In addition you are going to ask him to remain calm for part of the time and race at top speed at other times.

Do all that you can to acquaint a pony with similar conditions before expecting too much of him. It would be a help to take him to a small show in which you are not competing, just to get him used to the many distractions.

Gymkhana games take place within an arena or marked-off area of some kind. If your pony is not used to entering an arena, he may find this an unnerving experience, and if he fails to go in quickly, you might well be eliminated from an event. Try, therefore, to get him used to riding in and out of a roped-off area. Walk him in and out of it several times without running any races, so that he does not associate the arena with racing. If this happens, he will start to get excited the minute you enter.

Below: It is never too early to start! Even if you are not yet ready to compete in many mounted games, it is a good idea to go to some gymkhanas so that both you and your pony get used to the procedure.

Your pony will also be eliminated if he will not line up quietly at the starting line.

As soon as you feel ready, you can begin entering for local shows and gymkhanas. Contact the show secretaries and ask them to send schedules. Get as many of these as you can, so that you can choose those shows that have the best selection of games for you and your pony and you can space them out sensibly so you are not entering in shows on consecutive days. Consult with friends when making your choice; it is far more enjoyable to go to shows in which you know several of the competitors.

Note from the schedules whether you must send your entries in advance or whether you may enter for the classes on the day. If you have to send them, there will be a closing day for entries, so make sure you get your entry form into the post in plenty of time for this. Also read the rules so that you know them thoroughly.

The final fortnight

Once you know the dates of the shows, you can begin to plan a timetable of preparation for yourself and your pony. Hopefully the shows will mainly be in the Easter and summer holidays when the weather is a little warmer. This means you can pay rather more attention to the grooming of your pony's coat, as he has not so much need of the protective oils.

Try to groom your pony regularly and fairly thoroughly each day leading up to a gymkhana for at least a fortnight beforehand. It is no good thinking that a thorough going-over the day before the show will put a shine on his coat. This only comes through hard, regular groom-

ing, so aim to brush his coat for at least a good 20 minutes a day throughout that fortnight and for longer if possible. Pull his mane and tail too, if necessary – that is, if they are very thick and untidy. Aim to do a little each day rather than the whole job at once, or else the pony may get agitated. Only take out a few hairs at each 'pull' too; this will not only cause him less discomfort, but also, if you take out large chunks in one go, you could end up with an equally untidy result as you would have if you had left it alone. Remember you should never cut a mane or top part of the tail, though you can trim the bottom of a tail with scissors.

Check your pony's shoes and feet a week or so before a gymkhana. Long feet and loose shoes are dangerous, since they can cause a pony to trip or stumble. However, it is best to have new shoes fitted a few days before a show rather than the day before it. Should any trouble result, such as a shoe pinching, you then have time to put things right.

The day before

On the day before the show, you can shampoo the mane and tail. Even if the pony is a bay or chestnut, rather than a grey, the mane and tail will look better for a wash. Use warm water and soap, or horse shampoo. Rub the hairs between your hands in the same way you would your own hair and make sure you rinse away all traces of soap. Swing the bottom part of the tail in a circle (standing well to the pony's side so you do not soak yourself) to get rid of as much water as possible, then towel both the mane and tail dry and comb them out gently.

To bandage a tail Brush the top hairs and dampen them to make them lie flat. Put the end of the bandage under the tail.

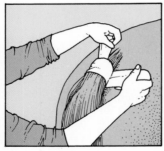

Twist bandage round tail, leaving a short length free. Turn this down and wind bandage around it, not too tightly.

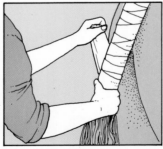

Continue bandaging down to bottom of the dock. Wind any remaining bandage back up the tail.

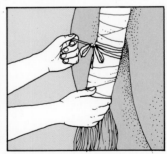

Tie the tapes on the outside and bend the bandaged tail so it is not completely straight. Slide bandage down tail to remove.

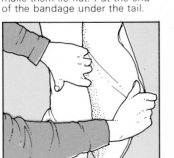

To put on stable bandages Wrap a large piece of cotton gamgee round the leg to act as padding.

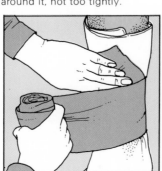

Begin bandaging just below knee or hock, winding it firmly but not too tightly. Take it over the fetlock joint.

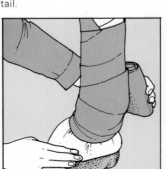

Twist bandage to wind it back up the leg. Continue bandaging evenly until you have reached the starting point again.

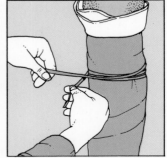

Tie the tapes securely on the outside of the leg (not the front or back). Tuck the ends of the tapes in to keep them secure.

You can put a tail bandage on while the tail is still damp; this will help to keep the hairs flat and maintain the shape. Never leave a tail bandage on overnight, though; it could damage the circulation in the dock.

If your pony has white socks or stockings, you can wash these. Use warm water and soap or shampoo, but this time scrub gently with a soft brush. Rinse thoroughly and towel them dry. Stable bandages will help to keep white legs clean. A badly stained grey coat, or the white parts of a piebald and skewbald pony might also benefit from a shampooing, but you must towel the coat as dry as possible. Never leave a soaking horse to catch a cold.

If you can stable the pony overnight before a show or gymkhana, you have that much more chance of keeping him clean than if he is turned out to grass. Make sure he has a good deep bed and a full hay net. Put stable bandages on all his legs to keep them clean and well-protected, plus a rug if the evening is chilly. If it is a warm night, there is no need for this, although a light summer sheet may help to keep the pony's coat clean.

The tack should be sparkling clean for the show. Clean it the day before and carefully inspect all buckles, studs and stitching to make sure they are thoroughly secure. Polish the stirrup iron and rings of the bit, and fit rubber bit guards to it. These big rubber discs lie outside the pony's mouth, inside the bit rings, and will protect the corners of the mouth from injury.

Get your clothes ready for the next day, too, and make sure they are all clean and well-pressed. Most gymkhanas ask that you should wear jodphurs, shoes (strong leather ones with a one-piece sole so they will not get caught in the stirrup iron) or boots, and a shirt and tie.

Most do not insist on a jacket. The important point is that you look clean and neat and tidy, rather than expensively dressed. Make sure your shoes are well polished.

The day of the show

You need to be up early. If your pony is being fed, give him his feed as early as you can, so he has time to digest it before you start getting him ready. He will need his usual thorough grooming. Then brush his mane and tail, put on a tail bandage and oil his hooves.

If you are taking him in a trailer or box to the show, get him ready for travelling. Bandage his legs with stable bandages, putting a good thick wad of cotton wool or gamgee under-

FIRST PRIZE

GYMKHANA ACTIVITIES

1. A well-turned out rider and neatly groomed pony wait for the start of a competition. If there is a long wait, get off your pony to give him a rest. **2.** The ambition of all Pony Club mounted games competitors; to be in the winning line-up at the Horse of the Year Show. **3.** Very occasionally, a particular mounted game may call for competitors to pop over a small jump. Jumping competitions are generally included in the day's events at gymkhanas. **4.** Competitors consult the schedule at a show. Remember always to be on time for your class.

5. The balloon race calls for speed and accuracy. Competitors have to burst a balloon with a pointed stick as they gallop past. **6.** Always make a fuss of your pony when he has performed. **7.** Taking a baton from a mounted or non-mounted person is a part of many games. Keep your eye on the object and do not turn so tightly that you knock the person over! **8.** A popular class on gymkhana schedules — the fancy dress event.

2

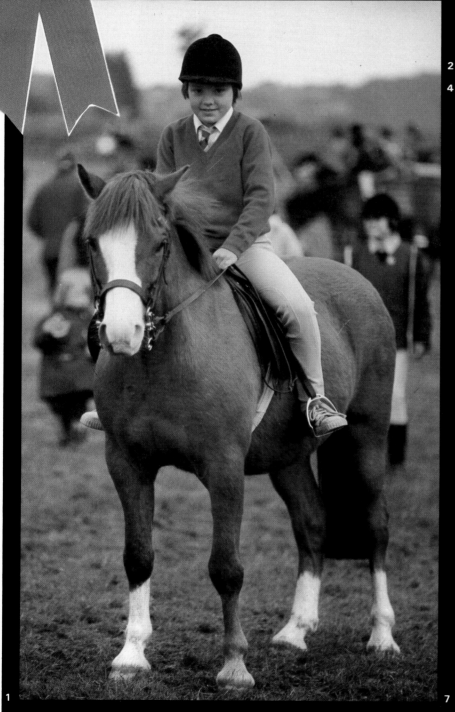

1

4

7

neath them. He should wear knee pads as protection against any knocks or bangs; if you think his hocks could suffer in the same way, invest in some hock boots, too. He should wear a stout, leather headcollar with a strong rope for travelling, while a light rug will keep him warm, if necessary, as well as keeping him clean.

Travelling to a show in a horse box means you have plenty of room to take all the equipment you need. This includes grooming kit – particularly a stable rubber to put a final shine on the coat, a hoof pick in case of emergencies and hoof oil and brush to give an extra gloss before the event. You will need a bucket – preferably a strong rubber one – to give your pony a drink during the day, and a haynet of hay for him to nibble. Take an emergency first aid kit, plus some cotton wool and antiseptic powder. An anti-sweat rug is a useful, though not essential, item of equipment, in case he breaks out in a sweat just before you want to leave. If you are hacking to the show, arrange for the equipment to be taken there for you in a car.

Allow yourself plenty of time to box your pony and travel to the show so that you arrive in good time. This is particularly important if you have to make your entries when you get to the show. Aim to arrive there at least an hour before the start of your first race. If you are obviously hurrying to box the pony, it will only worry and fluster him and either he will refuse to go into the box at all or he will be agitated and upset. This is just the way you do not want him to be – he should arrive at the show ground relaxed and calm.

At the event

On arrival, the first thing to do is to check to make sure the pony has travelled well and not suffered any injury. Providing he is happy to be left in the box, leave him there for the time being. If he is happier tied up outside, then do this.

After this, go over to the secretary's tent to confirm (or make) your entries and to collect your number. Check to see if events are running on time if the show has already started, so you can estimate when your first race should be. Walk round the competition arenas, so that you are thoroughly familiar with them and can be quite sure of the location of the collecting ring for your particular events.

About half an hour before the start of your first race, lead your pony out of the box and walk him about for a minute or two to stretch his legs. Remove his travelling gear, give him a brush over if necessary and then tack-up. Leave yourself plenty of time to do this quietly and calmly and thoroughly check the saddlery as you put it on your pony. After this give the pony a gentle work-out, both to limber him up and to settle him in the different environment. Cantering him around the practice areas with friends will not settle him; it is likely to get

Top: A New Zealand rug put over the pony's loins will help to keep this part dry during a rainstorm. **Above:** Ponies can be tied up to the side of a box in between races, providing you are sure they do not mind. It is best to take it in turns to keep an eye on them, though, just in case anything should happen.
Right: A helper checks a pony's hoof, perhaps to make sure the clenches have not risen suddenly indicating a loose shoe. Riders will find it a great help to have an experienced person with them at mounted games events. There are many occasions when you might want to leave your pony, while you check your entry in a class, for example.

him thoroughly excited and nervy, and it will be a great nuisance – even a danger – to others. You could even be sent home if you persist in doing this.

Go to the collecting ring when you hear your races called. Enter the heat you are told to – not the one you think you would like to be in – and ride it to the best of your ability. Should you have the misfortune to fall off, the rules state you can remount and continue the race from this point. If you are not hurt, it is a good idea to do this, even though you know you are not going to win. It shows an infinitely more sporting attitude than withdrawing from the ring with a sulky look on your face.

If you win (or in some cases come second) in your heat, you will be needed for the semi-finals and then, hopefully, for the finals. Dismount and give your pony a rest between heats. Similarly, if you do not have to enter later heats, but want to watch your friends compete, don't use your pony as a grandstand. Dismount and let him rest too.

Throughout the day your prime consideration should be the welfare of your pony, followed by consideration for the other people and ponies at the show. To ride your pony endlessly around between your races is unfair on him. If you are in several races, rest him whenever possible between them, tying him up in a shady place or else putting him back in his box.

Only do the latter, however, if it is a cool day or the box is parked in a well-shaded spot.

THE MOUNTED GAMES PONY'S YEAR

It is considerably more difficult to outline the timetable of events throughout the year for a pony competing in gymkhana events than it is for most other competition horses. This is because training is generally less exacting and rigorous, the season of events tends to be a little more erratic and, as most ponies are likely to be involved in many other riding activities, it is not so easy to focus attention on this one aspect.

The following timetable, therefore, is only a general one, used by a particular Pony Club.
Mid-autumn/early winter: (for ponies not in that year's team): Training sessions once a week.
Mid-autumn/early winter: (for ponies in the team that year): Complete rest out at grass, with shoes taken off.
Winter/early spring Practice session for the selected teams held once a

week. These are interspersed with informal competitions with other Pony Club branches.
Spring/early summer: Area meetings are held. Top teams qualify for zone finals. Practice sessions continue up to these meetings.
Midsummer: Ponies are rested from games practice. They now know the games so well, they will get bored and stale if made to do them repeatedly. They are hacked

out, attend Pony Club rallies and generally lead normal lives.
Late summer: Practice sessions stepped up to twice a week in preparation for regional finals.
Early autumn: Regional finals. Top teams qualify for the finals. Their ponies are given light work, with some continued games practice throughout the remainder of this period.
Mid-autumn: Finals.

Check to see that it is not hot inside – boxes and trailers can get insufferably hot on even moderately warm days. If the pony is very hot, walk him around until he cools off. On a rainy day, if you are not able to put him back in his box between events, cover his loins with a waterproof rug or mackintosh. If it is a very hot day and you have a long wait between classes, a sponge-down with cool water will refresh the pony. Give him a drink between classes, too, but restrict this to just a couple of mouthfuls of water. This is all he will need to make him feel better. If you were to ride a race just after he had had a long drink, it would make him feel very uncomfortable at best and, at worst, give him colic.

When your races are over, cool your pony

off if he is hot, give him a slightly longer drink if he wants one – saving a really big one for when he gets home – and then prepare him for travelling again. Make sure he has a haynet tied up in the box and then take him straight home. Again, it is not fair to make your pony wait around at the end of the day because you want to watch more events.

At home, unbox the pony straight away, take off his travelling gear and look him over to make sure he has no cuts or abrasions from the day's activity. If he lives out at grass, turn him out immediately, so that he can roll, have a good long drink and generally recover from his tiring day. A small feed might act as a reward for all his hard work and he will appreciate a rest from being ridden the next day.

CHAPTER TWO

HUNTING

HUNTING IS THE oldest of all equestrian sports and, although uncompetitive in itself, it is the forefather of many modern competitive ones. Ever since man first realized he could cover more ground, faster, and with the added advantage of the height given by sitting astride a horse, he has hunted animals on horseback. Wild boar, oxen, hares, foxes, coyotes, wolves, bears, stags, bison, tigers, lions and even elephants and giraffes all at some time or other have been hunted in such a manner.

In many instances, such hunting has been of necessity – to provide food or to protect family, livestock and crops; in many more it has been purely attributable to the excitement and thrill of the chase. Robert Surtees, the British nineteenth-century writer, creator of the world-famous, almost legendary character, Jorrocks, summed up one of the greatest attractions of hunting with the words that it was 'the image of war without its guilt and only five-and-twenty per cent of its danger'.

Hunting, as it is known today, originated in Britain. The pursuit of game for sport, using packs of hounds to find, chase and kill the quarry, was certainly well established in Britain by the time of the Norman Conquest. Although the 'sportsmen' of the day were said to resent bitterly the preservation of game and the Forest Laws the Normans were to introduce, these, in fact, did much to bring some order and organization into the hunting field. Hunting began to become an art and a science as well as a sport.

The principal quarry in those early days was the stag; the fox was looked down upon as not being worthy prey for the mounted followers of the hunt. It was not until the eighteenth century, when enclosures began to change the nature of the land – and thus also the business of riding across country after hounds – that foxhunting began to gain a stronghold. It was soon realized that the crafty nature of the fox presented hounds and huntsmen with a challenge that provided a fascinating day's sport for all, equally good, if not better, than that given by the stag or hare.

It was around this time, too, that hunting began to take its present form, with the founding of more organized 'packs' of hounds, each of them having clearly defined boundaries across the country

Left: Hounds, huntsman and whippers-in hack quietly to a meet through autumnal countryside. **Above:** Hunting of all sorts has always been a popular subject of artists. Here, a nobleman returns from a successful day's stag hunting.

within which they could pursue the sport. Many of the famous British hunts of today – such as those of the great hunting counties in the Midlands – were formed at this time.

Europe, the USA and Australia

Hunting from horseback has long been popular in Europe too – one of the best examples being staghunting in France. As with hunting in Britain, its roots go back over hundreds of years and, although hunting there has followed a somewhat chequered path through its history, there are now well over 100 well-established packs of hounds in France.

Hunting also has a wide following in the USA and Canada. Its origins in these countries can be traced to a certain Robert Brooke, the son of a British MP, who sailed across the Atlantic in the middle of the seventeenth century, taking not only his family and servants, but also a pack of foxhounds. Hunting was gradually to flourish, with the native grey fox being the early quarry, at least until the red fox – which is said to give better sport – was imported from Britain at the end of the nineteenth century.

The first packs of hounds were all owned privately; farmers often kept a few hounds for their personal sport. Towards the end of the eighteenth century, however, hunt clubs began to be formed, these, by and large, corresponding to the British hunting packs. The British influence, in fact, has been the chief one in US and Canadian hunting developments; throughout their history, hunts and hunting in the USA and Canada have been based on the customs, traditions and techniques found in Britain, although the vastly different types of country and life-styles have led to various changes over the years.

Australian hunting is based on British precepts, too. However, the quarry there is not confined to the fox; in some parts of Australia, kangaroos are the major quarry.

Hunting today

When used in the context of hounds chasing a quarry, followed by mounted followers, the term 'hunting' refers to foxhunting, staghunting, hare-hunting (harriers), drag-hunting and hunting with bloodhounds. Of these, foxhunting is by far and away the most popular in Britain, Ireland and the USA. There are more than 200 packs of foxhounds in Britain, for instance, while all other types of hunting mentioned have only a handful of packs around the country (three packs of stag hounds, packs of harriers, packs of draghounds and three packs of bloodhounds, one of which is in the Isle of Man).

Although foxhunting is also the most popular type of hunting in the USA, with more than 100 packs of hounds, drag-hunting also has a considerable following. It accounts for 15 to

20 per cent of all hunting activity. In western states where foxes are very rarely found, the coyote is hunted. These wild dogs usually run in pairs and are reputed to give a tremendous day's sport. 'Blank' days (see glossary) are rare, but so, too, is a kill, for a coyote will normally outrun the pack. The only time when a kill takes place is said to be when the coyote is 'sick or full of chickens'!

Stag-hunting is still the mainstay of hunting with hounds and horses in France as previously mentioned, but the French also hunt wild boar and hares from horseback. Foxes are generally shot. There are a few packs of foxhounds in Italy and Spain, and a pack of bloodhounds in Germany.

Procedure and seasons

All hunts have the same hierarchy – that is a Master (a position often shared by two or more people), a huntsman (who may also be the Master) and a couple of Whippers-in (see p. 46). However, the procedure for each type of hunting and the techniques differ greatly.

At a foxhunt, the hounds are taken from the meet, put into a 'covert' (a wood), or led across moorland, pasture or whatever the country comprises, and encouraged by the huntsman to scent out a fox. Once they have found a line, the chase is on and they will follow where the fox leads until they either catch it and kill it, lose the line (because of poor scenting conditions, or because the fox is particularly cunning) or run it to ground. If they run it to ground, it is usual to dig the fox out (unless the earth is thought to be very large), after which it must be shot before being given to the hounds. How long it takes for hounds to catch a fox varies every time they find one; it may lead them across country for most of the day and still remain free at the end, or they may catch it almost at once. The huntsman will then try to put hounds on to another line.

By and large, foxhunting comes under the auspices and jurisdiction of the Master of Foxhounds Association (there is also an affiliated US association). Most packs of foxhounds seek to be recognized and registered with this organization. Without it, they are not authorized to hold a point-to-point (see page 55), which is generally a major source of funds, nor may they purchase new hounds from recognized packs. This means that they are not likely to have really top quality hounds. The Master of Foxhounds Association lays down certain rules connected with hunting and if a pack is found not to be adhering to them, it can face severe reprimand or expulsion from registration. The first and most important of these rules is that the fox must be hunted in its 'wild and natural state' – no catching of foxes to turn loose when hounds arrive.

Hunting seasons naturally differ from country to country. The season for foxhunting in the UK starts on November 1 (after that date

Opposite top: Another old hunting scene. This time mounted huntsmen pursue a leopard in India. There is scarcely an animal that man has not hunted from horseback at some time or other. **Opposite centre:** A late nineteenth-century print showing a lady taking a fence in style while hunting in Connecticut, USA. Sadly, the graceful art of side-saddle riding is seen less often in the hunting field nowadays. **Above:** The anti-hunting lobby is nothing new. Here a hunt in Ireland is stopped by angry dissidents in 1881. **Left:** A more tranquil scene. Huntsman and hounds are followed by the mounted field on a fox hunt in North Carolina, USA.

Right: Snowy conditions do not stop hounds hunting, but they occasionally mean that followers have to take to their feet. **Below left and right:** Two hunting scenes from the USA showing very different types of country. **Bottom:** Yet more hunting country in the USA. Here hounds are being taken out for exercise during the non-hunting season. Like any dog, a hound needs daily exercise.

all foxes are deemed to be 'foxes' rather than cubs) and ends usually sometime towards the end of March or early April. Stag-hunting enjoys a much longer season than foxhunting. It starts at the beginning of August, with the hunting of the 'autumn' stags (these are the biggest); this continues until towards the end of October, at which time there is a rest period of about 10 days. From the beginning of November until the end of February hinds are hunted – this is the only period when it is legal to pursue a hind. After this, there is another ten-day break and then 'spring' stag-hunting carries through until the end of April.

Stag-hunting and harrier hunting

At a staghunt, the pack is split up and only about five and a half couple (11 hounds) are used at the beginning. These hounds, known as the 'turfers', seek out the stag. However, they have to find a specific stag; this is one that has been watched by men called 'harbourers' in the night and morning period immediately preceding the hunt. The harbourers will tell the huntsman the whereabouts of the stag and what sort of 'head' he has – its pattern of antlers and so on. The huntsman takes the tufters to this spot and they then seek out the stag; the harbourers go too, so that if, by any chance, hounds get on the line of another stag – not the one the harbourers have been watching – the huntsman can be alerted to call them off.

Once on the right line, the tufters may pursue the stag over a distance of five to six kilometres (three to four miles), at which point the huntsman will stop them and put the remainder of the pack on to the line. However, by law, he must allow the stag 20 minutes' grace from the time he stops the tufters to the time he turns the rest of the pack loose. Staghounds will generally follow just one stag for the whole day and it can give them hours of sport. However, it is not uncommon to kill more than one hind.

Hunting with harriers is different again; in fact many packs of harriers are hunted entirely on foot, since the way a hare runs when pursued makes this perfectly possible. Unlike a fox, a hare runs in a circle – albeit often a very large one – and, because they live and are hunted in scrubby moorland-type country, it is often possible to observe much of the day's sport without moving at all. Not all packs of harriers are hunted on foot though; in many cases both huntsmen and followers are mounted. The sport is good for the riders, because although there are constant checks (hares being pursued will suddenly stop and drop down very low on the ground, so that, quite often, hounds go right past them), it is usually very easy to find hares and the pack is never still for long as a result. Harriers, it is said, find more hares than foxhounds do foxes, but they kill less. Another reason why the sport is good for the mounted follower is that the nature of the country and the way in which a hare runs makes it possible to see exactly what hounds are doing and just how they are working. In fox-hunting, where much of the finding is in heavy woodland, it is seldom a mounted follower can really watch hounds at work.

Draghunting

Draghunting differs greatly from the types of hunting so far discussed, in that it does not involve the pursuit of a living quarry. Instead, hounds follow a pre-determined line laid by dragging a piece of material impregnated with a strong-smelling substance across the ground. Traditionally, aniseed was used, but today a chemical preparation is generally substituted. The line is discussed beforehand with the farmers over whose ground it is to be laid; sometimes the huntsman is aware of its route, while at other times he only knows vaguely where it will be. There may be just one line per day (but it will have a few checks on it when, for example, riders have to hack up a road) or there may be several, according to the country. Weather conditions will affect the strength of the scent and how long it remains pungent, in the same way that it does when fox or stag-hunting, so it may be necessary for the huntsman to cast around in the middle of a line until hounds pick up the scent again.

A day's draghunting is generally short but fast and arduous. It gives the mounted followers a good ride across country; the line may involve the jumping of 40 to 50 obstacles — many of them demanding.

Bloodhound hunting

Hunting with bloodhounds is different again, for here the quarry is a human. He is generally given about a 25 minute start, before hounds are put on to his line and each hunt is scheduled to last about 45 minutes. It is usual to have three such hunts in an afternoon's sport, each of which is anything from five to eight kilometres (three to five miles) long and which may involve the riders in jumping anything up to 30 fences each time. The runner picks his line carefully to avoid going over growing crops, and is in no danger from the hounds. When they catch him, they give him a thorough licking, but no more than that. Packs of bloodhounds are privately owned, and hunting is by invitation of the Master only.

Draghunting and hunting with bloodhounds is known as 'clean boot' hunting. Riders are always assured of an extremely good, fast ride across country, but in spite of this, most hunt followers would claim that the 'sport' lacks the thrill of the chase connected with other forms of hunting, where the line is unknown and the outcome uncertain. Fewer hounds are used — only four-and-a-half to five-and-a-half couple generally, as against $17\frac{1}{2}$ to $19\frac{1}{2}$ couple in the other types of hunting. Smaller packs are found to be more efficient.

Above: A small pack of stag-hounds on a country track in Ireland. The horses of the huntsman and whipper-in are heavily built, with plenty of stamina for a day of galloping and jumping. **Left:** A wonderful view of the hunted deer for a lucky foot follower.
Below: A rare sight; a pack of bloodhounds setting off to find their human quarry. There are only three packs of bloodhounds in the U.K.

The hunter

Any horse that carries its rider across country, following hunting hounds, may be described as a hunter. There is no specific breed known as a hunter in the way that there is a Thoroughbred, a Quarter Horse or a Percheron, for example, and a look around the members of any hunting field will show you that horses of all sizes and shapes can be hunted quite satisfactorily. Nevertheless, the fact that certain qualities and characteristics are known to be desirable in a horse to be ridden to hounds has meant a recognizable 'type' has evolved.

Certainly, in terms of appearance, nowhere are the qualities of a hunter better seen than in the show hunter classes held at major horse shows, though most of the horses in the show ring will never have seen a pack of hounds. The obvious reason for this is that the merest scratch or blemish, which is a natural hazard of riding fast across country, would spell the end of their showing career and dramatically reduce their value. Nevertheless, they must display those characteristics of conformation, movement, and, as far as can be judged in cold blood, temperament and good manners that are most sought after in a hunter. In some instances, they will have more 'breeding' than is necessary for many hunters – show hunters are nearly always near-Thoroughbreds – but, particularly for people not wholly familiar with the look of a good hunter, it pays to spend some time visiting the major shows to assess the general qualities displayed by these horses.

Before you buy a hunter, you should consider the type of hunting you will be doing and the type of country you are going to be riding across. These factors will inevitably influence your decision as to what sort of horse to buy.

For drag, bloodhound and stag-hunting, you need a horse with a considerable amount of blood (Thoroughbred) in its breeding. All three sports are speedy and the latter two involve a considerable amount of jumping as well. This means that a horse of tremendous stamina is required. Open grassland or moorland country calls for the same sort of horse, because again, the day's sport is likely to be fast. A light-weight, racing type is ideal.

In heavily-enclosed, highly-cultivated farming country, on the other hand, a shorter-striding, more strongly-built horse, with a rather more placid temperament, would be infinitely more suitable. The finer legs of the Thoroughbred horse are not as suited to travelling across heavy plough, nor would its more temperamental nature stand it in good stead when it was asked to wait its turn at an enclosed, narrow jump, or while hounds are taking some time to draw through a covert. Equally, speed is not such an important factor, for in such country hounds tend to run for shorter bursts at a time.

Left: A lightweight show hunter poses for the camera. He has a beautifully proportioned head, gracefully arched neck, good sloping shoulder and rounded muscular hindquarters — all desirable characteristics in a hunter. **Above:** The legs of a hunter are extremely important for they have to carry him, literally, through the season. The front legs shown here are clean (that is free from blemishes) with short cannon bones and sloping pasterns. The hooves look smooth and rounded, and not too big.

Horses wanted to follow a pack of harriers must also possess speed, stamina and good jumping ability. Although, like stag-hunting, it is conducted in moorland country, a follower with harriers generally has to be able to jump to keep up with the pack. One mounted follower said it was not uncommon to jump more than 100 stone walls in a day with the pack he was following. You would therefore need a good jumper and a good stayer.

Your own capabilities

There is often a strong temptation to buy a horse that is really too much to handle, partly because you like the look of it and partly because it is human nature not to admit the possibility that you will not be able to get the best from that particular animal. The hunting field is no place for the horse that is a handful; the excitement that to a certain extent infects all horses when they go hunting, will make the hot-headed horse behave even more badly. Not only will you not enjoy yourself, you are a menace and a positive danger to everyone else. In extreme cases, the Master may even tell you to go home.

Deciding on the type of hunting that attracts you and establishing the sort of country you will be riding across, you can turn to the essential qualities that a hunter should possess. These are overall good conformation, denoting some quality of breeding, a comfortable ride, soundness, jumping ability, good manners, pleasant temperament and courage. One further quality is not conventionally included, but it is a vital one if you have to transport the horse to the hunt in a horse box – a willingness to box and lack of fear when travelling.

The points of the horse

Overall good conformation means that the horse is well-proportioned and has a good 'outline.' This means that the animal looks as though he fits together well – his head is not too big for the rest of his body, his neck is not too thick and his back is not too long. Look for strong, smooth, well-rounded hindquarters that look as if they house good muscle and, therefore, power. The shoulder should be sloping and not straight. The last quality is often easier to assess from the saddle, particularly to the less experienced judge of horse flesh; you should be able to see more easily and also feel that he really uses his shoulders to the full extent. A good sloping shoulder will give you the feeling of sitting well behind the withers, rather than being poised over them.

There should be a good 'depth of girth' – that is, from the back down to the belly – to ensure ample room for the lungs to function. The legs obviously are of paramount importance. Look for strong, clean legs with good sloping pasterns (upright pasterns do not act as good shock absorbers which means that the

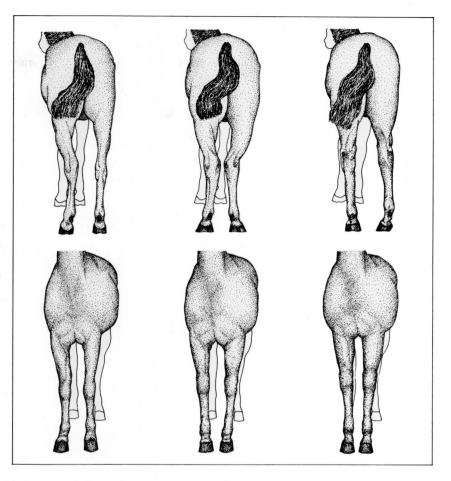

legs are more likely to be jarred when jumping or galloping on hard ground), well-shaped, correctly-angled hocks (not acutely bent or weak-looking) and well-formed, rounded, even feet. Beware of turned-in or turned-out front feet; besides possibly leading to unsoundness, they mean that a horse will have poor action.

The height of horse you are looking for will obviously depend on your own height and weight, but strangely enough, overall good conformation is more frequently found in smaller, rather than larger, horses. Many experienced riders consider 16hh is quite large enough to suit most people. In a taller horse, it becomes harder to find good conformation, and it becomes more expensive to keep.

A comfortable ride is tremendously important when you consider the length of time you might spend in the saddle during a day's hunting. Its key lies in the horse's action, so smoothness and evenness of pace are very important. Watch the action of the horse from the ground, making sure his leg movements are not particularly extravagant and his stride not too bouncy. Check in particular that he does not throw his front legs out to the side as he comes towards you and that there is no tendency to brush one leg against another. A horse that shows any signs of dragging a hind toe should be avoided – it can be a sign of future trouble. Reject a horse that leaves you feeling as if you have driven over rough country in a car with no springs.

Above: Some good and bad conformation points **Top row, left:** Good conformation. There is a straight line running from the point of the buttocks down through the hock to the hoof. **Centre:** The hocks are turning in – a condition known as cow hocks. For extreme hard work, such a horse would be best avoided. **Right:** The horse is bow-legged, that is his hocks turn out and his toes turn in. This puts a great strain on the ligaments of the legs. **Bottom row left:** Again, good conformation. A straight line runs from the point of the shoulder, through the knee to the hoof. **Centre:** The horse is pigeon-toed, which makes him prone to stumbling. **Right:** The front legs are set too close together making less room for the vital organs of heart and lungs. The horse is also likely to brush one leg against another which soon causes injury.

Soundness is of paramount importance in a hunter and probably something that you will have to leave to the vet to check. No right-minded dealer or person selling a horse will, after all, present one to a potential buyer with an obvious soundness defect or positive lameness. A basic unsoundness, however, can sometimes be detected if a horse is unwilling to jump and there is no apparent reason.

An ability to jump is important if you are hunting in country where to jump a fence means the difference between keeping up with hounds and getting left behind. When trying a horse, ride him over a few small jumps to begin with and see how he tackles them. He should clear them easily, almost just taking them in his stride and giving the impression that he has plenty in reserve. If you feel he has, try him over something bigger.

Horses to avoid

A hunter that does not have good manners and a pleasant temperament is a nuisance and a liability. Look at the horse's head and, most of all, his eye. Is it big and kind, or is it small and mean and constantly rolling to show the whites? Does he look gentle, or does he lay back his ears as you or anyone approaches? Many people will warn you off a horse with a pronounced bump on its forehead, saying this, too, is a sign of an uncertain temperament. The horse you are looking for should have a good, honest-looking, sensible head, with a kindly expression. Once astride his back, ride him directly away from his stable and yard. Does he go willingly, or is he nappy, agitated and cross? Check whether he is responsive to your aids, quick to answer your leg and generally listening to you as the rider. This perhaps has more to do with good schooling than good manners, but if you are looking for a 'made-hunter' (see glossary), it is important.

Courage and boldness are indeed important constituents of a hunter and perhaps the most difficult of all to assess at a trial. Up to a point you have to rely on experience – on the intuition a horseman will have as he rides a horse. If you do not feel you possess this, take someone experienced along with you when trying a horse. To a certain extent, you can test a horse's courage by its willingness and its performance in cold blood. A horse that will jump a big, or difficult, or tricky-looking fence when not following hounds, will certainly do so when the pack is in full cry in front of him.

Further precautions

It is always a good idea to ask to see a horse boxed and unboxed before buying him. If he arrives at your stable and is led out of his box, you will have no idea of any possible difficulties that might be encountered in getting him loaded. Should a prospective seller be unwilling to go through the exercise of boxing the horse, persist or do not buy the animal.

It goes without saying that any horse you are considering buying, should first be checked by a veterinary surgeon. But if you like the animal, make your offer (and remember most advertised prices are open to negotiation) subject to the vet's report. If you consider the horse a good buy, the chances are that other people will do so too, for good horses, particularly at reasonable prices, are hard to come by. If you dither over your decision, it may be too late. If, though, you are having difficulty in making up your mind – if you like some points, but are not so sure about others – it probably is not the horse for you.

Just how to find a good hunter, and even where to look for it, is not easy. Hunting friends will often know if a horse is up for sale in their hunt and they should be able to advise you as to its merits and demerits. Reading advertisements in horse magazines and periodicals is another way, but remember, if an advertisement states 'genuine hunter', check where it has been hunted. If it is not a part of the country with which you are familiar, either pay it a visit or find someone who knows about it. If it is vastly dissimilar to your country, the horse may not be what you require. Try also to

Opposite left: A veterinarian checks a horse's leg for soundness. Obtaining a vet's certificate for any horse you mean to buy is quite expensive, but vital. **Opposite right:** If your hunting country is well fenced, it is important to have a horse that will jump. Try him over a fence when you go to see him; if he will jump in 'cold blood', he will certainly do so when following a pack of hounds. **Below:** All hunters need and deserve a period of rest out at grass. If you look at a horse for sale during his rest period, take an experienced horseman with you. It is not always easy to spot the good or bad points of a horse when he is looking fat and rough.

find someone who knows the horse and has seen its performance in the hunting field.

Many of the best hunters, particularly in the past, have come from Ireland. International popularity has sent prices sky high. In addition, they have proved so successful at show jumping and eventing that they are being snapped up for these sports too. The Irish hunter was traditionally bred from an Irish Draught mare crossed with a Thoroughbred or near-Thoroughbred. It is said that the 'pedigree' of a half-bred Irish horse may not be as reliable as the sellers would have you believe, but the reputation continues to be well-founded; such horses encounter only banks, ditches and stone walls in Ireland but rarely show reluctance when faced with big timber fences found in other hunting fields.

Preparing for the season

The main task which faces the owner is to get the horse fit. A horse that has been taught to jump in cold blood will certainly do so out hunting. If he has been well-schooled, he should also behave well, so there is no great need for any special training. A young horse, however, should be introduced to hounds gently and sensitively (see p. 48).

Any horse that is required to work hard at its destined sport for a number of months each year needs a period of rest. The usual time for a hunter to have this is during the summer. Its length will depend on how hard the horse has hunted and the sort of condition he is in, but all will need a couple of months' complete rest without exception, this time being increased if, for instance, the horse concerned is in particularly poor condition when turned out. During this time they should be kept in a well-fenced field, where the grazing is good and where there is some shade provided by trees or a shelter. It is usual to take the hind shoes off, but to leave the front ones on, if the ground is very hard, to prevent the front feet cracking. The farrier should see the horse once a month to trim the feet and the owner should visit the horse once a day to check its condition.

Just when you bring a horse in from grass to prepare him for the oncoming season depends on when you want to have him fit. It will take a minimum of eight weeks to get a horse to hunting fitness and probably nearer 10 or 12 weeks to achieve tip-top fitness. Taking fox-hunting as an example, you would probably estimate backwards from the opening meet, but bear in mind that cubhunting (see glossary) starts before this. In some parts of the USA, where the winters are very hard, hunts begin hunting proper in the autumn, rather than in early winter as in the UK, and cubbing may start as early as July. In such instances there is generally a break in the early months of the year when hunting is impossible.

Traditionally, members of a hunt would go cubbing (which is the time young hounds are being introduced to hunting) only at the invitation of the Master. No-one, therefore, should go out cubbing without first telephoning the hunt secretary to ask permission.

If you want your horse to be reasonably fit for cubbing, you must take this into account when considering the time to bring him in from grass. Up to a point, going cubbing can be a useful part of the conditioning programme. If, for instance, you have a very strong horse, there is something to be said for having him only at fifty to seventy-five per cent fitness when you first venture out cubbing; you will have that much more chance of remaining in control. As a general indication, most horses would need about six weeks' work before going out cubbing. Remember, though, that it is not necessary to stay out for the full duration of the cub hunt if you feel your horse is not yet up to it.

Up from grass

If you bring your horse up from grass in mid to late summer, you might like to consider keeping him on a half-and-half system for the first few weeks. This entails keeping him in the stable by day and turning him out in the paddock by night. It is preferable to effect any change in a horse's routine gradually, while the use of this system also means he can get rid of any over-exuberance in the field without impeding the fitness programme. A young horse, in particular, may well have all sorts of psychological problems if he goes from perpetual freedom to perpetual confinement.

The reason for stabling the horse in the day and turning it out at night is simple, though the procedure may seem a slightly perverse one. Many horses can be adversely affected by heat and flies, which are frequently features of summer days. These can cause major problems with thin-skinned Thoroughbreds, who lose weight and condition and become agitated.

As soon as the horse begins work he must be fed, even if he has a grass belly. Corn feed is essential in helping to harden a horse and some people like to begin giving a couple of small feeds a day in the last week or so of the rest period, thus helping to prepare the animal for life in the stable. Do not be too surprised if he prefers to eat grass.

The business of getting a horse fit is divided into three principal areas – exercise routine, feeding programme and overall stable management. These are discussed individually, but remember that they have to be sensitively and sensibly combined over the conditioning period, if the maximum fitness is to be achieved with the minimum of problems.

Exercise

Throughout your conditioning programme, always aim to work your horse for six days a week and give him one day's rest. The first two to three weeks' 'work' means nothing more

---

UP FROM GRASS – SIX THINGS TO DO

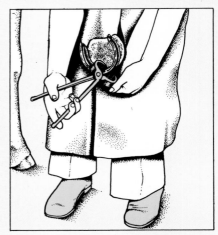

Call the farrier to check his feet and put on a new set of shoes. Ask for these to be fitted with stud holes if you think this is necessary.

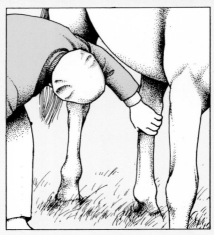

Check the animal over very thoroughly for bumps, swellings, scratches and so on. Pay particular attention to the legs, looking for signs of heat or tenderness.

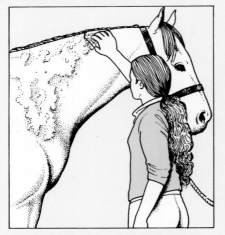

If the weather is reasonably mild, give him a bath. This is optional, but it is a good way of ridding the coat of parasites. Rub down and walk round until quite dry.

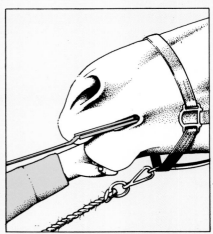

Check the teeth to see if they are long, uneven or sharp. If they are, they will need rasping so that the horse does not experience discomfort when eating.

Give a worm dose but make sure you keep him stabled the following night otherwise the worms will spread in his dung. Repeat every six to eight weeks.

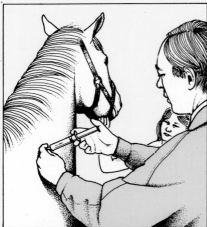

Ask your vet to come and give him an influenza injection. This provides year round immunity and can be combined with an anti-tetanus booster.

than walking. Do not be tempted to cut this period short, however boring it may become. It is essential in order to develop and harden the horse's muscles and readjust him to having a rider on his back, without either over-taxing his heart and lungs or running the risk of jarring his legs. Tedious though this walking period is, it is impossible to overstress its importance. If the conditioning is not done gradually and thoroughly, there is little hope of having a sound horse at the end of the hunting season.

The first walking sessions should last 20 to 30 minutes a day, sticking to roads or smooth tracks where there is no danger of tripping or stumbling over ruts. Make the horse work beneath you – he should not just be slopping along, even though he is only walking. Increase the time little by little, so you are up to about one-and-a-half hours by the end of the second week. Vary the time according to the horse's response; at no stage in the conditioning programme should your horse ever be really puffing and heaving, while, of course, you should never bring him back to the stable sweating heavily.

You may find that your horse, fresh from this period of rest, finds walking as boring as you do and may dance and prance around or strain to go faster. Sit still and quietly on his back and bring him back to a walk with the minimum of fuss – never be tempted to 'work off' his spirits by giving him a burst of a faster pace.

Trotting – the best stage

Sometime during the third week you can introduce gentle trotting into the routine, but, since all horses are different, the exact moment when this can begin will vary with each individual. As a rough guide, you can begin trotting when your horse is returning to the stable as fresh as he started, after a good 90 minutes.

It is the trotting movement that most jars a horse's legs, so ask him to trot slowly (but still working beneath you) to begin with and for bursts of no more than about 200 metres (200 yards). Include no more than four of these the first day. Never trot the horse right at the beginning of a ride; do at least a quarter-of-an-hour's good walking first. Do some trotting on the road and the remainder on softer, but still firm, ground.

After a few days of trotting, you can introduce some lungeing into the programme. It is best to combine this with some ridden work, perhaps reducing the riding time, resting the horse for a while, and then lungeing him for 10 minutes or so on either rein. By now, you should be aiming to give about two hours' exercise in all per day.

The routine continues in much the same vein in the fourth week. Trotting periods out on a ride can be longer, but remember never to do so much that the horse is really blowing. Find some long steady hills, walk up half-way

and then trot the remainder. Providing you never over-do this, hill climbing is excellent for hardening the horse's muscles and it is good exercise for his lungs as well. It is now also a good idea to include some ridden schooling work in the routine. Do some circling work at the walk and trot on either rein in a school, but again intersperse this with exercise and lungeing. Never let your horse get bored or stale.

From trot to canter

As with trotting, just when some gentle, steady cantering can be included in the routine will vary from horse to horse. Again, be guided by his condition after perhaps a two-hour ride which contained a fair amount of trotting, including one or two long spells uphill. If he arrived at the top of these with his breathing still fairly even and not strained, start to include some cantering.

Choose the ground carefully for your first canter – somewhere flat and firm that is not too

Above: Getting a horse ready for the hunting season means getting him fit, hardening up his legs and making sure his wind and respiratory system are in efficient working order. Much of this is achieved by regular steady exercise at a fairly slow pace. Road work is vital. Steady walking, and later jogging, along the roads will help to harden the legs and develop the correct muscles.

soft or dotted with pot-holes. Ask for a canter as quietly as you can; the horse will be just as excited and impatient as you. Indeed, his pleasure at this faster pace may well lead him to give a buck or two; just sit there quietly – he should soon settle down.

By the end of the sixth week you should be able to include three or four periods of steady cantering in a ride. At the end of this, though the horse will naturally be blowing, he should not be blowing overtly. You can begin to judge how fit he is by how long it takes him to recover. The fitter a horse, the quicker he recovers from any exertion. Keep all the paces steady; cantering should be nothing approaching flat out, and it should be at the pace you, not the horse, desire. Getting the horse to obey you is very important at this time; if the horse is not obedient now, he certainly will not be when he is fit. To this end, begin to ask more of your schooling sessions, including some sitting trot work (which is far more tiring, but more muscle-developing for the horse than the rising trot). Perhaps put him through an elementary dressage test, and ask for some cantering in circles with steady, smooth, controlled changes of leg.

The exercise routine continues in much the same vein through the seventh and eighth weeks. It is sometimes a good idea to box the horse to a different area for a ride now; it gets him used to the idea of going in a box before being asked to work and ensures that he will be well settled for travelling before it really matters to you. You can go out cubbing too, which will get him used to hounds as well as giving him a good work-out. If you think you are likely to encounter jumps, it is a good idea to pop him over a few small ones at home.

During the season

Throughout the hunting season, days' sport will be interspersed with exercise days. The routine of these will follow much the same as the ones in the latter weeks of the conditioning programme. Aim to give your horse one day's rest a week and on non-hunting days to exercise him for a good hour-and-a-half a day (the day following a hunt, reduce this to about half-an-hour's gentle walking). Exercise should include steady walking, trotting and cantering just as you have been doing. It can also include one good 'pipe-opener,' when you really let the horse have his head over a suitable stretch of ground. On mild days, and certainly on his rest day, he will probably appreciate a couple of hours turned out in the paddock, but make sure he is well rugged-up for the occasion.

Feeding

Feeding horses is an art and therefore cannot conform to hard and fast rules. How much to feed a horse depends not only on how hard he is working and his size, but also on his age,

temperament and individual appetite. Some horses are known as 'bad doers', meaning they are fussy eaters, on whom it is hard both to get and maintain flesh; others eat anything and always look well.

The feeding of any horse is tinged with a certain amount of trial and error. Although you should always ask about a horse's feeding habits when you buy him, up to a point you will have to experiment until you find what suits your horse best. Although it is usual to feed oats to horses in work, for example, some horses simply cannot be given them, since even a small amount will excite them to the point where they can become almost uncontrollable. Such animals have to be given a substitute protein ration, such as horse nuts (see above).

The most important aspect of feeding any

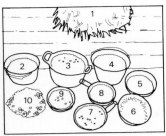

1. Hay, a bulk food which replaces the grass a horse would constantly nibble at if he were turned out in a field, or supplements meagre grazing. **2.** Sugar beet pulp is used to provide bulk and variety in a diet. It must be soaked for at least 12 hours before feeding or it will lead to indigestion and choking. During the soaking it swells enormously so will absorb a lot of water. **3.** Flaked maize is an energy-producing food and forms a horse's staple diet in some parts of the world. **4.** Oats are generally considered to be the best protein for horses. They should be bruised or crushed. Use good quality oats – clean and floury. **5.** Barley is fed whole or rolled. Rolled barley can replace oats in a diet. **6.** Chaff is chopped-up hay that is mixed with a corn feed to provide bulk and to prevent a horse from bolting the food. Chaff is best prepared on the premises using a chaff cutter and best quality hay. **7.** Bran is another bulk food that is usually mixed with the protein in a feed. Mixed with hot water to make a mash, it provides a laxative as well as an easily digested meal. **8.** Linseed, available in various forms, is fed to give variety in the diet, to improve an animal's condition and to make the coat shiny. **9 and 10.** Commercially prepared horse or pony cubes contain a balanced mix of protein and bulk feeds, although they are generally mixed with bran.
Bottom: A bale of horsehage (left) and a bale of ordinary hay (right). Despite the difference in size, they should last the same amount of time.

Linseed and barley are both fed boiled and are good flesh-producers. Horses generally find them very appetising. To prepare them, soak both feedstuffs for several hours, then bring to the boil and simmer for at least six hours. You will need to add more water as it is absorbed during the simmering process. Boiled barley is particularly fattening, so feed it carefully (no more than once a week). Linseed helps to give the coat a shine and can be fed twice a week.

Maize is fed flaked as another source of protein. Only small amounts mixed with the feed should be given, as it is both somewhat indigestible and can also lead to overheating. Sugar beet is another great favourite that is very fattening. It must be soaked overnight before feeding and acts as a good dampener for a feed. Horse nuts are commercially prepared 'cubes' which contain a complete, balanced diet, although most people like to feed bran with them. Several different preparations are available for feeding in varying conditions. They are extremely convenient and most horses do extremely well on them, but many people prefer to monitor exactly what their horses eat

Bran has virtually no protein value, but adds bulk to a feed and helps to make it more digestible. The best type to buy is 'broad bran'. The sweetness of molasses and black treacle can make a feed more appetising, while succulent fruit and vegetables – such as carrots (sliced lengthwise), cut-up apples, parsnips, turnips and swedes – are of benefit in the diet. You will need to experiment to find the kinds your horse likes best.

Hay is the dried grass fed to a stabled horse to take the place of the grass it would eat in the natural course of grazing. Its quality varies greatly; look for hay that is sweet-smelling and in no way mouldy, musty or dusty. Chaff is finely-chopped hay that is mixed with a corn feed to provide roughage, and to slow down the horse's rate of eating to aid digestion. Good chaff is increasingly difficult to buy; it is often more convenient to make it at home with a chaff-cutter to chop only good quality hay. Horsehage is comparatively new feedstuff, sometimes used in place of hay with horses suffering respiratory disorders and prone to coughing. This can often happen among horses required to do fast and strenuous work. Horsehage is made from grass, or grass and clover mixtures, in the same way as hay, but it is baled when the grass is half-dry. The bales are treated so that no heating can take place (but no chemical additives are used), before being pressed down to less than half their size and vacuum-sealed. This treatment ensures that the dried grass harbours no dust, and it is also claimed to retain a higher protein content.

Horses in hard work will also benefit from a daily dose of cod liver oil (a generous tablespoon) and some additional vitamin supplement. Many brands of the latter are available, each carrying instructions on dosage.

animal – a horse included – lies in what you observe. Notice how your horse reacts to the feeds you give him, as well as keeping a constant check on how fat or thin he is. It is such observation that will teach you the art of feeding.

Types of food

Before giving any guidelines about how much to feed and how to increase this as exercise increases, it is worth considering the various foodstuffs available. Oats are the most frequently used principal protein source. They can be fed whole, bruised (which helps digestion, particularly in fast feeders who may otherwise just swallow them whole) or crushed. If, however, they are crushed excessively, much of their goodness will be lost.

Above: It is a good idea to damp down hay before feeding to stabled horses. Running water over it from a hose pipe is usually adequate, but if horses show any signs of coughing, the hay should be dunked in a trough of water so it is thoroughly wetted, not just damp.

The principles of feeding

The principles of feeding in a conditioning programme are to give small corn feeds and a relatively large amount of hay when the horse first comes up from grass and to increase the corn ration gradually as work increases and the horse gets fitter while lessening the amount of hay. As a horse gets fit, he requires comparatively little bulk food in his diet, but a lot of protein to give energy. The bran ration, for example, will increase less in proportion than the oats or hard feed, but remember it is always important to feed some roughage (hay, chaff, bran and, to a certain extent, sugar beet). The ratio of concentrated feed to roughage should never be more than 60 per cent to 40 per cent.

When you first bring your horse up from grass, you will be giving him two small feeds a day. Start a horse of 15.2hh off on 900g–1.3kg (2lbs–3lbs) of corn a day, mixed with a similar quantity of bran. Over the eight weeks of the feeding programme, gradually increase this ration to about 4.5kg (10lbs) a day, but increase the bran amount to no more than 900g (2lbs) a day. Establish a basic source of protein (oats if they agree with your horse, nuts if oats do not)

and then vary it a couple of times a week just to ring the changes. You can do this by feeding any one of the protein sources already mentioned, although it should not be substituted for the full corn ration. Give half oats and, say, half boiled barley. Always damp down a feed; this makes it more palatable and also helps to eliminate any dust, which may be found in bran and poorer quality oats, for example. Use hot water in cold, winter weather.

Ideally, by the end of the sixth week of the conditioning programme, you should be dividing the feeding ration into three feeds a day. Purists claim that four feeds a day should be given, but three are quite adequate. Few hunting horses will suffer from three slightly bigger feeds a day.

When the hunting season begins, it is a good idea to give a horse a hot feed – perhaps twice a week – at the end of a day's hunting. It is both warming and digestible. The most usual form of hot feed is a bran mash, which is merely bran damped down with boiling water. This, however, merely acts as a laxative. A better version is a mash using the normal amount of oats, with the bran increased a little and the two mixed together with boiling water.

At the start of the programme, the hay ration for a 15.2hh horse will probably begin at about 9kg (20lbs). This can be gradually cut down to about 4.5kg (10lbs). Divide it into two, feeding some after exercise and the majority at night. Damp down the hay thoroughly if it is at all dusty (see left). If you are feeding horsehage, it is probably as well to divide the ration between this and hay. Although the former is very good, it can sometimes cause scouring. Some also claim it is very expensive to feed, but this should not be the case; not only is horsehage not much more expensive than top-quality hay, but there is also little waste. Horses will eat every scrap, while, since it is more compact than hay, far less drops down into the bedding to be trampled underfoot. Also, because of horsehage's higher protein content, it is sometimes possible to reduce slightly the hard feeds that are fed for protein. If you do find horsehage much more expensive than hay, you are probably not buying hay of sufficiently good quality.

The good horsemaster

The stable management or horsemastership of the conditioning programme is equally as important as the exercise and feeding routines. A horse that is not properly cared-for cannot be happy; if he is not happy, he will be neither well nor fit.

It is vital that you watch over your horse extremely carefully when you first bring him up from grass. It is in these early days, before he gets into the swing of the new routine, that minor things can go wrong. Check his feet and shoes daily, making sure that there is no hint of lameness, caused perhaps by a new shoe pinching or rubbing to produce a sore spot. As you pick out the feet each day, check to see that the shoes have not slipped or the clenches have not risen unduly. The horse will probably need a new set of shoes sometime in the fourth week and again towards the eighth.

Watch, too, for any signs of soreness on the head and round the back and girth region. Another reason for building up the amount of work given per day slowly is to give the horse's skin a chance to get used to wearing tack again and to harden up accordingly. If you know your horse has particularly sensitive skin, you can try helping to harden it by rubbing surgical spirit into danger areas a week or two before bringing him up from grass and on return from exercise when this begins. Use a string girth to begin with, rather than a leather one, which is more likely to rub, however supple it is. Put a numnah under the saddle to help to protect the back. Always keep your tack clean and supple and check it each time you clean it to ensure no stitching is coming undone or straps are not wearing thin under buckles.

Check the corners of the mouth each time you return from exercise to make sure the bit is not rubbing. Wash the bit when you come in to remove any saliva; otherwise this will harden and certainly cause rubbing. If you notice any slight soreness – excessive reddening rather than actual cracking – gently rub some grease, such as vaseline, over the affected part.

Feel the legs thoroughly each time you return from exercise to make sure there are no bumps, soft swellings or hot areas. Providing you stick to the slow, gradual programme recommended, you should have no trouble. If you do, however, but can spot it and attend to it in its early stages, there should have no long term damage.

You may well find that in the early days of coming up from grass, particularly if the horse is completely stabled, that he develops a cough. Providing that he still looks well – there are no other cold or 'flu symptoms, such as a runny nose, dull eyes and so on – this is probably a 'management' cough, resulting from a reaction to the changes in environment. Check first of all whether the animal is eating his bedding, as this will certainly result in coughing. If you are using straw as bedding, he may well be eating it; first of all try sprinkling it with disinfectant. For some horses this is sufficient deterrent, but many will merely scrabble around underneath the surface straw to find the palatable bits. The best thing then is to change the type of bedding, substituting either shavings, sawdust or even shredded paper.

The other thing to do is to check the hay for dustiness. If it seems the slightest bit unsatisfactory, wet it. This does not mean, as many think, dribbling a small bucket of water over a full haynet. Instead, positively saturate it, either by running a hose over it, or by dunking it in a bath of water. Hang it up to drain thoroughly, though, before putting in the box.

If your horse does develop such a cough, try to give him as much time as possible turned out in the paddock, particularly if the weather is not too wet or cold. Fresh air is the best cure.

The importance of grooming

Daily grooming of your horse does far more than improve the appearance. It helps to tone and harden the muscles, it stimulates the blood circulation to the skin and it massages the coat. Build up the grooming routine gradually; do not attempt to give your horse a full strapping in the first week you bring him in – he needs time to adjust to this gradually. You should begin to see some results towards the end of the second week and by the fifth or sixth week the changes should be obvious. The coat should be sleek and the muscles hard and well-formed, with no flabby areas along the neck, shoulders or hindquarters.

It is generally stated that a full strapping of a horse should take at least an hour, but few owner/grooms have this much time to spare each day for grooming. Make sure, therefore, that what you do really counts; brush the coat (with the body brush) as though you mean it,

Top: In all probability, this horse is merely enjoying a roll in the field. However, should he have colic (severe stomach ache) he must not be allowed to roll as it could lead to a twisted gut. Some of the symptoms of colic are discomfort and restlessness, looking round at or kicking his own belly and sweating. **Above left:** Coughing is an all-too-common complaint among horses. There are several reasons for coughing – colds, laryngitis, wind disorder, reaction to environment etc. You must determine the cause before treatment, but in almost all cases, a coughing horse should not be ridden. **Above centre:** Signs of laminitis, an inflammatory condition of the sensitive lining beneath the wall of the hoof which leaves the foot ridged and mis-shapen. It can be caused by too much hard, fast trotting on the roads. **Above:** Cracked hooves do not always lead to lameness but are a nuisance nonetheless. Pictured here is a sandcrack, which runs downwards from the coronet. It is not always visible at the top of the hoof but it spreads out further down.

not just glossing over the surface. Do all the grooming you are going to do at one time; do not spend the day popping in and out of the box, constantly bothering the horse whenever you have a minute or two to spare. He will get very bored with this and probably soon get niggly and bad-tempered, particularly when you approach with a brush in your hand.

Pull the mane and tail within the first few weeks of bringing him up from grass, doing this a little at a time if either or both are very thick. The mane may well stick up like a scrubbing brush when first pulled; damp it down over the neck, or in extreme cases, plait it loosely to encourage it to lie flat.

Rugging-up and clipping

Rugging-up is another subject to be introduced gradually. If you keep a summer-sheet on your horse when you first bring him in (and the weather is still warm), it will get him used to wearing a rug, and also will help to keep the coat clean and flat. An owner/groom, in particular, will find such labour-saving points invaluable. Keep an eye on all pressure points under a rug constantly to make sure there is no rubbing. Gradually increase the weight of the rug or the number of blankets underneath as the weather gets colder, or because you have removed the coat by clipping.

Points to watch for

Almost the most important aspect of stable management lies in the daily observation of your horse, as mentioned earlier. Unless you really know him well, you will not notice changes and it is catching such changes as soon as they happen, and taking the appropriate action, that will ensure you have a fit and healthy horse for the entire hunting season. If, for example, your horse begins to lose weight, do something about it immediately, but first of all try to determine why he is losing weight. Are you hunting him too hard? Are his teeth too sharp so that it hurts him to eat? Is the feedstuff you are giving him of a poor quality? Obviously you deal with each of these problems accordingly, but, if the answer to all of them is no, it may be that you are simply not giving him enough flesh-producing food. If you allow a horse to lose an excessive amount of weight during the hunting season, you will find it very hard to put it back on again and a thin horse cannot be expected to give a first-rate performance.

At the end of the hunting season, do not imagine you can return from the closing meet, turn your horse out in the field and leave him for the summer. Just as the conditioning programme has to be gradual, so must the 'let-down' process be, too. Gradually reduce the amount of feed, and the amount of exercise given each day and, as the weather gets warmer, reduce the number of rugs. If you try to rush

Above: Correct dress in the hunting field is deemed important among the hunting fraternity. In this hunt, the hunt staff wear a mustard-yellow coat which is fairly unusual.
Right: A lady wearing correct hunting dress, although she is holding a cane not a hunting whip. She wears a bowler, black jacket, shirt and white stock, white breeches, long black boots and string gloves.
Below: Hunting dress follows the same traditional style in the USA. Hunt staff and followers of this American hunt could easily be mistaken for British!

HUNTING DRESS

Above: A superb picture illustrating the correct, traditional dress of a huntsman in the hunting field. He wears a velvet cap, white stock, traditional 'hunting pink' or scarlet coat which will include the hunt collar and buttons, white breeches and boots topped with a mahogany-coloured band of leather and worn with spurs. It is obvious he is the huntsman because he carries the horn which he uses to encourage hounds as he hunts them, and attached to his saddle is a gun, which must be used to shoot the fox if it is dug out from its earth.

All hunts have their own individual design of collar and hunt button which distinguishes them from other hunts. These are worn by the hunt staff and selected members of the field invited to do so by the Master of the hunt.

The correct dress for ladies is shown opposite. Mounted male followers would wear either a black jacket and a bowler hat or a scarlet coat and a silk top hat. Like the huntsman's, their breeches are white and the long black boots have a brown band at the top.

Children should wear a neat tweed (or black) hacking jacket, a velvet cap, shirt and tie, jodhpurs and jodhpur boots or breeches and long boots. All mounted followers should carry a hunting whip. In the cubhunting season, 'ratcatcher's' gear is worn. Hunt staff will be dressed as usual, although probably not in their best coats and breeches. Other people can wear a tweed hacking jacket with a roll-neck sweater or a shirt and tie. They would wear a bowler hat or velvet cap and breeches and boots, but the overall impression does not have to be as smart as for hunting proper.

CLIPPING

Most hunters are clipped — that is all or part of their coat is removed — for the hunting season. Without a thick winter coat they can perform much better as they do not sweat up so easily. They are also easier to keep clean. If the winter coat is not removed, it will be impossible to get the horse fit, and he will never look really smart. Clipping also makes him much easier to cool off after

exercise, so that he can be rugged-up as soon as he is brought back to the stable.

There are various types of clip but the most usual for a hunter is a 'hunter clip'. This is shown very well above; the whole coat is removed except for on the legs and a patch under the saddle, where hair is left for protection. Some people prefer to remove the hair from the legs

altogether, making them easier to keep clean and examine for injury.

If your horse is going to spend the major part of most days out at grass (if you do not have sufficient time to exercise him for example) you should consider a trace or blanket clip in which less hair is removed. In particular the hair is left over the back and loins.

any of these procedures, you will have problems on your hands — the horse will either become sick or he will be generally upset and agitated. As the days become warmer, turn him out for longer periods in the paddock, but still bring him in at night and do not cut his food rations out altogether. By and large, the end of May or the beginning of June are the earliest times that it is possible to turn a horse out completely, with his shoes off.

The hunt hierarchy

The hierarchy of the hunt is as follows. The Master is the man or woman who has overall responsibility for all aspects of a hunt, including the kennelling of hounds and stabling of horses, arranging where and when meets will take place, liaising with farmers and landowners and so on. Nowadays, very few hunts have just one Master; two or more share the duties, each being responsible for a specific part of the country, and they receive considerable backing and help from the Hunt Committee.

In many hunts, one of the Masters will hunt hounds. If he does not do so, hounds will be hunted by a professional huntsman, who will be paid by the hunt. The 1st Whipper-in is also a professional. His job is to assist the huntsman during the hunt, while he may hunt hounds on days when the huntsman is indisposed for any reason. The 2nd Whipper-in is another member of the hunt staff, with similar responsibilities. The Kennel-huntsman looks after hounds in the kennels, though this job is often done by the huntsman. The Field Master, on

the other hand, is an amateur and a member of the Hunt Committee. He is responsible for organizing the mounted followers, generally trying to keep them in order and make sure any damage is reported to the farmer involved.

To be able to hunt, you must pay a subscription to the pack you would like to follow. The procedure for this is to contact the Secretary of the hunt and ask if you may join the hunt. Many packs are 'over-subscribed' — that is they are only prepared to accept so many mounted followers and they already have this number as subscribers. They will not take new members, therefore, until an existing member has dropped out. At one time, no subscription was paid to go cub-hunting, but in these days of financial pressure, many hunts do charge.

Hunting etiquette

Obviously, all mounted followers should show courtesy and respect to the Master(s) and all members of the hunt staff. This entails getting out of their way at all times (pulling over in a narrow ride, for example, to let them pass) and giving them all possible assistance when required. This could be anything from telling them which way the fox has gone, to holding their horses if they have to tramp through a wood where it is impossible to ride. Make sure other members of the field know if the huntsman is coming up behind them and wants to get past and always turn your horse's head towards hounds. To allow a horse to kick a hound is one of the most unforgiveable sins of all in the hunting field.

A Master of Foxhounds, is always addressed as 'Master' and it is obvious politeness to say 'Good morning, Master' to him or her at the meet. Should they be present when you are leaving the hunt in the afternoon, you would also say goodnight (after midday, it is always goodnight).

The most important thing to remember when hunting is that you are a 'guest' of farmers and landowners and it is only through their generosity that you are able to hunt over the land at all. Show respect for this – never ride over sown fields or growing crops, but keep well to the edge of the field. In excessively wet conditions, try to avoid galloping full tilt across grass fields, too; the damage a number of galloping horses can do by cutting up the ground is considerable. Never leave gates open, especially when there is livestock turned out in the field and, should you have the misfortune to crash into a fence and break it, do your best to repair the damage at once and notify the Field Master immediately. The really con-

scientious will get to know the farmers over whose land they ride, at least by sight, so they can acknowledge and thank them when they see them.

Be courteous to the other members of the hunt, too. Never barge past people, particularly in a narrow ride. Wait your turn at a jump and do not push to the front of the queue; when it is your turn to jump, make sure you have given the person in front ample time to land and move away from the fence. Take your turn in holding gates open for the rest of the mounted field and remember to thank those who do the same for you. If you are the last through a gate, wait until the person holding it has shut it.

Never ride past someone who has fallen off; stop and make sure they are all right. Similarly, if you see a loose horse, do not go galloping on regardless, leaving others to catch it. Try to catch it, or if other, more experienced, people are already doing so, keep your horse still to avoid exciting the loose horse still further.

Some people find jumping a great temptation in the hunting field and are inclined to jump everything in sight. You will never see a wise, experienced rider doing this; he jumps only when necessary. If there is a choice of places to jump an obstacle, such as a post and rails or a hedge, he will choose the place where the ground offers the best take-off. Similarly, this person will only gallop full tilt when it is absolutely necessary – that is, when hounds are in full cry in front of him. At other times, he has consideration for his mount. He always rides slowly and steadily across heavy plough, knowing that to gallop in such heavy going will soon result in sprained tendons or other leg problems. Thus he is always present at the closing meet of the season, when other people's horses are lame or otherwise debilitated.

If you know your horse to be a 'kicker' – or to be the slightest bit unreliable when other horses are around – the usual practice is to plait a red ribbon into his tail. However, this does not lessen your responsibility; if your horse kicks another horse or rider, you will be the one to blame. In such circumstances, keep well to the back at all times and avoid any crowded places, such as narrow gateways. If you suspect your horse kicks, it is infinitely better to try to cure him of this habit before bringing him out with hounds. The habit is prone to develop in a young horse and can generally be overcome by hitting the animal hard with a riding crop whenever it occurs. He will soon learn that lashing out with the heels produces a reaction.

For yourself, remember that you are part of a group – a piece in a jigsaw. People who hunt as individuals, rather than as a thinking part of a much bigger whole, are a nuisance and a danger to themselves and others. When a farmer refuses to have the hunt across his land, it is often because of just one person like this. Finally, learn as much as you can about the arts and techniques of hunting. Those who have even a little knowledge about the way hounds work will not only make more sensitive members of the mounted field, but also will enjoy their hunting infinitely more than the untutored.

The young horse and hounds

The first principle every rider should bear in mind when introducing a young horse to hounds is that the hunting field is not the place to try to further his knowledge in any other way. In other words, do not bring a horse out hunting until you are confident that he is well-schooled and well-mannered. If you are going to ask him to jump, he should already have been taught to do so – a farmer's fences should not be used as schooling obstacles. Teach him how to stand and move when you want to open a gate from his back, too, before he has to do this in the hunting field in the company of others.

HORSES AND HOUNDS

Opposite, top left: Hounds wait patiently to move off. **Opposite, top right:** A red ribbon tied round the tail of a horse indicates that he has a tendency to kick. It does not absolve the rider from responsibility but it does act as a warning to others. **Opposite centre:** The Eskdale and Ennerdale hounds being exercised across bracken-covered moors. **Opposite, bottom left:** The Tiverton Stag hounds. **Opposite, bottom right:** A young horse being introduced to hounds at the kennels. Few people have the opportunity to do this, but it is a great help in overcoming any initial fear. **Above:** A familiar sight for hunting people. Mounted followers keep a respectable distance behind hounds and huntsman. **Left:** A hunt in a famous hunting area – the Cotswolds in Gloucestershire.

As with everything to do with horses, it is best to introduce a young horse to hounds gradually. First just take him to the meet, let him get used to the conditions and then take him home again. When he has got used to this experience, you can begin to follow the hunt, but only for an hour or two at first.

The way a horse is introduced to hounds can affect his behaviour out hunting for the rest of his career. If you rush him through the initial stages, allowing him to get constantly over-excited, this is the way he will be likely to remain. An over-excited horse generally means an uncontrollable one and not one, therefore, on which you can expect to relax and enjoy your hunting. Go to mid-week meets if at all possible; there are always fewer people there than at the weekend. There is something to be said, too, for not having a young horse at the peak of fitness at this time; it is demanding a lot of a youngster to expect him to behave in a mature fashion in these exciting, strange circumstances, particularly if he is also full of oats.

Both at the early meets and then when you begin to follow, keep your horse a little way away from the remainder of the field. Many people are of the opinion that it is the close proximity of other horses that causes a horse to become excited – not hounds hunting in front of him. If he gets excited when you are standing still waiting for hounds to draw through a covert, walk him around slowly. Do not think that a gallop across the field will settle him down; it will merely unsettle everybody, while, if the huntsman has asked for quiet so that he can hear hounds working, it will make you extremely unpopular too.

Many people like to use cubbing as an opportunity to introduce a young horse to hounds. There are obvious advantages in this – generally the going underfoot is better at this time of year, there are fewer mounted followers so fewer horses to excite him and the hunting day is much shorter. On the other hand, cubbing often entails long periods of standing around, which a youngster could find very boring and unsettling.

If you decide to introduce your young horse to hounds during the cubbing season, also remember that you are still hunting and therefore the guest of the landowner. Do not think that simply because you are cubbing rather than hunting proper, you can allow your horse to misbehave, or use the field where the mounted followers are waiting as a schooling ground.

In the same way that horses prone to kicking wear a red ribbon in their tails as a warning to others, a young horse should wear a green ribbon. But again, this does not absolve you from any responsibility over the way he behaves or misbehaves. Whether you are introducing a young horse to hounds out cubbing, in the hunting season proper, at the meet, or by joining the mounted followers later, the message is the same. If he acts in an over-excitable fashion and behaves badly – take him home.

THE HUNTER'S YEAR

The hunter's week

Before examining how a hunter's year could be organized, it is useful to consider a possible programme for a hunter's week. The programme here is based on the assumption that the animal is being asked to hunt twice a week, so bear in mind that you should not be riding him too hard on those days, even if he is fit. It is assumed, too, that one day's hunting is on Saturday (the most usual hunting day) and the other is Wednesday. This will vary from hunt to hunt, but it is an easy matter to adjust the programme accordingly.

Monday: Give your horse his usual exercise of about one-and-a-half hours, including some roadwork, walking, long steady trotting and gentle cantering. Include one 'pipe-opener'.

Tuesday: Exercise the horse as above. Prepare for the following day's hunting. Shampoo the mane and any white patches on the coat, white socks and stockings. Rub them all as dry as possible. Put on a tail bandage during the day, but remove in the evening. Put on stable bandages overnight to keep the legs clean. Clean and check your tack and put out your hunting clothes.

Wednesday: Give your horse an early feed — no later than 7.00 am to 7.30 am. When your horse has finished eating, groom him and put on a tail and stable bandages. A good tip to help repel the mud, or at least make it easier to get off, is to rub over all the areas which will be affected (under the chest, belly, round the inside of the hindquarters and inside the top of the legs) with vegetable oil. Do not put this under the stable bandages, however; rub it over the legs when you have removed the bandages at the meet. Some riders prefer to put udder salve on the legs, as this can act as a mud fever preventative.

Put on the horse's travelling gear. Make sure you allow for the return journey in the evening, when the temperature may well have dropped. Then put the tack in the box, together with a full hay-net for the homeward journey, an elementary first-aid kit, some water and a bucket. When it is time to leave, box the horse in the usual way.

After the hunt, make sure you arrive back at the box with a cool horse, rug him up and bandage the legs — on top of any mud — and give him a third of a bucket of water. This is sufficient to wash his mouth out and refresh him, but it is better to leave a proper drink until he has returned home, by which time he will be more relaxed and less excited. Tie up

the hay-net for the homeward journey.

At home, let him have a longer drink and then give him a small feed — just a couple of handfuls of oats, mixed with some bran, all dampened down well. It is better to hold over the main evening feed for an hour or two.

When he has finished the small feed, begin the job of cleaning him. There is disagreement as to the relative merits and demerits of trying to remove the mud the same night, or leaving it to dry and then brushing it off the next day. To remove it immediately will probably mean washing it

off, so, if you know your horse is susceptible to mud fever, it may be better to leave it rather than to wash the legs. On the other hand, waiting means that you cannot check his legs thoroughly to make sure he has suffered no cuts or abrasions, while some types of mud simply will not brush off even when they are dry. In any event, you will find it easier to wash the mud from the belly and round the stifle area; these are sensitive places and most horses will not tolerate the hard brushing necessary to remove the mud from them.

Use warm water and a hose,

if possible, to wash off the mud. If you use a bucket and sponge, the water will soon get muddy and you will end up by simply spreading more mud around. Wash the tail if it is totally clogged. The idea is to remove as much mud as is practical, without taking so long that the horse gets restless and irritable. Rub all washed areas as dry as you can with towels or clean sacking, paying particular attention to the heels, and inspect the animal thoroughly for any injury.

Rug-up the horse, and if it is a very cold night, put on some stable bandages to keep him

warm and cosy. Give him his evening feed now — preferably a hot mash (see p. 42) — tie up the night's hay ration, then leave him for the night.

Thursday: Check the horse over again thoroughly in the daylight before feeding. Brush off any remaining mud. If he had a fairly hard day the day before and the weather is reasonable, it is better to turn him out in the field for a few hours, rather than riding him. Make sure he is well rugged-up, though. If the weather is bad, do not leave him standing in his box all day. Instead, lead him out, well rugged-up, to

stretch his legs and to give him a bite of grass.

Friday: Give him about one hour's steady exercise, then follow the procedure for getting ready, as Wednesday.

Saturday: As Wednesday.

Sunday: As Thursday.

The hunter's year

The calendar of events outlined below applies chiefly to the foxhunter, as this is the type of hunting in which most riders will be participating. The stag-hunting season is considerably longer, which means that you would need more than one horse if you are going to follow to the end of the season. The fact that stag-hunting lasts for nine months of the year means that there would not be enough time to get a horse fit and give it a period of rest, while it would be worn out by the end of the season.

Adapt the programme below to suit your hunting season.

Late summer: Bring the horse up from his rest period at grass. This will allow at least a month's cubbing before the hunting season proper starts.

Late summer-mid-autumn: Follow the conditioning programme, as on p. 37.

End autumn-mid-spring: Foxhunting season. Follow the weekly procedure outlined **left**, adapting it as necessary.

Mid-late spring: Follow a gradual 'run-down' process, heading towards the resting period. Gradually cut down the feed and slowly reduce the amount of exercise. Decrease the number (or weight) of the rugs as the weather gets warmer. Turn the horse out in the paddock for part of each day as soon as possible.

Early summer: Turn out the horse during the day and bring him back into the stable at night. If the weather is warm and the horse is being badly bothered by flies, reverse this process, turning him out at night and bringing him in by day. Ride him gently if you wish during the early part of the month, but aim to turn him out completely, hind shoes removed, by mid-June.

Midsummer: Total rest out at grass. Arrange for at least one visit from the farrier to trim the feet and visit the horse yourself each day to check him over for injury. Remember that, in order to get the maximum benefit from this rest period, the grazing should be good and there should be adequate protection in the field from excessive heat and flies, as well as any wind or rain. There must be a constant clean water supply; if this is provided in an old bath or similar receptacle, make sure that there are no sharp edges around it. Scrub it out regularly (at least once a week) before filling it with fresh water.

GLOSSARY

blank: To draw a blank means hounds fail to scent out a quarry. A blank day means hounds did not find (a fox) all day.

to bolt (a fox): Action sometimes taken when a fox has run to ground or is lying in a drain. A terrier is put into the earth or drain to force the fox out.

brace (of foxes): Two foxes. Foxes are always counted by the brace.

to break: A fox or hounds leaving a covert.

brush: A fox's tail.

bye-day: An extra hunting day, additional to those advertized on the *hunt card.*

cap: Sum of money paid by mounted non-subscribers when they follow a particular hunt. Can also refer to special collections made from subscribers (see *wire fund*).

carrying a scent: Refers either to country where the scenting conditions are good, or to a hound that still 'uses' its nose when the pack is running.

check: Temporary pause when hounds lose the scent.

couple: Two hounds. Hounds are always counted in couples.

covert: A wood.

cry: Noise made by hounds while following a scent.

cub: Infant fox. Foxes are usually born in the spring and, after November 1 of that year, they are known as foxes.

cub-hunting, cubbing: The hunting of fox cubs, done before hunting proper starts, as a means of introducing young hounds to the sport. Usually begins some time between mid-July and September, depending on the harvest.

deep: Ground which is very soft or heavy underfoot.

drag: Refers to the line laid when drag-hunting.

drain: An underground drain or pipe, used as a hiding place by a hunted fox.

to draw: To draw a wood describes the action of the huntsman as he takes hounds through a wood to find a fox.

earth: A fox's home. It is burrowed underground.

earth stopper: Person employed by the hunt who blocks up the entrance to earths at night before a hunt, while the fox is out hunting.

field: The mounted followers at a hunt.

Field Master: See page

'Forrard': Term used by the huntsman to encourage hounds onto a scent.

full cry: When hounds are in full pursuit of their quarry and are *giving tongue* accordingly.

giving tongue: Describes the cry made by hounds when on a scent.

gone away: Said of a fox that has left the covert and is running.

gone to ground: Said of a fox that has taken refuge in an earth.

harbourer: Person who watches a stag the day before a hunt so as to advise the huntsman of its whereabouts.

'Holloa': Loud cry made by anyone who sees the hunted quarry, as an indication to the

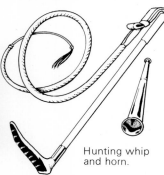

A member of the field giving a 'view Holloa'.

Returning home after a blank day.

Mounted mask..

huntsman which way it is running. Sometimes known as 'view holloa'.

horn: Copper instrument about 20cm (9in) long, used by the huntsman as he hunts hounds. The different calls he blows indicate different activities. For example, there is

a call to indicate gone to ground, going home, and so on.

hound couples: Two collars attached to one another and used to keep two hounds together.

hound jog: Describes the slow trotting pace of horses following after hounds as they

Hunting whip and horn.

A couple of hounds.

travel along the road.

'Hounds, please': Cry passed through the field to warn them that the huntsman and hounds are coming up behind and will want to get past.

hunt card: Printed card sent to subscribers to inform them

of the venues of forthcoming meets

hunting pink: Colloquial term to describe the scarlet coats worn by some male hunt followers and the members of the hunt staff.

hunting whip: A specifically designed whip, with a long leather thong at one end and a slightly hooked bone handle at the other. The handle is used for closing gates.

hunting year: The hunt year runs from May 1st to April 30th. Subscriptions usually fall due at the beginning of the year.

hunt servants: The huntsman (if a professional), kennel-huntsman and whippers-in (see p. 46).

(the) kill: When hounds catch and kill the quarry they have been hunting.

to lay-on: Said of the huntsman when he attempts to put hounds on to the scenting line. Also describes the point when the main body of staghounds are released on the line (see p. 32).

'Leu-in': Term used by the huntsman as he encourages hounds to draw through a covert.

made-hunter: Term used to describe a horse already experienced in hunting.

mask: A fox's face.

meet: The appointed venue where hounds, huntsmen and field gather at the beginning of a day's hunting.

nose: A hound with a 'good nose' describes one that picks up a scent easily.

open country: Term used to describe hunting country with little or no woodland.

opening meet: The first *meet* in a new hunting season.

pad: A fox's foot.

rat-catcher: Informal dress worn by riders when cub-hunting.

stag: A male deer that is four years old or more.

stern: The tail of a hound.

taking your own line: Said of a mounted follower who goes his own way out hunting, rather than remaining with the rest of the field.

'Tally-ho': Cry given by someone who sees the fox when he knows the huntsman is not far away.

tufters: Staghounds used at the beginning of the day to seek out the stag.

vixen: Female fox.

to walk (a hound puppy): Members of the hunt often look after foxhound puppies in the first few months of their life, before hunting training commences. This is known as 'walking' a puppy.

whippers-in: See p. 46.

wire fund: Money generally collected from all mounted followers to help towards the cost of mending fences or repairing other damage done by the hunt.

CHAPTER THREE

CROSS COUNTRY

THOUGH HUNTING (SEE p. 28–51) is a non-competitive equestrian sport, it nevertheless awakens and kindles the competitive spirit of all keen horses and riders who participate in it. Not surprisingly, therefore, it has given birth to competitive sports, principally hunter trials, team chases and point-to-points.

Hunter trials

A hunter trial is primarily a speed and jumping test, held across natural country, usually over a distance of about 2.5 to 3km (1½ to 2 miles). The jumps are, by and large, akin to those found in the hunting field – including such things as hedges, ditches, various post and rail fences and perhaps a stile – rather than the daunting obstacles of an event course. A rider may also be asked to open, go through and shut a gate while riding the course, while it is not unusual to find a heavy ploughed field separating jumps.

Hunter trials are usually looked on by competitors as a good schooling ground for a hunter or as a useful introduction to cross-country jumping for a novice eventer; the rider, for his or her part, has an opportunity for light-hearted competition. Prize money is low and certainly no one is riding for a financial reward. Having said this, however, it is undoubtedly true that hunter trials, in common with most other equestrian sports, have become more competitive in recent years. Fences which, it seemed, were once held together with bits of old string and rusty nails, are now professionally constructed and incorporated into well-planned courses. As the level of competition rises, it is not uncommon also to find the odd event-type obstacle, a water trough for example, particularly in open classes.

Team chasing

Team chasing is related to the hunter trial in its organization. It is certainly the newest of all cross-country sports. A competition in which teams of four (or occasionally five) ride together around a cross-country jumping course, it first saw the light of day in the early 1970s, when the British rider Douglas Bunn staged the first Team Cross-Country Ride at his All England Show Jumping Course at Hickstead, Sussex. The idea was that teams of four

Above: This photograph, taken in 1936, shows the rider wearing an ordinary jacket — a sight seldom seen in the point-to-point field today. Jockeys are more usually dressed in specially selected bright racing colours. **Left:** A confident competitor in a team chase competition leads the other members of her team over a post and rail fence and then through a shallow river. Team chasing is among the newest of competitive equestrian sports but already it has a large following.

Top: A print dating from 1860 depicting one of the early point-to-point races. It provides a good illustration of how riding styles change over the years. Today's riders hold their horses on a short rein, and the short length of their stirrup leathers allows them to stand up and crouch forward on their horses' necks. **Above:** Another 19th-century print showing a race taking place in France.
Right: The amateur nature of point-to-pointing makes it a friendly as well as a competitive sport. Here a rider displays obvious concern as a colleague takes a tumble.

would ride round a prescribed cross-country jumping course and the time of the third person home would be the decisive score. The winning team would be the one with the fastest recorded time.

As a sport, team chasing achieved instant success. The team factor had a great appeal for riders, who often found that encouragement from other riders helped them to ride more boldly across country than they would if tackling a course alone. In fact, this was to become something of a hazard, since the sport began to be something of a break-neck race. In an effort to lessen this, many team chases now include what is known as a dressing fence. This is a fence which at least three members of the team must jump together, rather than in single file. A fence judge will add on an appropriate number of seconds if the riders are straggled out instead of jumping at the same time. A particularly good place to install a dressing fence is at the last jump of a course, when riders, in sight of home, tend to urge their often tiring mounts onward particularly enthusiastically.

The jumps in a team chase will comprise a number of straightforward hunt-type fences, intermingled with more difficult event-type obstacles. At present, there are no official restrictions regarding the height of the fences in a team chase course as there are in eventing, so it is not unusual to find quite high fences, at least in open events. Courses can vary in length from 3 to 5km (2 to 3 miles) with anything from 18 to 35 fences, according to the standard of competition.

Both hunter trials and team chases are usually staged by individual hunts who tend to impose their own rules. These are generally simple, for it is a point of these types of competition that they are not bound round with complicated rules and regulations. They cover, for instance, the line that must be taken between the set markers of the course. There will be a number of classes, catering for all standards of horses – novice, open and perhaps an adjacent hunt class – and riders.

Like hunting, hunter trials and team chases are held by courtesy of farmers and landowners, for courses have to be built over their land. Because of this, they generally take place at opposite ends of the hunting season – in the autumn and early spring – when the harvest is generally in, the lambing season is over and the ground is not wet enough to be permanently damaged by galloping hooves. This means, however, that such events are always at the mercy of the weather and it is not unusual to find them cancelled because of very wet conditions.

Point-to-points

Point-to-points are very different from hunter trials and team chases. They are concerned primarily with speed; although the course includes a number of jumps, they are first and foremost a race. Competitors in each 'class' race directly against one another, all at one time, rather than having their time recorded as they ride the course individually.

Point-to-points originated in Britain in the eighteenth century, when hunting folk, ever-boastful of their horses' prowess, would race their mounts from sight of one village steeple to another. Hence the sport's other name – steeplechasing. The races also became known as point-to-points because they were just that – a race run from one point to another. It is from this somewhat informal beginning that the whole of modern racing has evolved, a field that has many different aspects and in most instances is dominated by professional trainers and jockeys. Point-to-point racing only (together with hunter chasing) is the sole amateur-dominated aspect of racing and, as such, is a sport open to any horseman or woman who is sufficiently interested and brave to want to participate in it.

All hunts affiliated to the Master of Fox-hounds Association or its US equivalent (see p. 31) may hold a point-to-point each year; in Britain, all are anxious to do so, for it is the hunt's main source of revenue. All potential competitors have first to gain a certificate from their Master of Foxhounds, which states that their horse has been hunted at least eight times in the preceding season. The races themselves are generally held from the spring through to early summer.

The rules and regulations imposed at point-to-points come under the jurisdiction of the National Jockey Club. Should a hunt deviate from them, the point-to-point would no longer be 'recognized' and any horse that runs at an 'unrecognized' meeting is henceforth disqualified from racing at other meetings. It is also stated that only amateur jockeys may ride and that no horse may be professionally trained – that is, trained by someone who makes his living by training racehorses. Only the owner, his or her groom, or in some instances the proprietor of the stable where the horse was kept during the hunting season, can have anything to do with the training of the horse.

This does not mean that the world of point-to-point racing is not a training ground for future racehorses. Many successful point-to-pointers will progress from there to hunter 'chasing' (a steeplechase held at a National Hunt Meeting but also open only to horses qualified in the hunting field and ridden by amateur jockeys) and then into the hands of the professionals.

Hunt races

'Amateur' racing is subject to different interpretations in various countries of the world. In the USA, for instance, steeplechasing is described as being amateur, while point-to-

Le Petit Journal

LES COURSES DE STEEPLE
Le saut de la rivière

points are different from American Hunt Race meetings.

Hunt Race meetings are run under the rules of the National Steeplechase and Hunt Association and the prize money is considerable. Professional jockeys and trainers may participate together with amateurs. Races are held over brush, timber and the flat. As in Britain, point-to-points are staged by the various hunts as a means of raising funds and are generally held at the end of the foxhunting season. Some point-to-points hold races over timber for 'lightweights', 'heavyweights' and ladies. Others are more akin to the hunt meetings, with races over brush fences, timber fences and on the flat. Still more, determined to ensure the amateur status of their meetings, have cross-country races in which competitors choose their own line between designated points, the course not being marked by flags. It is not uncommon at these events to see real 'hunters' participating – a sight that has become uncommon outside the USA.

Above: A steeplechase at Auteuil, France, in 1903. The 19th and early 20th centuries saw the establishment of racing as a major sport.

Physical fitness

Aspects of training these competition horses are discussed on p. 59–64, but it is vital to realize from the start that the rider must be just as fit as his horse. Riding a fast team chase, or a point-to-point race, is an extremely exhausting and tiring physical exercise for the rider, as well as the horse, and it would be a great pity to get your horse to a winning level, only to find that you are not up to riding in the event yourself. Riding every day is not sufficient to get you into tip-top shape; you will need to do something else to develop stamina, such as jogging, riding a bicycle or swimming.

The competition horse

As all the areas of cross-country competition riding mentioned in this chapter spring di-

rectly from hunting, it should follow that a good hunter should be able to participate in each of these events. In the case of hunter trials, this maxim still applies. No one would buy a horse purely to carry them to victory in this sport. They would be looking, first and foremost, for a good horse to hunt through the season. If it proved to be a good, bold jumper, they then might consider entering trials with the intention of having some additional fun and sport.

The same is probably true of team chasing. Any horse that performs well out hunting, will jump in cold blood and behaves itself whilst galloping along in the company of others, is suitable for the sport. However, in comparison with many other equestrian sports, team chasing carries extremely good prize money, which, not unnaturally, has led to an upsurge in the numbers of people taking part and to a

Below: Two members of a team in a team chase event take a wide brush fence together during a competition. The fence is a particularly attractive one for a horse to jump as it is wide and very solid in appearance. It will be the time of the third member of the team to cross the finishing line that gives the overall score.

constant raising of the standard of competition. Better and better horses are therefore needed for success. Having said this, however, it is still the 'hunter-type' of horse that is required – a horse with overall good conformation, natural jumping ability, boldness, courage, obedience.

A successful team chaser will be one that can gallop fast, but, even more importantly, the horse should be a really good, bold jumper. The fences in a team chase event are often higher, though not usually so complex, as those found on a three-day event course. It is quite possible, for instance, to be confronted with a really high wall; if a horse cannot jump this, it does not matter how fast he can gallop.

Speed in a horse is synonymous with 'blood' and the sort of horse you will probably be looking for will be a Thoroughbred, a seven-eighths or possibly a three-quarter bred. Temperament is extremely important – you want a horse with a good, 'steady' character, rather than one that is extremely temperamental. Thoroughbreds can often be a little too highly-strung for this kind of sport.

Good event horses (see p. 78), too, do not necessarily make good team chase horses, although since both have to cover a cross-country jumping course at speed, it would be reasonable to assume that this would be the case. The reason for this is that horses in team chase events are usually asked to go considerably faster than eventers. By the same token, a point-to-pointer will not necessarily make a good team chaser. In the latter instance, although the horse must have the ability to gallop fast and jump at speed, he must think about the fences sufficiently to ensure he clears them, for they will generally be unyielding if a horse hits them. Although point-to-point fences are solid, it is often possible to brush through the top

Below: A typical fence to be jumped at speed in America's timber races. This picture was taken at the famous Maryland Hunt Cup Timber race in 1980 when the race was won for the first time by a lady rider.
Bottom: A point-to-pointer being given a good gallop during his training and conditioning programme. The sandy soil provides ideal ground.

part of them – a completely impractical course of action with a thick timber post and rails or stone wall.

As far as point-to-pointing is concerned, it is no longer enough to have a horse that is simply a good hunter if winning is the main object. Whereas people used to point-to-point their hunters, they now hunt their point-to-pointers – and they only do this because a horse must have hunted to qualify for entering a point-to-point. Point-to-points in the main have become an end in themselves and, as such, are far divorced from the hunting field. Anyone interested in buying a horse for point-to-pointing is looking for a racehorse, not a hunter, and a racehorse means a Thoroughbred.

What to look for in a point-to-pointer

A point-to-pointer must possess three major characteristics. He must be able to jump; he must be able to move fast; and he must have the stamina to match the demands made on him over a reasonably considerable distance. Jumping in this instance means being able to take solid brush fences, standing at 1.3m (4ft 6in) high, at speed – that is in his galloping stride so that they barely slow him down. Being able to move fast and possessing stamina must go hand-in-hand; it is no good having a horse that can gallop flat out over 1km ($\frac{1}{2}$ mile), only to drop away after that, since point-to-points are run over nearly 5km (3 miles). What you are looking for is a horse that can maintain a good steady gallop over, say, 4km (2$\frac{1}{2}$ miles), keeping sufficient in reserve to enable him to sprint home over the final 1km ($\frac{1}{2}$ mile).

As even Thoroughbreds vary greatly in appearance and conformation, to give even general guidelines on the sort of appearance or build required is almost impossible. Look at the horses being walked round the paddock before the start of a race at a point-to-point: no two will be alike in size, shape or apparent temperament. You will see small horses of little more than 15hh and others of 17hh; they will have neat little heads and pricked ears or big, rather coarse heads and big floppy ears; they will have fine, slender legs, as if chiselled out of marble, or strong thick ones that may be quite lumpy and blemished. Some will be plodding round, their heads almost on the ground; others will be dancing and prancing. It would be a lucky person, rather than a fine judge of horseflesh, who, with no knowledge of the horses' form, could tell you at this stage which would be the winner! So what should you look for?

The best practical advice for someone completely new to the sport, who would like to own a point-to-pointer and possibly ride it themselves is to buy a horse that has already raced and, ideally, has shown some form – that is, has been placed in a few races. Horses are not allowed to run in point-to-points until they are five years old, and they are generally considered to be at their peak from eight to 11 years, so look for a horse of about this age.

Even though it is not uncommon to see unlikely-looking horses (i.e. those with pretty poor conformation) in the winner's enclosure, it is still advisable to look for a horse with good conformation. A long, sloping shoulder indicates the horse will possess considerably more freedom of action and length of stride than a rival with a short, upright shoulder. Similarly, a horse that has ample lung-space – where there is really room for the lungs to expand – should be able to perform better than one whose lungs are cramped. Look, though, for a horse with a good deep chest (from back to belly) rather than a wide one. A wide chest necessarily means that the forelegs are set wider apart, which restricts the horse's freedom of action.

As propulsive power comes from the hindquarters, it is sensible to look for a horse with good, strong, rounded hindquarters. A good depth – from the thigh to the hock – and a stifle joint that is set well forward usually denotes an ability to move fast. Hocks should be strong and broad. In the front legs, a long canon bone, which thus means long tendons, could lead to tendon trouble, as a bigger area is open to strain. As always, the horse's action is important; a long-striding horse with easy, rhythmic paces is the sort that usually wins races.

It is a good idea to check the horse's pedigree. If he has some successful racing blood in his ancestry, there is always the chance that some will have filtered down the generations to course through his veins. But remember that, like everything to do with horses, there is never any certainty. If a horse turns out to be a brilliant point-to-pointer, this has almost as much to do with luck as it has to do with knowledge and experience.

Training for competition

The hunter sets the basic norm in the training of a horse for cross-country competition. As already stated, horses ridden in hunter trials, as well as those entered in team chases, are likely to be used primarily for hunting. Though this is not the case for point-to-pointers, they still must be hunted in order to be able to compete in point-to-points. It is necessary, therefore, to follow the basic training outlined on p. 37–44 to get the horse hunting fit. Nevertheless, the particular training required for each of these sports incorporates slight differences.

The hunter trial horse

Hunter trials are probably the most informal of the cross-country competitions. If, therefore, a horse has been hunted regularly in good jumping country, very little additional training will really be needed.

However, it should be remembered that

Above: This horse has achieved a really strong forward spring from his hocks, giving him the necessary height and width to clear this hunter trial obstacle. Note how his back legs are now fully extended and how his rider is leaning well forward, so as to avoid impeding his head or action in the slightest way. **Right:** A straightforward parallel rustic poles and rails fence. The stout pole on the ground would help a horse to judge its take-off point accurately. **Far right:** A pair of young competitors, their ponies looking alert and in good condition.

hunter trials usually take place at opposite ends of the hunting season. If you are competing in the spring trials, your horse will be hunting fit and is likely to have had plenty of jumping practice during the season; thus, you should be able to enter him in hunter trials with no further preparation. However, you should not have pressed him so hard throughout the season that he is not up to galloping fast round a hunter trial course. Remember that a tired horse will always find extra reserves out hunting, which he may not be able – or prepared – to produce when asked to perform in cold blood.

If you want to enter your horse for autumn trials, then you will have to alter your training programme in order to get him fit earlier. A horse that is expected to take you, at speed, round a hunter trial course, which may be at least 2.5km ($1\frac{1}{2}$ miles) long and have a minimum of 20 obstacles, must be physically prepared. This means he must be as fit as you would wish him to be at the opening meet of the season; in other words, he should have a good eight weeks' conditioning behind him.

As he will not have had the benefit of several months' hunting, which would give him considerable jumping practice and should ensure that he is obedient and responsive, it will be necessary to incorporate more schooling work and some jumping into your conditioning routine. Aim to include at least three schooling sessions in your weekly programme for about three weeks before the first hunter trial. These need not be extensive – 20 to 30 minutes is enough to begin with – and, providing that the horse has been well-schooled, they need not be very demanding. Their purpose is to get the horse moving forward freely with his hocks well beneath him, to ensure that he is answering your leg and that he is generally responsive and obedient.

Jumping rehearsals

Jumping practice should obviously be over the natural obstacles you are likely to encounter in a hunter trial, rather than show jumps. Make sure you include ditches, since these are a favourite feature of hunter trial courses and the type of obstacle that horses will quickly baulk at unless they have encountered them previously. If your horse refuses at a ditch, do not turn him round to attempt it a second time, but simply keep urging him forward. Be prepared for an enormous leap, even if it is only quite a narrow ditch; horses always seem to be convinced that a ditch harbours unspeakable terrors and they thus launch themselves well into the air to make sure they avoid them. You will find this gets less overt as they become more familiar with this sort of obstacle.

If there is a steep slope down to the ditch with a similar bank the other side, try to encourage your horse to go down the slope before making his jump. Again, be prepared for a big leap and keep your weight well forward so that

CROSS-COUNTRY FENCES

1. A table fence — that is a flat structure resembling a rectangular table, situated between post and rails.
2. A slightly unusual obstacle; a huge galvanized iron drum used to fill a gap in a hedge.

3. A staircase fence constructed from good solid poles.
4. A classic tiger trap that is often constructed over a ditch.
5. A low stone wall bounded by heavy post and rails.
6. This fence could cause more trouble than the others, despite its simple appearance. It is merely a stout pole suspended over a water-filled ditch.
7. A fence made of heavy wooden sleepers with a post and rail on top.

8. Heavy wooden poles piled horizontally on top of one another.
9. Wooden poles of the same length arranged vertically. The sloping angle makes it easier to jump than a perfect upright.

you do not hinder his landing or jab him in the mouth. If you allow your weight to fall backwards in the saddle, you will make it extremely difficult for him to negotiate the bank on the other side.

Many hunter trial courses will include a stream that you have to splash through, though probably not the more daunting jumps into a stream or shallow lake found in an event course. This can be another stumbling block unless your horse is thoroughly used to it. When hacking, take every opportunity to splash through puddles rather than going round them even if they do make your horse's legs dirty. Then find a stream that is very

shallow, but wide enough for your horse not to be tempted to jump it. Examine the bed of the stream to make sure that there are no sharp stones, unstable patches of ground or holes that could cause injury. Urge your horse forward gently; be prepared to be patient, since you may meet with considerable resistance at first. Once in the stream, make him stand in the running water for a minute or two. Then walk on through, turn round and ask him to walk through again.

Another obstacle you may encounter is a hedge with a ditch on the far side, which the horse will obviously be unable to see. He will not know, therefore, that you want him to really spread himself out over the fence, so you must ensure he does this by approaching the obstacle with a long, easy stride, maintaining sufficient impulsion to carry him well forward over the fence. If you allow him to hesitate at the take-off, he may make a higher, more upright, jump that could land him in the ditch. If, on the other hand, the hedge has a ditch in front of it, which the horse can see, steady him before the fence so that he is able to judge his stride for the take-off. It may be that by putting in a short stride just before the fence, he can meet it in just the right place. Do not steady him too late though; if you interfere with his mouth in the last few strides, you could throw him off balance altogether.

Many hunter trials now include a few event type fences. These are obstacles you would not normally expect to find out hunting – a water trough, for example, or a wooden hayrick. It is as well to prepare your horse for such a possibility by including the jumping of a few such unusual obstacles in your training sessions.

Include some opening and shutting of gates in your training sessions to ensure that both you and your horse are really adept at it. This should present no problem to an experienced hunter, but it is something that could make a vital difference to your time. Precious seconds – even minutes – will be lost if you fumble and hesitate unnecessarily.

The team chaser

'Any horse that is thoroughly fit and has been hunted hard over good, fast country that includes a number of different types of fences, can enter a team chase event, with no further training.' So says one of Britain's leading team chase riders. He also believes that it is unnecessary to practice with the other horses and riders in the team, providing that the team walks the course together and works out a strategy in advance.

The recipe for success is therefore twofold. Your horse must be extremely fit and also he must have had considerable and varied jumping practice. Fitness is of the essence; winning teams go very, very fast and a team chase could be nearly 5km (3 miles) long with 35 big fences. These are demanding and testing conditions for any horse. If you are not intending to hunt your team chaser, or are thinking of entering the autumn events that take place before the hunting season gets under way, you must follow a rigorous programme to get him fit and you must ensure that he is thoroughly familiar with the types – and heights – of fences he is going to encounter. The basic conditioning programme should be extended by another two weeks to a month, especially if you are riding to win.

Continue the routine you have been following over the last few weeks, extending the time spent exercising to about two hours a day, if

possible. This should include hacking out on roads, some steady cantering and a fast sprint over a short distance, plus some schooling and jumping practice. You can also include some interval training (see p. 92).

If you are a novice in team chasing, make a point of going to a few events as a spectator and walking the course, so you can see the types of fences included. Then make sure you include similar obstacles in your jumping practice sessions.

If you have a chance to practise with your fellow team members, be certain to take advantage of this, particularly if you can try your horses out over a few jumps together.

Top: In a team chase event, members follow each other over a post and rails into a fairly long stretch of water, a good illustration of how important it is to accustom your horse to water before a competition.
Above: In order to prepare horses for jumps involving water, spend time letting them wade or stand in a running stream. The cool water is also very good for their legs during a rigorous conditioning programme.

MAKING A BRIDGE

Forming a cross or bridge with your reins can help to control a pulling horse. First knot the reins.

For a single bridge, pass the right rein through your left hand.

Take hold of the right rein further down as shown. If your horse is not a bad puller, this will be sufficient to hold him.

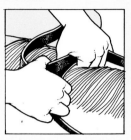

If you want a stronger hold, hold the reins in a double bridge. To do this, pick up reins in a single bridge, then take both in your right hand.

Press your knuckles down on the horse's neck and lean your weight on them. Your fingers will shut securely round the reins.

Riding with bridged reins is far less tiring when galloping, as you can support your weight on your hands. Lift them slightly to slow down.

However, this is frequently impractical; few farmers will welcome you galloping over their land for 'practice', so probably the only way you will get to jump together is if one or other of you has a few wide natural jumps erected in a field that he owns. In many instances, it will be the first team chase you enter that acts as your training ground.

If everyone knows his horse well, you should have a good idea of which one will want to go in front and which would prefer a lead. You can judge from your hunting experience; if you like to tuck in behind a reliable horse and rider when you come to a fence out hunting, you will certainly want to be a follower in a team chase. On the other hand, a bold, strong horse that tends to pull if he thinks he is going to be left behind could be just the one to lead the team to victory.

The point-to-pointer

Whether you want to get your point-to-pointer fit for the opening meet of the hunting season or not until shortly later depends to some extent on whether you mean to race him in the very earliest point-to-points of the season, or whether you are going to wait until the later ones. A horse has to be hunted eight times in the season in order to point-to-point. Here, the weather may play a part, for it is not uncommon for hunting to be cancelled if hard frosts make the ground unsuitable for riding fast. Bearing this in mind then, it is probably wise to hunt a point-to-pointer as much as

possible before this is likely to occur. On non-hunting days, take the horse for a hack as you would a hunter (see p. 40); his feeding could also be the same as for a hunter in work.

Specialist training

More specific training for the forthcoming point-to-point season should generally begin about a month before the first race you plan to enter. In this instance, hunting fit is not racing fit, as many riders seem to imagine; even a horse that is sufficiently fit to be hunted twice a week is not fit enough to race round a point-to-point course, galloping all the way, and it would be cruel to expect him to do so.

The first thing you must find before training in earnest can begin is a suitable place for galloping your horse. Look for a large grass field that is reasonably flat. The ground can undulate a little (point-to-point courses are not flat), but make sure there are no bad ruts or uneven stretches where the horse could trip or stumble. The ground should be well-drained; if it is very muddy you will cut up the turf and could also damage the horse's legs. You must of course get permission.

Twice a week ask your horse to gallop round the field, aiming to maintain a steady pace for about 2.5km ($1\frac{1}{2}$ miles). Galloping in this instance refers to a good, fast hunting canter, rather than a flat-out gallop. You certainly should never push the animal to his limits. Over the next month, gradually increase the speed and move up to a good 3km (2 miles).

Look also for a fairly steep grassy hill, and on one day of the week – not the day you are working in the field – ask the horse to sprint up it. Moving fast uphill puts less strain on a horse's legs than galloping on the flat, as they do not pound into the ground in the same way. However it does demand quite a lot of the cardiovascular system. It is good exercise, therefore, for hardening the legs and developing the heart muscles. The aim is to harden the horse's legs (without straining them), to get the tendons used to fast work, and to really develop the breathing apparatus – that is, to make sure the lungs and heart are working as efficiently as possible. Do not ask your horse to move fast downhill; it puts a great strain on the legs.

When you have been galloping steadily over 3km (2 miles) for a couple of weeks, begin to ask the horse to really stretch out over the last 0.8km ($\frac{1}{2}$ mile). Again, never push him to his limits; you should always feel that he still has something in reserve. Also keep an eye on how quickly he recovers from the exertion. Recovery should take a shorter and shorter time and its rate is a good indication of how fit the horse is.

If there is a good long stretch of firm sand on a beach not too far away, it is well worth boxing your horse there and giving him a good gallop along the sand. Having selected the part of the beach along which you intend to gallop, walk all the way along it first. There may well be some sharp item buried just beneath the surface at some point, or there may be places where the sand is less firm than you think. Such conditions could do serious damage to a galloping horse. How frequently you use a beach in this way will obviously depend primarily on how convenient it is; once a week (substituting it for one of the other galloping sessions) would be ideal. Try to find the extra time to walk your horse through the shallows as well; sea water is extremely therapeutic for horses' legs.

Intersperse the galloping exercise with days of ordinary exercise – one-and-a-half to two hours' hacking on roads and tracks. Include as much trotting as possible, particularly up hills.

Over the jumps

If your horse has raced in point-to-points before and has done plenty of jumping out hunting, it will not be necessary to give him much jumping practice. Try to find some proper point-to-point jumps and then pop your horse over these a couple of times a week or so before a race as a reminder. Ensure that he takes these jumps at speed, but not flat-out.

Go round the edge of the field at a steady canter and then accelerate as you go into the jump. If one of the practice jumps is an open ditch, so much the better. This will help prepare you and your horse for meeting ditches in a race. There is no need to tackle an open ditch differently from any other fence; if you are going at a good, steady gallop your horse should be well able to stretch out over it.

If your horse has not raced before, but can jump (and has been doing so happily out hunting), introduce him to point-to-point fences gradually and carefully. If at all possible, it is best to begin by jumping with a more experienced horse. Before tackling the real fences, try jumping some hurdles, perhaps laced with brush, approaching them at a good hunting canter, rather than the faster, racing gallop. Let the other horse lead you over the first time, but thereafter try to jump side-by-side. You want to get your horse used to jumping with others next to him, as this is what he will encounter in a race, and you certainly do not want him to get used to always following another horse over a jump!

Remember, though, that, as a novice, he will not be used to galloping into a fence of this height. He will expect you to steady him up as you would usually do to allow him to adjust his stride for his approach and take-off. There is no time for this in a point-to-point; a horse must be able to gallop over the fences, almost taking them in his stride. Teach your horse this gradually; if you rush him you could severely shake his confidence.

Once an inexperienced horse has got the hang of jumping fast and is taking the point-to-point fences well, reduce jumping practice. He does not need constant reminding; this will make him bored and possibly careless.

Knowing your horse

Throughout training, if possible, turn your horse out in the field for a couple of hours or so

Below: Practising with others can be a great help, particularly if you are all members of the same team. It not only gets your horse accustomed to jumping when there are other horses nearby, it can also act as an encouragement. Here the rider will swing right-handed after the first jump to take the second small obstacle, and will have practice in persuading her horse to ignore the other horse on her left. Like-minded riders can often help one another by offering constructive criticism during these practice training sessions.

on his rest day. Try also to turn him out every day, when the weather permits, for about half an hour to let him have a little grass and freedom. This alleviates the boredom of being cooped up in a stable for some 22 hours a day and thus helps to keep a horse generally interested in life. Some very 'corned-up' horses, however, are too excitable to turn loose in a paddock, since their over-exuberance could lead to serious injury. In such cases, lead them out (in a bridle) for half-an-hour or so, letting them have the odd nibble of grass.

It should be emphasized that the training of a horse for racing of any kind varies enormously, since it depends on the individual horse's temperament. It is therefore impossible to outline a training scheme that will suit every horse, as no two animals are alike. The key is to know your horse and to judge from your own experience what exercise he needs. A lazy horse will need more galloping to keep him in condition and concentrating on the job in hand than a nervy, athletic one. No more than, say, one-and-half hours' ordinary exercise each day is enough to keep the latter fit, while he certainly will not need to be galloped twice a week and sprinted once a week. Similarly, horses vary enormously in their immediate pre-race requirements. Some will need a good gallop on the morning of the race to wake them up; others would just become excited by this and would be in no state to run a race. You must, therefore, temper any training routine to suit your particular horse and, again, you can only do this successfully by knowing him – his habits, temperament and athletic ability – extremely well.

Coping with bad weather

The timing of the point-to-point season means that training often has to be conducted through the inclement weather of a hard winter. In heavy frost or snowy conditions, follow your routine as best you can. Remember the aim is always to keep the horse moving; to keep his muscles and joints thoroughly exercised. Snowy weather presents less problem than hard frost, since the latter makes the ground too hard for galloping. It is quite possible to canter on grassland that is covered in snow – in fact, this is infinitely better than cantering when it is wet, since heavy rain may well make the grass extremely wet and slippery. Do not attempt to gallop fast on snowy ground; instead ride at a steady canter, but go on longer – up to about 5km (3 miles) rather than 3km (2 miles). Never ride on snowy roads to get to your grassy area though, unless they have been salted or gritted; the surface just under the snow will be like a skating rink and a horse will certainly slip and fall. If necessary, get a supply of salt and use it to clear a route to the grassland. It would be a good idea to lead your horse over this, rather than to ride him, risking damage or injury through slipping.

In heavy frosty conditions, you must do the best you can. This will probably mean putting down a large circuit of straw and riding your horse round it. Alternatively, find an indoor school you can use, just to exercise your horse, to stretch his legs and at least maintain his level of fitness. Lungeing, however, should not be used as a way of keeping a horse exercised. Working in small circles is not something that is generally required of a racehorse and it can put considerable strain on his legs and joints, since they are not used to this. It is also not always easy to control an extremely fit animal at the end of a lunge rein. If he does get out of control he could very easily injure himself. By and large, it is infinitely better and more effective to control him from on top – sitting on his back.

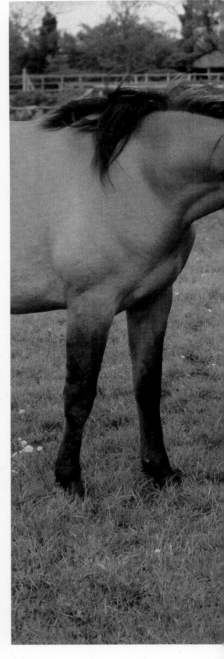

Feeding

Feeding a horse expected to compete in hunter trials and team chase events does not differ much from the feeding routine of a hunter. The fitter you get a horse and want him to be, the more hard feed he needs, but remember that he must be getting enough exercise to balance his food intake. If he is not given sufficient exercise to burn off protein, he will quickly get 'above' himself and start to misbehave on a ride.

Excessive amounts of protein also lead to health problems. The chief one is often known as 'Monday morning sickness' and it shows itself in partial paralysis of the horse's hindquarters or in sudden lameness coming on during exercise. The answer is the correct amount of exercise, rather than that of cutting down the feed. You cannot expect to maintain a high level of fitness in a horse if you reduce his protein intake dramatically. In the case of team chasers, particularly those expected to compete frequently and win, it will probably be necessary to increase the hard feed above that of most hunters. Reduce the amount of bulk feeds you give as you increase the

Left: All horses appreciate a spell of freedom in the paddock each day, although if they are in hard training they should not have access to such lush pasture as this. Providing they regard you as a friend and not someone whose presence always means hard work, you will have no trouble when you want to catch them.
Above: Stabled or thin-skinned horses will need the protection of a New Zealand rug if they are turned out — even for a few hours — in cold weather.

Left: The point-to-point season is not always noted for the brilliance of the weather. Training horses in such wet, muddy conditions can prove very difficult.

protein foods. It is most important to maintain the correct balance and to make adjustments according to your horse's condition.

The feeding of any competition horse can be very tricky – even more so than usual. You can only hope for a non-fussy feeder that eats the feed put in front of him, regardless of the work he is doing. You will be lucky if he does; it is a characteristic of many racehorses, for example, that they go off their feed as you begin galloping them. This is just when, of course, you want to increase their food intake, rather than reduce it.

If your horse does go off his feed, there is nothing you can do but tempt him with tasty tit-bits. If you know he has a penchant for barley or maize, work some of this into his feed. Tempt him with sweet foods – sugar beet or molasses (molasses is less fattening and

therefore better for a horse in hard work). Try turning him out for an hour or two each day, both to calm him down (it is the excitement that has taken him off his feed) and to let him have some grass.

If your horse does not go off his food, begin to increase the hard food as you begin the hard training. A point-to-pointer in training should have almost as many oats as he will eat (unless, of course, he is really greedy). This generally means somewhere between 6.3kg to 7.2kg (14lbs to 16lbs). If your horse does not react well to being fed oats for any reason, and has to be fed cubes instead, give him those specially prepared for racehorses. As always, reduce the amount of bulk food, such as bran and hay, relatively as you increase the hard feed. Give the usual vitamin supplement and cod liver oil (see p. 41), while it sometimes

CLOTHES AND COLOURS

Above: Markings and designs used in racing colours, recognized by the Stewards of the Jockey Club. These colours were put onto an organized basis in the second half of the eighteenth century to overcome the confusion that had reigned hitherto. Nowadays, no two runners will ever display the same combination of markings and colours. Riders at point-to-points do not have to register their colours. If you have the same colours as another competitor, you will probably be asked to wear a different coloured hat.

Right: Riders may wear an ordinary jumper, with a distinctive sash, and a protective reinforced hat. Many point-to-point riders prefer to wear 'blouses' made of a lighter material than wool, and they often wear special padding underneath as protection in case of a fall. Competitors in hunter trials generally wear an ordinary polo neck jumper, although some hunter trials demand that a hacking jacket and shirt and tie or hunting stock be worn.

helps to feed a milk supplement as well, as an extra body-builder and energy-giver. The cheaper powder sold for calves is just as good as the milk supplement prepared especially for horses.

As you are feeding comparatively little hay, it is important to make sure it is the best obtainable. Should your horse begin to cough and you think this is an allergic reaction to the hay, either switch to horsehage or make sure that you soak the hay thoroughly before feeding (see p. 43). If the cough persists, seek veterinary advice immediately; you cannot race a coughing horse, whatever the reason for his complaint.

Even more than usual, the key to successful feeding of horses in hard competition lies in patient observation of both them and their feeding habits. Keep a constant, watchful eye on their condition, noticing any changes. Take note, too, of what foodstuffs they particularly like and feed these (in moderation) if they suddenly go off their food. It is important that such horses have sufficient protein for the work expected of them, but it is equally important that you do not pander to their feeding whims to such an extent that they begin to put on extra flesh. A fat horse can never be a fit horse.

Preparing for competition

Preparing a horse for hunter trials and team chases varies very little from the day-to-day routine described for pre-competition or pre-hunting days. You obviously want the horse to look his smartest, which means regular grooming beforehand, and possibly shampooing any white parts of the coat the day before the event. An application of vegetable oil (see p. 50) could save you a major cleaning-up operation after the race, but it is really necessary only if you think the conditions are going to be very muddy. Similarly, the entry procedure follows that outlined in Chapter One. Collect the schedules for as many events as possible before deciding which ones to enter. Then either make your entries by post or on the day.

Competitors in hunter trials can usually wear cross-country-type riding gear – that is, breeches and boots, a coloured jumper and an ordinary velvet cap, though many competitors now prefer to wear a skull cap. Check the schedule, however; some hunter trials still require you to wear a jacket with a shirt and tie or stock, rather than a jumper. In team chasing, it is usual for members of a team to wear the same jumpers, so combine to choose the colour or pattern you want for your team. Make up a name too; listen to the others called over the loudspeaker at a team event and you will see the kind of names teams make up. Often they are quite amusing, or at least somewhat informal – reflecting very much the spirit of team chasing. It is a relaxed sport – a good ride across country, where enjoying yourself is infinitely more important than winning.

The procedure for entering a point-to-point is essentially the same as for other types of competition, although there are one or two more things to bear in mind and do. Similarly, it is a good idea to work out some sort of programme for your horse between races; one suggestion is given on p. 69, but remember again that this will vary from horse to horse.

Entering a point-to-point

The first essential is to obtain the certificate which states that you have hunted the requisite number of times from the Master of your hunt and to send this off for registration. If another person is going to ride your horse in a point-to-point, he or she must have a card from the local hunt secretary showing that a hunt subscription has been paid. If they are not able to hunt throughout the season, most hunts will make a concession, so that point-to-point riders do not necessarily have to pay a full hunt subscription.

The closing date for entries for most point-to-points is a week beforehand and you can enter for as many races as you like. Most people prefer to enter two or three races at this stage, leaving them with the choice of which race to run when they get to the meeting and can sum up the competition. It is also often a good idea to enter at more than one point-to-point meeting on the same day. Since the state of the going can so easily be affected by the weather, you may well find that on the day of the race one course will suit your horse far better than another. Courses also vary tremendously; at some you will find the fences are infinitely easier than at others. Consider, too, whether your horse prefers to gallop left- or right-handed; courses go in different directions at different point-to-points and it is sensible to enter those your horse will favour whenever possible.

In most cases it is possible to walk the course the day before and all jockeys should certainly do this before riding a race. Check the ground for undulations or unevenness across the course. Take note of places where these occur and try to plan a route that keeps you on the flattest ground possible, even though this may have to be adapted in action. Note any patches of the course where the going is particularly soft, and avoid these – unless your horse likes soft going. If you cannot avoid the soft spots, remember to steady your horse at these places, rather than have him flounder and perhaps pull a tendon. Check the take-off at each fence, so that you can select the best spot for you and your horse in each case.

You must decide, too, on what colours to wear. These do not have to be registered if they are to be used only in point-to-point races. If you find on the day that some one else has exactly the same colours, then borrow a different colour hat. You must wear a skull cap and not an ordinary velvet cap.

Once the point-to-point season begins and you are racing on various Saturdays, you will need to devise a different programme for your horse from that one you have been following so far. A possible outline is given on p. 71.

At the event

The routine for taking the horse to an event – whether it is a hunter trial, a team chase or a point-to-point – is exactly the same as travelling anywhere in a horse box and trailer. Make sure your horse is properly equipped for travelling and that you have taken all the ancillary and spare items of equipment he may need during the day. In these instances, an anti-sweat rug is an important item; your horse will normally be very hot immediately after the competition and will need an anti-sweat rug to allow him to cool down without catching cold.

At a hunter trial and a team chase, either make or confirm your entries with the secretary. In either case, you will need to go to the secretary's tent or caravan to pick up your number, to find out the estimated time of your class and when you are to go in the list of entries.

Below: HRH Princess Anne wearing an ordinary white shirt and hunting stock, fairly formal clothing for a hunter trial.

Walking the course

In some cases it may be possible to walk the course the day before the event, but for many riders it is more convenient to do this on the actual morning. Make sure you arrive in plenty of time to allow this. Walk the whole way around the course, examining the approach and landing to the jumps. Note any that are particularly heavy, or likely to get sticky later on in the day, and make a note of the point to steady your horse as he comes into such obstacles. Note, too, any hidden ditches on landings, which will denote fences that you must ride your horse towards strongly, giving him sufficient impetus to land well over the jump. Check for uneven ground or any places where the course allows you to take a shorter line and thus save time. Plan your whole route, including the approach into each fence so as to jump it in the spot you think best. If the ground looks heavy in front of any fence, plot an alternative line of approach in case the take-off area has become churned-up by the time you get there. Make sure you have noted the position of all the flags that mark the course; you must pass the stipulated side of these or else you will be eliminated.

In a team chase you should follow the same procedure, but in this instance you will naturally discuss such matters with your team mates, plus deciding on who will take the lead at certain fences, whereabouts to approach them, and so on. Having decided on a group strategy, remember it and stick to it when actually riding the course.

Getting into action

With luck, you will be drawn to ride well down the list of competitors, so you will have the chance of watching others in action before you. You can learn from this which are the tricky parts of the course and which obstacles are troublesome; it is very often the ones that looked quite straightforward when walking the course that cause the most trouble. Time a few horses over the course too, to see how long it is taking them to ride. If you have hunted regularly, or know your horse well, you should know the approximate speed in which he is capable of going round the course without becoming distressed. If you are riding in an autumn hunter trial, and you do not feel he is really fit, it may be necessary to pull up and give him a breather half-way round the course – there is no point in over-taxing him; it just means you will not have a horse for the hunting season in front of you. Decide just where you mean to give him this little rest, and then do so, making sure you are not in the way of anybody riding the course behind you.

Stick to your plan of campaign as you ride the course, if at all possible. It is not always easy to do so in the thrill of the competition, but, if it was carefully thought out beforehand,

ASPECTS OF CROSS COUNTRY RIDING

Left: Competitors walk the course before the start of a hunter trial. **Below left:** Co-ordinating racing colours ready for a point-to-point. **Below right:** Two lady riders weigh out with the clerk of the scales. **Bottom:** A competition horse being walked round a carefully prepared track for gentle exercise. **Opposite, top:** Two riders take a wooden tiger trap in a team chase event. **Centre:** A large field in a hurdle race. **Opposite bottom:** The certificate that must be completed before a horse can run in a point-to-point.

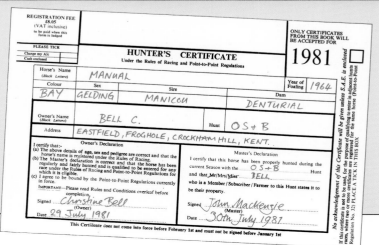

it must be advisable to follow it. The main thing to remember is never to risk injuring your horse by making him do more than he is capable of – either because of his sheer ability or because he is not sufficiently fit. If, on the other hand, you come within sight of the finish and your horse is going strongly and well, push him on over the last few fences – success may be yours.

After you have ridden, dismount and take off the saddle. Put on an anti-sweat rug, if necessary, and walk the horse round to cool him. You may sometimes have quite a long wait before the results; if you know you are not in the running, take your horse home.

Point-to-point procedure

At a point-to-point, you must declare that your horse is going to run with the clerk of the course three-quarters-of-an-hour before the scheduled time of the race. The jockey must 'weigh-out' with the clerk of the scales – that is, he has to be weighed with the saddle, saddle cloth and breast plate to ensure that the horse is carrying the correct minimum weight. This is laid down in the official regulations for a point-to-point; a horse that has won previously is penalized by having to carry extra weight.

About 35 minutes before the race, tack-up the horse and thoroughly check all your equipment again, looking for loose stitching, or thin spots in the leather. If you find any, discard that piece of tack and substitute another; a point-to-point race is not the place to trust to luck. Tacking-up is probably best done in the horse box; your horse may by now have sensed the atmosphere of the racecourse and could be getting excited and fidgety. It is therefore easier to tack up in a relatively confined space. Depending on the weather, put rugs on over the tack – obviously using your best, cleanest rugs, rather than dirty stable ones. It can often be bitterly cold at point-to-points and it is important to keep a horse warm and happy before the start of a race.

The horse is now ready to go into the paddock. All horses must be paraded there for a quarter of an hour to give spectators a chance to see them all and decide which one to entrust with their bets. An official will say when the horses must be mounted, after which they are taken down to the start of the race. This generally entails a good canter along the track down to the start, which gives the horses time to stretch out and prepare themselves for the ensuing race. It is customary at this time to take them to a fence to show it to them, although this is not – or should not be – essential.

You will find it a great help, particularly if you and your horse are fairly new to point-to-pointing, to study the other horses running in your race. Watch them at other point-to-points, so that you get to know those which race well and which are good jumpers. Tuck in behind

69

one such when you come to race yourself and try to avoid any that you have noticed have a tendency to fall or suddenly run across the track in front of a fence as they approach it. On a novice horse, try to give him a view of the fences as he comes to them; in other words, do not be so tucked in behind another horse that the fence comes as a surprise to your mount. If you find your horse at the front of the field, but he is galloping and jumping well, stay there, rather than pulling back in an attempt to let someone else make the pace. And if you find yourself up with the leaders with your horse going well underneath you, in sight of the finish, push on for all you are worth.

Once again, it is vitally important not to overtax a horse, particularly in the early point-to-points of the season. If you feel him tiring, even if you are only half-way round a course, pull him up then, rather than run the risk of a fall. A tired horse will become careless and may hit a fence hard. Even if this does not bring him down, it can shake him severely and the memory could affect him the next time you take him out.

Should you be unlucky enough to have a fall with a novice horse, you must be prepared for his confidence to be shaken. Do not run him in another race before you have done some very careful schooling over your practice jumps. See if you can persuade someone with an experienced horse to accompany you at such sessions; giving you a lead over the jumps will show your horse that everything is all right and should do much to restore his confidence.

If and when you find yourself in the first four home in a race, you must take your horse to the unsaddling enclosure. The jockey now has to be weighed-in; the horses must not leave the enclosure until they are told to do so by a steward. If you do, you might be eliminated. Put an anti-sweat rug on and have someone walk the horse round within the enclosure to cool and calm him after all the excitement. Take him home as soon as you can and make much of him. All competition horses should be examined very carefully for injury. If there is any sign of heat or swelling on the legs, bandage them carefully before settling the horse for the night.

Below: A nasty fall at the water jump during a race in Czechoslovakia. The horse's hindlegs appear to have slid beneath him (below left); he stumbles forwards with the rider still on his back (below right); but recovery is impossible (bottom).

THE CROSS COUNTRY HORSE'S YEAR

Hunter trials/team chasing
If you want to enter your horse for hunter trials or team chases towards the end of the hunting season, his year will be much the same as the hunter's (see p. 50). If you want to ride him hard in these events, do not expect him to do more than one day's hunting a week in the last two or three months of the season. To expect him to carry you out hunting twice a week and to go like the wind around cross-country jumping courses for the next month or so is too much to ask of any horse.

The week before a competition is again similar to a hunter's week, except that you could not expect to hunt hard in the middle of a week and then ride to win in a hunter trial or team chase at the weekend. If you want to ride round the course gently, resting your horse as he needs it, then that is another matter. A not too strenuous mid-week hunt could be good preparation.

As discussed previously, if you want to enter the earlier hunter trials or team chases, you will need to bring your horse up from grass a little earlier. For these horses, the year could run along the following pattern:
Midsummer: Bring your horse up from grass and follow the outline on p. 59 to p. 62 to condition him and make him fit. Remember to include some

schooling sessions and jumping practice in the programme to prepare him for the ensuing events.
Early-mid autumn: Competition time. Do not attempt to enter more than one a week. If you are riding really fast in team chases, two over a three-week period would probably be sufficient.
Late autumn-early spring: Hunting season. In the latter part of this, hunt only once a week if you want to enter further competitions.
Spring: Competition time.
Late spring: Decrease food rations and amount of riding, turning the horse out for longer and longer periods during the day. Aim to turn him out completely by end May
Early summer: Complete rest at grass with front shoes taken off and no riding at all.

Point-to-pointing:
The following programme presumes that you want to begin racing at the beginning of the season. If you decide to enter later point-to-points only, adjust the timings accordingly.
Early autumn: Bring the horse up from grass and follow outline on p. 52 to get hunting fit.
Late autumn-early winter: Hunting season. Aim to follow for the necessary eight days during this period.
Winter: Begin point-to-point training as outlined on p. 62 to p. 64. If you have not managed to hunt eight times,

finish quota as soon as possible.
Spring: Point-to-point season. Never enter for more than two point-to-points in a three-week period.
Late spring: Let the horse down gradually, over a month, decreasing his food ration and the amount of ridden work. Turn out in the paddock during the day whenever possible towards the end of this period.
Summer: Complete rest at grass.

The point-to-pointer's week: Below is a possible routine for a point-to-pointer during the racing season. Remember you will have to adjust this to suit your particular horse. It begins with the Sunday before a race the following Saturday.
Sunday: Rest day. Turn the horse out in the paddock for an hour or so if he reacts well to this. Otherwise lead him out to graze on grassy verges for a similar length of time.
Monday: 3km (2 mile) canter.
Tuesday: Ordinary hack for 1½ to 2 hours, trotting up hills.
Wednesday: 3km (2 mile) canter with a fast finish.
Thursday: Gentle hack for about 1 hour, mostly walking.
Friday: Fast sprint up grassy hill. Cool off and return home. Make a written list that evening of all the equipment you need to take to the race, including a spare bridle, girth and any other critical item of tack. Take a spare set of shoes, too; there

is generally a farrier in attendance at a point-to-point who will fit them for you. Take an elementary first aid kit.
Saturday: Assemble and check thoroughly all the equipment on your list and pack it into the horse box. Give your horse a pipe-opener in the morning if he is the sort that needs it; otherwise leave him quietly in his box until it is time to get him ready to leave. Allow yourself plenty of time to travel to the meeting. Follow the procedure outlined on p. 50 when you get there.
Sunday: Many horses tend to fret a little the day after a race, so it is not a good idea to leave them standing in the stable, even though it is a rest day. Walk them out for half-an-hour to stretch their legs and stop them fretting, then turn out in the paddock for half-an-hour or so. It is sometimes advisable to cut down the food rations slightly, but make sure they are as appetising as possible.
Monday: Keep on light rations and take for a gentle hack.

If the horse is to race again the following Saturday, follow the procedure outlined above for the rest of the week. Presuming he is not racing the next Saturday, give him a week of fairly light hacking work, with a fast sprint on the Friday or Saturday. The next week, give him a good 3km canter on Monday and Wednesday, with a fast sprint on the Friday.

CHAPTER FOUR

EVENTING

THE FEDERATION EQUESTRE INternationale (International Equestrian Federation), the controlling body of most equestrian sports, describes the three-day event as 'the most complete combined competition, demanding of the rider considerable experience in all branches of equitation and a precise knowledge of his horse's ability, and of the horse a degree of general competence, resulting from intelligent and rational training'. This description may sound daunting, but it certainly does not deter today's young riders; this tough sport, which demands a high level of expertise in three different fields of equestrianism, has become one of the most keenly contested areas of all equestrian competition. The reasons for this lie in the satisfaction of training a horse and the thrill of the competition itself, for the financial rewards in terms of prize money are small.

The birth of eventing

Modern eventing, known also as horse trials and, at one time, combined training, is one of the newest equestrian sports. Yet it originated when the great Greek soldier and horseman, Xenophon, was training horses and men to ride into battle. Xenophon realized that a horse had to possess seemingly endless resources of speed and stamina. In addition, the animal had to be supple and agile, while he also had to be totally obedient. These are the self-same qualities needed in a top eventer today.

It was not until the beginning of this century, however, that eventing, as we know it, emerged as a competition and only over the last 30 years has it risen to its current popularity. Its immediate precursor was the long distance, military 'endurance' ride, practised from the late 17th century up to the beginning of the 1900s by the cavalry arms of the French, German, Swedish and American armies. These rides seem to have varied in distance from 30km (18½ miles) to about 720km (450 miles); although they did not involve jumping, many were conducted at an extremely fast pace. The emphasis was undoubtedly on endurance.

Gradually, however, horsemen became aware of the importance and desirability of other attributes and disciplines in their horses. The agility, supple-

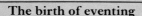

Left: One of America's lady event riders,
Torrance Watkins, takes a post and rails in fine style.
International rules decree that steel crash caps must
be worn by competitors during the cross-country section.
Above: An officer of the 20th Hussars rides into
battle. Ideally his horse would have been as fast, strong,
supple and obedient as the eventer of today.

Above: Eventing is an inter-national sport. Here a competitor is about to enter the dressage arena during the 1980 Equestrian Federation of India's National Championships in Delhi. **Top right:** Another competitor at the National Championships of India puts his horse at a formidable drop fence during the cross-country section. **Above right:** Early days at the Badminton Horse Trials. Copper Coin, with Pamela Moreton, has taken an enormous leap over the water jump. Even then (1956) the sport had a wide spectator following.

ness and obedience necessary for dressage, to-gether with jumping ability, were also sought. Thus eventing, which combines these skills with a test of speed and endurance, began to emerge. The French were the first to stage a competition with the *Championnat du Cheval d'Armes* held in 1902 as a military exercise. It was divided into four separate phases – a dressage test followed by a steeplechase, then a 50-km (30-mile) ride over roads and tracks, and finally a show-jumping competition.

From then on, eventing gained more and more recognition, it was included in the 1912 Olympics when ten nations took part. The sport was dominated by the army until after the Second World War, when two significant events led to its blossoming. The competition was extended to include civilians and the second was the interest taken in it by the Duke of Beaufort in Britain. In an exceptionally generous move, the Duke suggested that a three-day event should take place in the grounds of his home at Badminton, in Glou-cestershire.

The original idea was to stage the event in 1949, 1950 and 1951 in order to find riders and horses for the 1952 Olympic Games. So popular was the competition, however, that it has been held annually ever since, and the name Badminton is now wholly synonymous with the world of eventing. To win Badminton,

which is now classed as a championship inter-national event, is to win one of the most coveted and prestigious equestrian trophies of all.

Eventing is now a truly international sport and there are few nations that do not compete in it. This is especially the case in the USA, where the sport has gained great popularity over the last 10 to 15 years. American riders now rank among the best in the world, while the Ledyard three-day event, held annually in Boston, rates as one of the most important dates in the eventing calendar, comparable with Luhmuhlen in West Germany and Badminton and Burghley in the United Kingdom.

Eventing today

Events, or horse trials, can last for one, two and three days. All include tests of dressage, cross-country jumping and show-jumping. In a one-day and usually a two-day event, the dressage test comes first, followed by the show-jumping, with the cross-country phase last. Any horse that is eliminated in the show-jumping – where the jumps are higher than those of the cross-country – may not compete further. In a three-day event, dressage still comes first, but the cross-country is held before the show-jumping, and is itself preceded by two roads-and-tracks sections (see p. 75) and a steeplechase course

Above: Two of the most famous names of eventing — Lt. Col. Weldon and his horse, Kilbarry. This picture was taken during a cross-country practice session of the 1956 Olympic team.

— the whole being classified as a speed and endurance test, together with ability and capacity. The show-jumping, held on the final day of the event, is described as a test of soundness and precision. It is designed to show that the horses are still sufficiently supple, sound and obedient — and possess the necessary energy and courage — to jump a reasonably demanding show-jumping circuit.

The cross-country phase is generally the most important part of the trial, and the most exciting from a spectator's point of view. The official horse trial rules state that 'the relative influence on the whole competition exerted by the dressage should be slightly more than that exerted by the show-jumping, but considerably less than that exerted by the cross-country'. The inclusion of these three distinct phases is in no way haphazard; instead it represents an endeavour to put together the 'complete test' of horse and rider. In the case of three-day events, that complete test becomes a supreme test.

The dressage test shows that an extremely fit horse, capable of cross-country jumps at speed and jumping artificial fences in a show ring, is nevertheless sufficiently supple, flexible and obedient to his rider to perform a series of 'controlled' movements in a small area. The show-jumping phase that follows in a one- or two-day event, will prove to the judges that the horse is (or is not) fit to go round the cross-country course. In a three-day event, as mentioned, the cross-country phases are held on the day following the dressage and will comprise a ride over roads and tracks that has to be completed in a given time, followed by a fairly fast ride round a steeplechase course, followed by another section of roads and tracks, before the gruelling cross-country jumping course. This is not only a test of the horse's stamina, but also of his ability as a jumper, for the fences of the cross-country, although not necessarily very high, are nevertheless extremely solid, often very wide and frequently awkwardly placed. Boldness and courage are essential qualities, as are trust in, and complete obedience to, the rider.

One- and two-day events are, in fact, quite different to the three-day variety. They are held at novice, junior, intermediate, open intermediate and advanced levels (see below). To qualify to enter in a two-day horse trial (even at novice level), a horse and rider must first have completed at least two official one-day horse trials. In three-day events the categories are different — there are championship three-day events, standard three-day events, novice three-day events and junior three-day events. Each of these lays down various rules and regulations governing qualification for entry.

Scoring and grading

Event horses are awarded points when they are placed – or win – an event, then graded according to the points they have accumulated. The points awarded range from six to 50 for a win (according to the standard of the class), down to one to 20 for sixth place. The horses are then graded as follows: Grade I: Horses which have been awarded a total of 51 or more points at official horse trials and three-day events; Grade II: Horses which have been awarded a total of from 16 up to and including 50 points; Grade III: Horses which have been awarded a total of less than sixteen points. These grades are categorized into standards as follows: Advanced Class: restricted to Grade I and II horses; Open Intermediate Class: open to all grades; Intermediate Class: restricted to Grade II and III horses; Novice Class: restricted to Grade III horses; Junior Classes: open to horses of the appropriate grade ridden by juniors. A rider is classified as a junior from the beginning of the calendar year of his fifteenth birthday until the end of the calendar year of his eighteenth birthday.

The scoring at horse trials is deliberately complicated to reduce the possibility of errors and anomalies creeping into the final scores. At the end of the dressage phase, the competitor with the lowest score is the leader. In the cross-country and show-jumping phases, penalty marks are added to that score as they are accrued, so that the final winner will still be the person with the lowest score at the end of the three phases. If two or more competitors are equal, the result will be decided by the best cross-country score – the competitor with the lowest number of jumping and/or time penalties. If the event is still tied the competitor with the lowest dressage score wins.

Dressage

Dressage tests, even in advanced classes, are not as exacting as the requirements of 'pure' dressage (see p. 130) and most competent riders should find them comparatively simple. Obviously the requirements vary within the different classes outlined above, with the novice being the shortest and most straightforward test and the advanced the longest and most difficult. (Copies of current tests can be obtained from the relevant governing body.) All tests are divided into a series of movements, for which the judges will award a maximum of 10 marks. These are totalled and subtracted from the maximum possible marks to give a result in penalty points. Judges are looking first and foremost for obedience, and then for such things as straightness of entry, when the competitor first comes into the arena, good balance and regularity of paces, smooth transitions, correct bends round corners and on circles and acceptance of the bit throughout.

In novice tests, horses must be ridden in an

The three principal competitive elements of eventing. **Above:** The dressage test. **Above left:** The show jumping phase. **Left:** The cross-country jumping course, incorporating (**above centre**) the roads and tracks section. These three separate elements present a complete test for horse and rider. The dressage test comes first and is followed in one and two-day events by the show-jumping. If horse and rider perform to the required standard in the show-jumping ring, they then go on to compete in the cross-country phase. In a three-day event, which is described as being the supreme test for horse and rider, the dressage test if followed by the cross-country sections, with the show-jumping phase being held on the final day. The horse is tested for his suppleness and obedience in the dressage, his speed, endurance, courage and jumping ability in the cross-country and his final fitness and agility in the show jumping.

ordinary snaffle bridle, although flash, grakle or drop nosebands are allowed. In intermediate or advanced tests, a simple double bridle may be used if preferred. On no occasion are bit guards, whips, martingales or boots and bandages of any sort allowed. At an advanced level, competitors must wear spurs.

Cross-Country

The extent of the cross-country phase varies according to the type and standard of the event. In a one-day event, there is only a cross-country jumping course, while at a two-day event, there is also a roads-and-tracks section and a steeplechase course. A three-day event has a considerably extended roads-and-tracks element that is always divided into two phases, to be held before and after the steeplechase. The cross-country jumping course is also considerably longer.

Detailed rules and regulations cover the nature of the cross-country fences, for it is here that riders and horses are tested to the extreme. It is stated that the 'obstacles must be solid, fixed and imposing and should be left as far as possible in their natural state, but where natural obstacles are used, they must be reinforced if necessary'. Height and width restrictions are imposed on all obstacles. Though by show-jumping standards these are quite low, they can appear enormous to a tiring horse and rider and are often not placed in easy jumping conditions.

Competitors should ensure that they are thoroughly familiar with the height and width restrictions governing the standard of class they are entering. They should know, too, the time allowed for each section (the rules give a distance per minute allowance) so that they can ride accordingly. If they exceed the time allowed they will be given penalty points; if they exceed the time limit, which is generally twice the time allowed, they will be eliminated.

Penalties are also given for refusing at fences, running out or circling at an obstacle and falling (horse and/or rider). Elimination occurs the third time a horse refuses at any one fence, for taking the wrong course, or for passing the wrong side of a boundary flag.

Show-Jumping

In three-day events, the object of the show-jumping phase is 'solely to prove that, after a severe test of endurance, the horse has retained the suppleness, energy and obedience necessary for him to continue in service'. Though the course is never extremely demanding – as tricky or twisty as you will often see in a show-jumping event – it can often cause a lot of trouble. Horses used to galloping boldly forward over cross-country jumps can sometimes experience difficulty in the restricted confines of a show-jumping arena, unless they have been prepared to cope with such circumstances.

The event horse

There is no simple formula for choosing the perfect event horse. Indeed, having the right type of horse may not have as much bearing on your ultimate success as the way you treat, train and ride him. However, the age of a prospective event horse should always be taken into consideration. Horses may not be entered in official horse trials until they are five years old (six for three-day events). Many experienced event riders like to buy a horse younger than this – either a completely un-broken horse or a three-to-four-year-year-old, broken in but not schooled seriously.

If you are a novice, you may not want to be responsible for the great majority of the horse's training yourself, although bear in mind you could be guided by an experienced instructor and trainer, which would mean that you were 'trained' together. Should you decide there-fore, to buy a slightly older horse, be very care-ful. You must first try to discover why the horse is being sold – is it because his previous owner did not really rate his chances as a good eventer, or that he had some fundamental bad habit that could not be cured? A four- or five-year-old that you feel comes from sensitive owners, has been lightly ridden and introduced to the hunting field, is an ideal to look for.

Most successful event horses are three-quarter bred, seven-eighths bred or pure Thoroughbred. This is because the character-istics associated with such breeding are among those sought after in an eventer. Many people, however, feel that a pure Thoroughbred could be too excitable and 'hot-natured' to be a top-class eventer – unlikely, perhaps to settle sufficiently to perform dressage well, or likely to become upset by a minor error on the cross-country course. For this reason, they prefer horses with some solid 'hunter' blood in their close ancestry. Whatever the case, base your judgement on the horse itself, rather than on its parentage.

An event horse must be 15hh or over. Again, many riders feel that somewhere around 16hh to 16.3hh is the perfect height – above this, good conformation is harder to find, while training can become more difficult, particularly for women. Somewhat unusually, sex should also be taken into consideration. Often, geld-ings are preferred to mares, since it is argued the former are more reliable and less tempera-mental. Conformation is, as always, important.

As you look at the horse, you should also be aware of a certain presence – something a little extra that makes him stand out from other animals. You are looking for an even, kind temperament, but you want a horse that is obviously on the ball – that reacts, for example, to any sudden movement around him. A horse with a dull temperament will not be a good event horse; he will not instantly catch the eye of the dressage judge, nor have the extra reserves of energy that keep him going even when he is tired. You want a horse that appears to be dominant rather than submissive – that has at least some mind of his own rather than doing what he is told but without much enthusiasm. A dominant horse may refuse to do what you ask of him to begin with, but once

Right: A three-quarter or seven-eights Thoroughbred cross horse that could make an ideal eventer. It has a good front, a short back and nice, clean legs with good sloping pasterns. Its only fault is that its hindquarters look a little on the weak side.

you have established who is the master, and he puts his trust in you, that boldness will work to your advantage.

The importance of movement

Never judge a horse simply on how he looks when standing still. The way he moves is even more important; and ideally you are looking for a horse that is so beautiful in movement, he takes your breath away. This does not mean that movements should be extravagant; excessive pointing of toes or throwing about of legs is a suspicious sign and means that the horse should usually be avoided. Look for a horse with good natural balance at all paces. A good walk is very important, while the trot should display a springy, even stride. The horse should canter correctly in three-time.

When you ask for a little more of the horse at each pace, see whether he lengthens his stride or merely moves his legs faster. It is a lengthening of stride you want. Certainly you are looking for a comfortable ride, but does he feel strong and powerful beneath you? Do the paces feel 'elastic', like a coiled-up spring? A good length of stride is extremely important – a horse that covers the ground with long, easy strides will not tire nearly as quickly as the horse whose legs have to work much faster.

Jumping ability

Hopefully, any horse you consider buying will have been taught at least elementary jumping, so you can assess his capability to some extent. This is not easy – some authorities will tell you that you can judge ability from the way he tackles small obstacles – that if he jumps these badly, he is not likely to be better at tackling larger ones. Others say many horses think small fences are not worth troubling about and jump them badly. Also, a horse will probably jump familiar fences efficiently, but he may not react in the same way to the unknown.

If you feel your mount has jumping ability and yet he jumps small obstacles carelessly, take him over something larger and see how he tackles it. Try setting up a few jumps at varying distances from one another, altering his usual routine. See if he goes into these willingly, naturally shortening and lengthening his stride to cope with the variations in distance. Remember you are looking for a horse that jumps both boldly and cleverly; your horse must be bold enough to tackle the awesome jumps on the cross-country course and clever enough to avoid or jump himself out of any difficulty.

If the horse has had a reasonable amount of experience at jumping, try him over a few natural obstacles of the type you might encounter in an event. He should be unperturbed by strange-looking jumps; if he is worried, try to assess whether this is natural caution about something he has not previously encountered. This would be something you can

correct with careful training.

It is also important to see how a horse copes with the mistakes he makes. If he hits a fence, ride him round and take it again. He should have learnt to jump higher to make sure he does not touch the fence. Watch, too, to see if he can get himself out of trouble if he approaches a fence incorrectly – coming in too close to it, for instance. What you hope he will do then is to fold his front legs up beneath him tightly and really propel himself upwards and forwards from his hocks.

Be very wary of a horse that refuses or runs out at any of the fences you are asking him to jump, especially if they are comparatively small. A horse should be able to take them from an awkward stride or almost a standstill if necessary. Refusal to do this could mean that he already has bad jumping habits, which are very difficult to eliminate. It could also indicate a basic unsoundness, the pain of which is making him reluctant to jump.

No horse is perfect. If you look hard enough you will always find something wrong – a conformation defect, a distrustful expression or an unwillingness to jump certain obstacles. You must decide whether that defect is so fundamental that it will affect the horse's performance or something that can be overcome by sensitive handling and careful training.

Top left: A very nice looking horse that could make a good eventer. It is a three-quarter bred with the look of a natural athlete. It has a good front with lovely sloping shoulders, strong-looking hindquarters and a good 'outline'. **Top right:** On appearance, this does not look a good potential eventer. It is far too heavy for the work; it has a big head and a short neck which will impede smooth movement and good balance; it has a straight shoulder – note how 'upright' its front legs appear to be – a flat back and weak quarters; its hocks are also too straight, which means it may not have the upward spring and impulsion that comes from well-bent hocks. **Above:** Before buying a horse, watch how he moves at speed. Look for a long, easy stride that covers considerable ground with each step. Short, choppy strides will quickly tire both horse and rider.

Above: The hunting field is the ideal training ground for a potential eventer. If ridden sensibly, he will get a feel for galloping across country taking natural fences in his stride.
Right: All riders — however experienced — will benefit from regular lessons from a qualified instructor. Choose someone conversant with the eventing disciplines, who can help you realize your horse's full potential.

Training the eventer

While a horse must be fit to enter any horse trials, and absolutely at the peak of his fitness for a three-day event, the conditioning and preparatory programme is not directed solely to this end, particularly if dealing with a novice horse. In this instance it must include training to ensure that the dressage work and the jumping ability are up to the required standard. Before you can plan your programme, therefore, you have to decide how much training your horse needs and to what level. A young horse of four or five will have to be worked extensively to develop his dressage, while he will also need considerable jumping training and practice. With an older, more experienced, horse of, say, 10, the emphasis will be more on getting the animal really fit. In this instance, the horse should hopefully be classed as Grade I, so he will have a thorough basic grounding in dressage and already be thoroughly experienced in tackling cross-country and show-jumping event courses.

A good eventer should be at the peak of his career at the age of 10 to 12; it is during this period that he should be competing in championship three-day events. It is vital not to hurry a horse in his early years. It may destroy his confidence and his legs, for instance, will not fully harden until he is six or seven.

Basic training

Assuming you have bought a four-year-old horse that has been well broken-in and taught to jump, your initial aim will be to enter him in a few novice events the following year.

The best exercise and training you can do with your horse in his first winter is to take him hunting. (Remember to tie a green ribbon into his tail to indicate to others that he is young and inexperienced.) He needs to be reasonably fit for this, but not necessarily at top hunting fitness, for you should not hunt him hard. The idea is to instill an idea in him that riding across country, popping over the odd jump, is something to enjoy, rather than something to be looked upon as hard work. Take care of your horse in the hunting field; do not gallop on hard, sticky or rough ground; do not ask him to jump anything really big and do not ask him to jump at all unless you are satisfied that the conditions are thoroughly favourable. Asking too much of him at this stage could cause physical injury or mental upset.

Towards the end of the hunting season, begin to include some formal schooling sessions in between hunting days (aim to hunt just once a week). Always ensure that your horse enjoys his training. Never over-face him, so that he gets wary of your demands, and never overdo a training session, so that he gets stale and bored. An event horse must enjoy himself to be successful, and he must have complete trust in you, knowing that what you ask him to do is always reasonable. Never sacrifice the thoroughness of training because you want to see quick results. It is infinitely better to delay your entry into competition than to enter before the horse is really ready and thus run the risk of ruining him. Resolve too, to maintain a high standard of riding throughout your training; it is easy to become sloppy and careless

unless you constantly concentrate on what you are doing, yet it is vitally important that you give clear, concise aids and ride with sympathetic hands, particularly if you are training a youngster. Have regular lessons from an expert to make sure your riding is up to scratch and your training following the right lines.

The accent in these early training sessions is on schooling, not in trying to get your horse fit. Aim to school on three days out of the seven and never for more than about 20 minutes at a time. It is then reasonable to ask for total concentration. After such a session, hack out for about three-quarters of an hour, to show your horse that life is not all work.

Schooling – the first aims

Your first aim is to get the horse moving forward freely and happily on a light rein. Do not worry excessively if his head is not correctly positioned at this stage or about whether he is thoroughly on the bit. These are things to perfect later. Ask for walk and trot, looking for good steady, rhythmic paces in which the legs are really working and the horse is going calmly. Work at rising trot at this stage – sitting trot puts too great a strain on the muscles of the back and could cause hollowing – and ride on the outside diagonal. Sit for the first few strides when you ask for a trot from a walk and for the last few strides when returning to a walk.

It is best to school in a large rectangular area, rather than by circling. You want to ensure that your horse is able to go straight before asking for continual bend. Try to get him into the habit, though, of going round the corners correctly, asking for the correct bend and making sure his shoulder does not fall into the inside of the track during the turn.

Keep the work to walk and trot to begin with, looking for a general willingness and desire

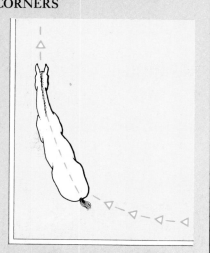

RIDING CORNERS

It is tempting to cut across corners in a rectangular school or manège, but to do so will soon make your horse unbalanced. **Above left:** You should ride a corner so that your horse's body bends in an arc. **Above right:** Bad cornering; the horse's hind-quarters have been allowed to fall outside the track. **Left:** The rider is controlling her horse through the corner so that there is no change of pace or tempo.

to please and an understanding of moving forward freely. When he is going forward well at a walk and trot and taking the corners reasonably accurately, try to instill in him the idea of moving in a straight line as well. This sounds easy, but any rider knows it is not as simple as it seems. Most young horses have a tendency to move in a slightly crooked fashion and you have to work to ensure that the hind feet exactly follow the tracks of the front feet. This means positioning his spine so it is parallel to the side of the school or the outer line of your rectangular area. Remember that horses are narrower across the shoulders than they are across the hindquarters; therefore, if your horse's side is parallel to the wall or side of the track, his hindquarters must be inside his forehand. What you must do, therefore, is to bring the shoulders very slightly inwards by gently squeezing on the inside rein, while supporting this action with the outside rein.

It is very important to get into the habit of thinking of the outside rein as a supporting rein; many riders forget this and, as a consequence, their horse's shoulders fall in, there is an awkward bend along the neck and the last thing the animal is able to do is to move forward in a straight line. As you apply this rein aid, keep your horse moving straight forward by exerting slight leg pressure. If you do not use your legs, the rein aid would make the horse slow down.

LEG YIELDING

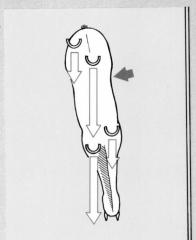

One of the first exercises used to teach a young horse the important principle of moving away from the rider's leg. It is an elementary lateral movement in which the horse is asked to move both forwards and sideways. His neck and body are bent slightly in the opposite way from the direction he is moving. The rider asks the horse to move away from an active leg aid and then controls that movement with the opposite hand. The horse's quarters impose the direction, but they should be preceded by the shoulders. The solid arrow shows the position of the active leg.

Canter and leg yield

When you are happy with progress at walk and trot, start asking for a gentle canter. In these early stages, do not fuss too much about applying the right aids to ask your horse to strike off on a given lead; instead, when you come to a corner of the school (at a tròt), sit down in the saddle and give a sharp kick. Encourage him forward with your voice, too. If he does strike off on the correct lead, let him canter at least down the long side of the school and then bring him back to a trot. The important thing here is that you bring him back to a trot, not that he should drop back into it of his own volition because you are not pushing him forward. If he strikes off on the wrong lead, let him canter for a little way to establish his stride, and then bring him back to a trot and try again. Do not pull him up immediately, as it will confuse and upset him.

Remember that all your flat work must be conducted on both sides evenly. All horses will have a preference for one side and, at the canter, there is always one side on which you can be assured of getting the right lead. It is vital to eliminate such a preference, otherwise the horse will develop lop-sidedly.

The other thing to ask of your horse at this stage is to begin to leg yield – that is, to move away from your leg. Your horse may have been taught to do this, or he may do it almost naturally; horses differ markedly in their sensitivity to this movement. It is important, though, that you feel the horse is going forward well in walk, trot and canter on a light contact – in other words, that he is answering your forward leg aids, before asking him to move away from your leg.

Once you feel your horse has begun to understand what is required, try walking down the centre line, taking one forward step and then asking your horse to move away from your leg for one step. A horse will naturally fall towards the track from the centre of the school, so this makes it easier for him. Do the exercise in either direction, taking no more than three or four forward steps, interspersed with three or four sideways steps. Do not prolong the exercise and follow it with a good strong trot round the school to remind the horse of the importance of moving forward on your command.

Turn on the forehand and lungeing

Teaching a turn on the forehand is another useful exercise for getting the horse to move away from your leg. It can also help you to realize how the outside hand can be used as a supporting aid, while aiding you to gain control of the animal's hindquarters (opposite). It certainly is not such a good exercise as others for suppling the horse and strengthening his muscles, but it serves a useful purpose in the early training.

Whether you include any lungeing in your schooling sessions, or use it only for exercise, will depend on whether you are for or against its use for general schooling. It can be used to develop a horse's balance and to supple him; to make his paces regular and rhythmic and to help to develop the correct bend on a circle. On the other hand, it is often difficult to make a horse really work with his hindquarters properly engaged beneath him.

If you do decide to give your horse some lungeing exercise, work on a large circle, rather than a small one which can put an unnecessary strain on the joints of the legs, and lunge for no more than 10 minutes at first. Try to make your horse really work on the lunge, lengthening his stride when you ask him, rather than merely going forward faster.

An important , but often overlooked, aspect is to teach your horse to stand still when you ask him to do so. From the very first time you go to mount him, make him stand still while you mount and remain still until you ask him to move forward. When you bring him to a halt from a walk, always make sure he stands quite still for as long as you require. Sit on his back for four or five seconds before dismounting, to get him into the habit.

You will find that these processes can be covered in about six weeks. By the end of that time, your horse should be moving forward well at all paces, answering your aids instantly, leg yielding happily and standing quite still whenever you ask him. Incorporate some circling work, too. Remember, again, that you are not seeking total perfection at this stage. If he appears willing to please and seems to be enjoying himself – then you have achieved your first, most important, aim.

Left: The position at the halt is extremely important and nothing wins or loses points more quickly in a dressage test. A horse should halt squarely — that is with front and back legs together, his weight distributed evenly over them. This means his hind legs must be brought well under his body. He should keep absolutely still, his head held so that there is a straight line down his neck and right through his spine. His neck should be arched and his head held quite high and well flexed from the poll. He should be ready to move instantly, but smoothly, at a signal from the rider, so he must look bright and attentive.

THE TURN ON THE FOREHAND

An exercise that should be included in the early part of the training of a young horse. It teaches him to move away from an active leg and is useful, therefore, for instilling this basic principle. It should not be necessary to include this exercise in later schooling.
Below: Stages of a left turn on the forehand — the quarters turning to the right, pivoting round the near-foreleg. To ask for this, sit tall and centrally in the saddle, very

slightly incline the horse's head to the left and use your left leg strongly against his side. Support your rein aid with the right rein to prevent the shoulders dropping away and keep your right leg against the horse's side to prevent him moving backwards. When he has completed the turn so that he is facing in the opposite direction, ask him to walk forward immediately.

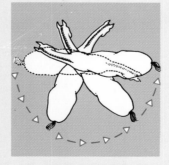

Left: Diagram showing the progression of a horse's body in the turn on the forehand. He pivots round the inside foreleg, his quarters moving in a circle around the front legs. Thus the hind leg on the same side as the pivoting foreleg must cross over *in front* of the other hind leg, (see picture 4 below).

Below left: A medium walk. In this the horse's stride should appear free, with a good amount of spring or energy. The hindlegs are fully engaged so that they are active beneath him. **Below right:** An extended walk. To the uninitiated, this can appear almost the same as a good medium walk. However, the legs should really be striding out to cover as much ground as possible. The hind feet should touch the ground well in front of the prints left by the front feet. **Bottom left:** A medium trot. Like the medium walk, the pace is active and springy with the impulsion coming from the hindquarters. **Bottom right:** An extended trot. Again each stride should cover as much ground as possible. The horse lengthens his neck to achieve this, but the rider must maintain a good steady contact.

The start of training

After the initial schooling sessions have been completed, turn your horse out and give him a complete break for about six weeks. From the time he comes back into work again, it will take at least 12 weeks to prepare him for an event.

The first task is to plan a specific training programme. In this you must develop the horse's flat work, make sure his jumping ability is up to the required standard and get him sufficiently fit to enter an event. Thus your programme must include schooling work, jumping practice and conditioning exercise to harden the legs, develop the muscles and ensure his heart and lungs are working efficiently. As always, aim to work your horse for six days and to give him one rest day, during which he should be turned out for at least a couple of hours.

It is a good idea to sketch out a 12-week programme on paper and then to note any changes you find necessary. Such a permanent record is invaluable in helping to devise future programmes, both for this particular horse and for new ones. Remember that the programme must include a sensible feeding and stable management routine as well as the exercise aspects.

For the first week of bringing your horse up from grass, do no more than walk him for half an hour or so a day in the same way as for a hunter (see p. 38). Towards the end of the second week, include some trotting work. In the third week you can begin to include about 20 minutes' schooling, coupled with half-an-hour's light exercise at the end of this. In the fourth week you can extend the schooling to about half an hour – the maximum period for intensive schooling. Later, you should also include some jumping practice, too. The time to reach these various stages depends on how long he has been out of work. If your horse has had a longer rest, you need to increase the length of time devoted to walking and trotting before starting formal schooling and jumping.

You should familiarize yourself thoroughly with what is wanted in the novice dressage tests, that you fully understand the definition of such terms as medium walk, working trot, counter canter, and so on. In order to get as close to perfection as possible in these move-

ments, you should ask your horse to perform more advanced movements as well. These will give him the necessary balance, suppleness and mastery.

Circling work should now be featuring in your schooling sessions. Make the circle large to begin with – about 20m (65ft) in diameter. This means the horse will not have to bend too much to follow the circumference, so you can also concentrate on his paces. Work at all paces at the sitting trot and begin to ask your horse to accept the bit and position his head correctly. Remember to work evenly on both sides, changing the rein by turning and walking across the centre of the circle.

Start to ask your horse to lengthen his stride. Keep a light contact on the reins and squeeze your calves alternately against his side. At a walk, for example, when you feel the inside hind leg come forward, squeeze with your inside leg, then squeeze with the outside calf as he steps forward with his outside leg. The speed of the walk should not increase, but you should feel the legs really striding out beneath you and you should be aware of more ground being covered. As you squeeze with your legs, squeeze gently with your hands too, so that he is not tempted to increase the pace. You should develop a 'squeeze-release-squeeze-release' rhythm.

As you ask for a lengthening of the stride, make sure that your horse does not throw his quarters or shoulders to the outside or inside of the arc of the circle. Remember to use your outside hand to support the outside shoulder and your inside leg to maintain the correct bend.

Besides this your constant aim is now to get the hindquarters well beneath your horse. He can only do this if the joints of his hind legs and quarters are sufficiently supple. Use your exercise periods to help you with this; trotting up a gentle hill, in particular, can help with engaging the hind legs more effectively, as the greater part of the horse's weight is over them. In any event, try to vary the location of your schooling sessions, so that they are not always held in the same place. This will help to keep your horse on his toes and interested.

Also, as you progress to the stage where your horse is getting fitter and more full of himself, try not to be tempted to go for a calming hack before schooling. The dressage test comes at the beginning of a horse trial, and so you want to instill the idea in your horse of doing this sort of controlled work before going for a good ride across country.

Get into the habit of doing as much as possible of your schooling work at the trot, for this is the basis of good training. Asking for variations of stride at a trot will help greatly in suppling and balancing the horse. You may also find it easier to keep the horse going forward well whilst fully accepting the bit than you do at either a walk or a canter, as it is often easier to maintain controlled forward impulsion at the

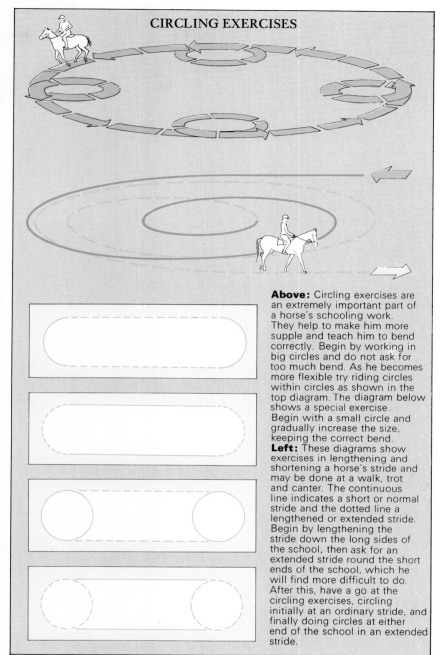

CIRCLING EXERCISES

Above: Circling exercises are an extremely important part of a horse's schooling work. They help to make him more supple and teach him to bend correctly. Begin by working in big circles and do not ask for too much bend. As he becomes more flexible try riding circles within circles as shown in the top diagram. The diagram below shows a special exercise. Begin with a small circle and gradually increase the size, keeping the correct bend.
Left: These diagrams show exercises in lengthening and shortening a horse's stride and may be done at a walk, trot and canter. The continuous line indicates a short or normal stride and the dotted line a lengthened or extended stride. Begin by lengthening the stride down the long sides of the school, then ask for an extended stride round the short ends of the school, which he will find more difficult to do. After this, have a go at the circling exercises, circling initially at an ordinary stride, and finally doing circles at either end of the school in an extended stride.

trot. Work at the extended trot will help to promote freedom of movement in the hindquarters and the shoulders, really suppling the muscles. Having developed good extension at the trot, you will again find it easier to ask for this at a canter.

Lateral work

Now is the time to include some more active lateral or two-track work into your schooling sessions. Leg-yielding and turning on the forehand, though fairly elementary exercises, also come under this heading.

The lateral work you are chiefly concerned with includes the movements in which the horse steps forwards and sideways at the same time. Do not attempt it until you are satisfied that your horse has thoroughly grasped the knack of going forwards freely. Lateral work helps tremendously in suppling the horse and strengthening the muscles, particularly those of the shoulder. It also encourages him to bend and it improves the flexibility of the joints. This improvement makes it easier for the horse to bring the hind legs beneath him.

The first movement to teach the horse now is the shoulder-in (see p.152), which is the foundation for all other lateral movements. Done correctly, it will certainly bring increased suppleness by loosening up the shoulders and strengthening the hind legs, which will give them greater mobility. It is important that the hindquarters should not swing off the outside of the track when the shoulders are brought in towards the centre; if this happens, the benefit of the exercise will be lost, for the horse will not be bending his body correctly.

The initial tendency is generally to get too much inside bend – that is overt, incorrect bending of the head and neck. This is often caused by the rider using the inside rein too strongly, and not supporting it with the outside rein. You must use your outside hand to control the bend and the horse's energy. Keep your inside rein low to prevent the neck from becoming rigid and maintain a constant squeeze-release action so that the head does not become 'set'. Do not ask for too much bend at first; just ask for a little and make sure the outside shoulder does not fall away. As the horse reponds to this, start to use your inside hand to ask for more bend of the head and neck.

Ask the horse to maintain a shoulder-in for three or four strides, then straighten him for several strides. Come down the other side of the school and ask for the movement again. Straighten him again and change the rein, really asking him to lengthen his stride so that he stretches forward. Repeat the exercise on the other rein; points to bear in mind are that the horse is bent away from the direction in which he is travelling and that the speed and tempo of pace should be maintained before, during and after the exercise.

From a shoulder-in, you can progress to a half-pass (see p.158). This is another exercise that helps greatly in bringing the horse's hind legs beneath him, thereby lightening the forehand. It also demands greater agility from the horse as he really has to flex and stretch his hind legs to effect the movement. Unlike the shoulder-in, his body is now bent in the direction in which he is travelling, but, in common with the shoulder-in, you might find it hard to maintain the correct bend initially.

Counter-canter

By now, your horse should be easily able to canter on a given lead as you request. Normally you will ask him to lead with the inside leg when riding round the school or in a circle, but advanced dressage tests ask for a counter-canter to be ridden in the second loop of a serpentine.

The counter-canter is not only an excellent exercise in obedience, but also very useful as a suppling and balance exercise. It can help to straighten a horse that has a tendency to go crooked or to fall into the inside at a canter, but it should not be introduced into the schooling until the horse is going well at an ordinary canter – that is, his paces are even and balanced and he will strike off on a correct lead when asked. To ask for a counter-canter, reverse the aids you would normally give.

After this, try cantering a figure of eight, beginning with a circle of true canter and then asking for the second circle in counter-canter. Then progress to serpentines (the movement asked for in an advanced test), cantering the first loop in true canter, the second in counter-canter and then asking for the second circle in counter-canter. Then progress to serpentines

DRESSAGE TERMS

There are 10 dressage movements required in eventing dressage tests up to an advanced level. The definitions are as follows.
Medium walk: The horse should walk forward freely, but actively, with the hindlegs well engaged beneath him. The stride should be evenly spaced and he should maintain a straight line. The rider should keep a light but steady contact with the mouth to keep the head still.

Extended walk: The horse's strides should still be regular but he should cover as much ground as possible. This means a **lengthening** rather than quickening of stride, in which the hind feet come to the ground in front of the print left by the fore feet. The rider maintains a steady contact with the mouth, but lets the

horse stretch his neck a little further forward.
Medium trot: The horse moves forward freely and actively again, with his hind legs well engaged beneath him.
Working trot: This is generally defined as being a 'tempo between the medium and collected trot.' It is a little livelier and springier than the medium trot, with the horse showing greater flexion from the poll.
Extended trot: This is similar to an extended walk in that the horse lengthens his stride. This necessitates greater impulsion from the hind-quarters and free use of the shoulders, together with a stretching of the neck. The rider must maintain steady contact in order to keep the horse straight and to ensure a rhythmic stride.

Working canter: A pace between the medium and collected canter. The horse will move freely and rhythmically, showing perfectly balanced, even paces. He should move in a straight line with the impulsion coming from his quarters.
Extended canter: The stride is lengthened so as to cover more ground, but should remain even and light. The horse goes forward calmly, extending his neck to achieve the pace.
Counter-canter: The only difference between a counter-canter and an ordinary canter is that the horse leads with the outside, rather than the inside, leg. When riding on the right rein, for example, it is usual to lead with the off-fore; in a counter-canter, the rider asks the horse to canter with the near-fore leading. It is a fairly advanced movement, asking

for considerable suppleness from the horse, as his body will not be bent to the line of the circle.
Shoulder-in: A lateral or two-track movement, in which the forehand is taken off the track to the inside of the schooling area to move along a separate parallel track. The inside foreleg has to cross over the outside leg and the horse is bent round the rider's inside leg, so that he is bent away from the direction of the movement. Hindlegs stay on the same track, moving directly forwards.

Half-pass: A two-track movement in which the horse moves forward in an oblique line, his body remaining parallel to the side of the schooling area. The outside fore and hind-legs cross over in front of the inside legs, but the forehand should lead the movement.

Above: A fine display of an extended trot during a dressage test ridden by Andrew Hoy of Australia at Fontainbleau in 1980. Note that this rider has decided against riding his horse in a double bridle. Instead he has opted for a simple egg-butt snaffle and cross-over noseband. This picture also gives you some idea of the careful scrutiny of the judges, tucked quietly away in their judging 'box'.

(the movement asked for in an advanced test), cantering the first loop in true canter, the second in counter-canter and the third in true canter. Make the loops very wide at first.

Most horses will find the counter-canter difficult to begin with, particularly since it should look as smooth and balanced as a conventional canter. Many animals will increase their pace in an effort to maintain balance and it is not unusual, too, for the hindquarters to come off the track. If you allow this to happen, the horse's balance will be upset, rather than improved. Aim to improve the pace gradually over the training period, never rushing at it; the canter is exciting for a horse and the work should be conducted as calmly as possible.

Varying the routine

All the schooling exercises discussed above are spread out over your whole schooling pro-

gramme leading up to your first event. Intersperse them throughout with jumping practice and ordinary hacking, and never let your horse get stale. It should not be necessary to have more than, say, four schooling sessions a week, although you may have to adjust this to suit your horse. If you find yourself having difficulty with one particular movement, leave it and come back to it later. If possible, take professional lessons from an expert trainer.

Over the weeks leading up to an event, make sure you have worked the horse in all the movements required in the dressage test, but only run through it completely once or, at the most, twice, some time before the event. If you ride the test over and over again, your horse will soon know it and begin to anticipate the movements. Not only will it take the sparkle out of the test on the day, but he may well begin to anticipate your next aid before it comes and could well begin a new movement in the wrong place.

87

Above: There really is no excuse for letting a horse refuse a jump, particularly a fairly small one. It is very bad to allow a young horse to get into the habit of refusing, and providing you ride him sympathetically and never overface him, there is no reason why he should. If your horse does refuse, ride him round in a small circle and come into the jump from just a few strides away. Never let him get away with refusing; he must jump the fence before the session ends

Jumping

In the early days of jumping practice, even if you are confident in your horse's jumping ability, merely ask him to pop over a few small, scattered fences – low logs or cavaletti – taking them from a trot. The aim again is to get him going forward freely over his jumps with no hesitation or fear. Remember to shorten your stirrup leathers by a few holes when you begin, particularly if you come to it straight after a dressage schooling session. Always ask him to jump from an easy stride on a loose rein (so that you have light contact). You want him to *bascule* over the jump now, rather than jump it flat; this means snapping his front legs up in front of him as he propels himself upward and forward, then dropping his head and neck when he has cleared the top of the fence, so that in effect he 'see-saws' roundly over the jump. Taking off from an easy stride should help him to achieve this.

Introduce some combination fences into your practice session at an early stage. These encourage the horse's athletic action and encourage him to use more of himself, thereby improving balance and suppleness. Experiment with numbers of different types, but keep the fences low. Increase the width of the second fence, rather than raising either of them at this stage. If you increase the number of fences in a combination to three or four, keep the first and third to low cavaletti, so that they act mainly as a guide for the horse to balance and adjust his stride.

Try never to let a horse run out at a fence; if you allow him to get away with it just once, you may be stuck with the habit before you know where you are. The same thing applies to a refusal; young horses should simply not be allowed to stop and the way to ensure that this never happens is never to overface them. Raise fences and increase the width so gradually that the horse hardly notices it, and so that you can be sure you are not asking him to do too much. If your horse does run out, show him how this displeases you by giving him a sharp smack with the whip, then take him at it straight away with no fuss. Thereafter take him over it again and again, several times, so that he is in no doubt of what you want – and who is in command.

Just as you do not want a horse to stop at fences, so you do not want him to rush them. If he gets into this habit, it will be impossible for him to be properly balanced; nor will he be able to adjust his stride, and this the event horse must learn to do. Combination fences, particularly those on the circle, will help correct this fault. Keep him trotting at the jumps, rather than cantering, if rushing is a problem.

Try to get into the habit of letting the horse judge his moment for take-off, rather than kicking against his sides when you think it is right. He will do a much better job if left to himself and, as there will be many occasions when you will have to rely on him to get you both out of trouble when you come into a cross-country jump, it is best to establish this ability now. By doing plenty of groundwork over low fences and combinations, you should have no problem in leaving it to him when the jumps are bigger. Indeed, the less you interfere with him, the happier he will be, secure in the knowledge that he is not going to be hurt by a jab in the mouth, or an untimely dig in the ribs.

Include some individual spread and upright fences in your jumping practices, teaching your horse to come into both types of fence at an oblique angle. Also try riding towards the jump so that you have to turn shortly in front of it and then jump at an angle. Then jump at an angle from a straight approach and turn immediately after the jump. Jumping at an oblique angle allows a horse to regulate his stride, so that he approaches the jump correctly, without having to alter the length of his stride. Thus, if you arrive at the take-off point awkwardly, you can often correct for this by taking an oblique line from that point to the fence.

Vary the distances at combination fences; you will find, for example, that if you have two upright fences forming a combination, the distance apart to allow for one stride would be greater than if the second fence was a spread. Equally, the distances should vary as the heights increase. At first, set the jumps at the distance that allows your horse to take natural, comfortable strides. When he is jumping these well, alter the distances, so that he has to put in a couple of short strides instead of one long one. Remember to leave it to him to make the adjustment; do not try to interfere with his mouth or to adjust his stride on the approach.

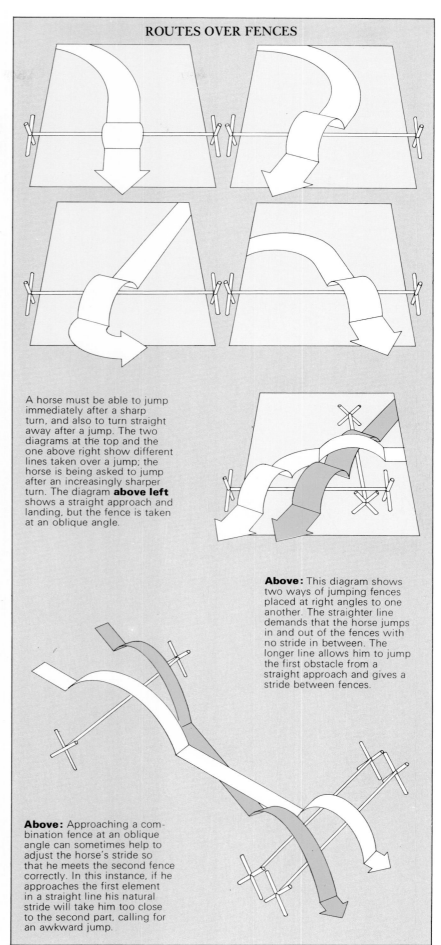

ROUTES OVER FENCES

A horse must be able to jump immediately after a sharp turn, and also to turn straight away after a jump. The two diagrams at the top and the one above right show different lines taken over a jump; the horse is being asked to jump after an increasingly sharper turn. The diagram **above left** shows a straight approach and landing, but the fence is taken at an oblique angle.

Above: This diagram shows two ways of jumping fences placed at right angles to one another. The straighter line demands that the horse jumps in and out of the fences with no stride in between. The longer line allows him to jump the first obstacle from a straight approach and gives a stride between fences.

Above: Approaching a combination fence at an oblique angle can sometimes help to adjust the horse's stride so that he meets the second fence correctly. In this instance, if he approaches the first element in a straight line his natural stride will take him too close to the second part, calling for an awkward jump.

Further jumping exercises

After a time, you can begin to try your horse round various 'courses' of jumps, including different types and distances, with bends and turns incorporated. This is the ideal way of starting to introduce your horse to the different types of jumps he will encounter in a cross-country – but, again, take care not to overface him. Legs should be protected by leather brushing-boots and over-reach boots.

Get your horse jumping ditches, banks and other natural jumps easily. Then find some typical event fences (see p. 99) and begin training over them. When you first ask him to jump a fixed, solid fence, make sure it is low, so that if he does hit it, he will learn that the fence is solid without causing himself too much injury or upset.

An event horse must become confident and adept at jumping 'drops' – that is jumping from one level of flat ground down to another – and similarly up onto a bank or a raised piece of ground. In an event, a drop can measure about 1.5 metres (5ft); putting a horse at this could be disastrous if he had no previous experience of how to tackle it.

Sit very quietly, but keep urging him forward firmly all the time, using your leg, reinforced with a stick if necessary, and reassuring him with your voice. Do not turn away, however long it takes to persuade him to jump; he will go eventually, probably with a big leap. Be prepared for this and make a great fuss of him on landing. Then ride round straight away and ask him to jump down again, then again, until the lesson is firmly planted in his mind.

Water is a feature of all event courses and you must now teach your horse to jump over a small obstacle to land directly in the water and also to jump out of it. Work at it gradually, making sure he is wading through the water (see p. 61) confidently first. Then erect a small jump, such as a cross rail, a few trotting strides away. Wade through the water on to dry land and ask him to trot over the jump. Turn round, trot over the jump and then wade through the water. Move the jump a little closer, but so it is still one stride away from the water. Then put the jump on the edge of the water so that he either jumps directly into the water, or jumps out of it. If possible, it is a good idea to place the jump actually in the water, too, so that he has to take off and land in it.

Live rehearsal

Entering your horse for one or two small hunter trials before you go in for an event will help to prepare him for the cross-country jumping phase. Never be tempted to bring on a young eventer by going in for a team chase though; you do not want to give him any taste of being led over jumps by another horse, nor do you want him to think the whole thing is a race to be galloped round in the fastest possible time.

If a horse tries to take the tricky fences of a three-day event at fast speeds before he is really experienced, it will inevitably result in disaster.

In the same way that the odd hunter trial will be good practice for a novice horse, so will small show-jumping competitions. Make sure that in both cases, you are not asking him to jump anything higher than about 90cm (3ft); you certainly do not want to overface him during a competition.

Fitness

Schooling sessions and jumping practices should be interspersed with days of hacking – the time spent on this varies depending on whether you are also including a 20-minute dressage session or a jumping practice on the same day. By working your horse for about an hour-and-a-half per day in the latter weeks of the schedule, he will be fit enough to compete in a one-day event at novice level – in which the

Above left: Fences with a considerable drop on the landing side are common in most event cross-country courses. Notice how the rider has given the horse his head and although she is sitting slightly further back than usual, is in perfect harmony with her mount. **Left:** Jumping down into water can be an unnerving experience for a horse. It is essential, therefore, to practise this before entering an event. **Above:** Jumping out of water up onto a bank. Make sure you are thoroughly conversant with jumping both on to and off banks as they are favourites with cross-country course builders.

cross-country course will be only about 1.6km (1 mile) long.

In your first novice event you should be prepared not to go the whole way round the cross-country course. Riding an exacting dressage test, followed by a twisting show-jumping course and then a gallop across country over some tough jumps is a lot to ask of a young horse at his first event. Pull up if you feel your horse is not going well and easily. Of course, there is always a temptation to push on, knowing that it is timing that decides the winner, but it is not worth it. Going too fast can make a young horse careless and you cannot afford to be careless over fixed cross-country obstacles. A bad knock is almost bound to hurt him, possibly badly, and it will certainly shake his confidence, both in his own ability and in you.

When you begin to up-grade your horse and think about entering three-day events, the emphasis in training shifts slightly. By now his dressage work should be fairly polished, while

he will have had plenty of cross-country experience, so that, although these aspects must not be entirely neglected in training, they need less emphasis. Now, it is getting the horse fit that is of paramount importance; to compete in a three-day event, a horse has to be very fit indeed.

Devising a fitness programme is an exacting task; you have to ensure you can achieve the maximum level of fitness – the hardening of the muscles and the development of the horse's wind (breathing) – while maintaining perfect soundness and keeping the horse in a calm, reasonable frame of mind. Many event riders will develop this fitness in much the same way as that outlined for a point-to-pointer, by allocating perhaps a couple of days a week over a period of time to galloping. Gradually, the length of each gallop and its speed are increased. Others prefer to use a system known as 'interval training' (see p. 92). They prefer this because they believe continuous galloping can over-excite a horse, making him think every time he is asked to go fast that he must go flat out. This can easily lead to leg injury if, for instance, he gets over-excited on rough ground. The counter argument is that, providing a horse is well schooled and obedient to his rider and the progression to galloping is gradual, there is no reason why this should affect him. It is also incorrect to assume that a horse brought to fitness through interval training is necessarily going to have harder and sounder legs than any other fit horse. By and large, however, it enables a rider to get his or her horse extremely fit in less time than the more conventional methods, while it is not necessary to have large areas of ground suitable for galloping at your disposal. Choose for yourself which system suits you best.

Interval training

The principal of interval training is to exercise your horse in short bursts (of two to three minutes, working up to six to 10), each followed by a short rest period, at the end of which you ask him to work again. The second work period should come just before he has fully recovered from the first, so that his lungs and muscles have to stretch to make that little extra effort.

The conditioning programme to prepare a horse for a three-day event is spread over 14 to 17 weeks. You will know, through knowing your own horse, whether he will need more or less time to get to a peak of fitness, but always build an extra two weeks into your conditioning programme. This will allow for any setbacks, such as the horse suffering a minor injury. For the first fortnight he must only be walked, beginning with about half-an-hour and gradually working up to an hour. In the third week, the interval training can begin; this is generally conducted on a four-day schedule.

Begin the interval training with trotting. Find a suitable stretch of ground and trot for two minutes, then rest for three minutes before trotting for two more minutes and then resting again. Ask the horse to work at the trot, lengthening and shortening his stride. When you give him a rest, however, he should really rest. This is important; if he dances and prances around, get off him and let him have a mouthful of grass so that he learns to relax.

It is likely that your horse will be blowing quite hard after this first exertion. The idea is that you begin the next period of work just before he completely recovers. If he is still panting hard, it will be asking too much of him to continue immediately; if he has recovered completely you have lost the benefit of the training. In either case, change the length of the periods of rest (or work him slightly more or less hard) to suit your particular horse. As ever, it is very important not to rush this period of slow work; it is this slow, methodical process

Right: A rider checks her watch during a three- or four-minute break in an interval training session. Interval training is based on the principle of working a horse intensely for short periods then resting him for a similar length of time, asking him to resume work slightly before he has recovered his normal pulse and respiration rates. In this way, he is continually being stretched just a little bit further.

that really hardens his legs and wind, and gives the muscles a chance to develop and strengthen properly.

Maintain the trotting pace during interval training for three to four weeks, but you can gradually ask for longer periods interspersed with fewer breaks. Remember you do the interval training on every fourth day; intersperse it with normal hacks, and odd dressage and jumping sessions on the other days. Turn your horse out for an hour or two each day whenever possible.

Around the sixth or beginning of the seventh week, you can begin interval training at a canter. Begin with three three-minute periods of work, interspersed with breaks of three minutes. As soon as your horse shows signs of almost full recovery after his first three-minute break, increase the next work period to four minutes. Then increase all the work periods to four minutes, keeping the rest periods at three.

You must learn now to canter (or gallop) at a predetermined speed. As previously mentioned, the various phases of the cross-country section and the show-jumping in a horse trial have a distance-per-metre (yard) allowance, and you want to be sure you can pace your horse exactly to this. Begin with a slow speed – say about 400m (437 yds) a minute. Measure off this distance on a flat piece of ground and mark it in some way with stakes or flags. Canter round the field, then time yourself with a stopwatch over the measured distance. Be aware of the feeling of the speed. If you complete the distance in less than 60 seconds, try again, dropping your pace; if you are slower, increase the speed. Gradually, over the weeks that follow, increase your speed over this measured distance until you reach the speed decreed for your particular standard of competition.

At the climax of your interval training, you should be galloping for at least a six-minute period, followed by a three-minute rest, followed by two five-minute gallops separated by a one-minute break. Obviously you could plan this slightly differently to achieve the same result; two longer periods of gallop, separated by a longer break, will produce a similar effect. As always, adapt the programme to suit you and your horse.

If possible, vary the venues of where you do your interval training so that the horse does not get used to always galloping in one place. Try to find some good uphill slopes and use these. Work at different speeds – perhaps riding for a minute or two longer at a slower tempo, particularly if you feel he is slightly excitable and needs calming down. Remember that the work periods are opportunities for schooling too – for varying the pace and asking for lengthening and shortening of strides. As he gets fitter you can include 45 minutes or so of hacking around your interval training. Always walk home to cool the horse and to make him understand the necessity of calming down after a strong gallop.

Below: Exercising on uphill stretches is an important part of a conditioning programme. It puts far less strain on a horse's front legs than moving fast downhill, helps to build up the muscles of the hindquarters and aids development of the respiratory system.

SUCCESSFUL EVENTING

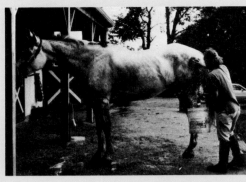

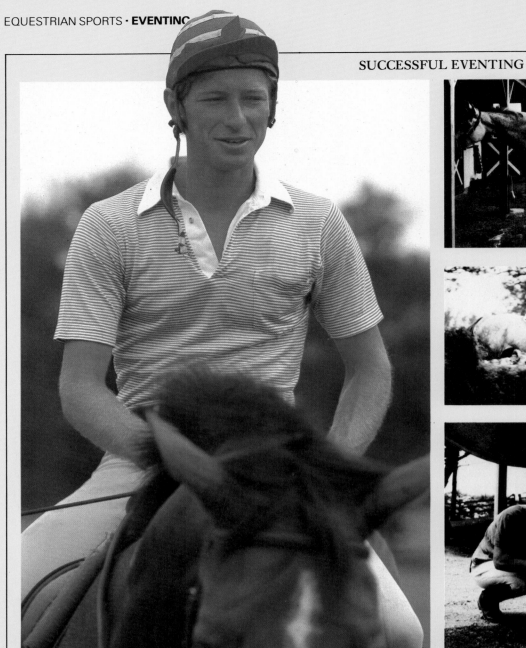

Above: Bruce Davidson has played a prominent part in eventing for some years. He won the World Championship at Burghley in 1974 and was a member of the World Team Champions the same year. He came first in the Pan American Games in 1975, was a member of the winning team at the 1976 Olympic Games in Montreal and winner of the World Championships in Kentucky in 1978. **Above right:** Preparation and action — Davidson's great horse Might Tango, with whom he won in Kentucky. **Right:** Schooling a young horse over a log fence.

Bruce Davidson's Suggested Interval Training Schedule

Your horse is now basically legged-up. You've completed five weeks of your conditioning program and you're ready to begin interval gallops. You have 10 galloping days until your first event. Start easily and remember always tailor your work to your own horse's needs and your terrain.

March 7 Tuesday	Gallop three 3-minute works at 400 meters a minute (3,600 meters)
March 11 Saturday	Gallop three 3-minute works at 400 m/m (3,600 meters)
March 14 Tuesday	Gallop three 4-minute works at 400 m/m (3,600 meters)
March 18 Saturday	Gallop three 4-minute works at 400 m/m (4,800 meters)
March 21 Tuesday	Gallop two 4-minute works and one 5-minute work at 400 m/m (5,200 meters)
March 24 Friday	First school over cross country fences
March 25 Saturday	Walk
March 28 Tuesday	Second cross country school — over a course
April 1 Saturday	Gallop three 5-minute works at 400 m/m (6,000 meters)
April 3 Monday	Gallop one 5-minute work and two 6-minute works at 400 m/m (6,800 meters)
April 5 Wednesday	Gallop five minutes at 400 m/m, break,
April 6 Thursday	gallop five minutes at 400 m/m and one minute at 500 m/m, break,
April 7 Friday	gallop five minutes at 400 m/m and one minute at 600 m/m (7,100 meters)
April 8 Saturday	Walk
April 9 Sunday	Touch up stadium jumping
April 10 - 14	Your first event, *Dressage day and stadium jumping
April 15 Saturday	Cross-country
April 18 Tuesday	Relaxed program
April 22 Saturday	Resume schedule Gallop three 5-minute works at 400 m/m (6,000 meters)
April 26 Wednesday	Gallop three 6-minute works at 400 m/m (7,200 meters)
April 27 Thursday	Gallop one 6-minute work at 400 m/m, break,
April 28 Friday	gallop five minutes at 400 m/m and one minute at 520 m/m, break;
April 29 Saturday	gallop five minutes at 400 m/m and one minute at 640 m/m (7,560 meters)
	Repeat April 22 program
	Walk
	Touch up stadium jumping
April 30 Sunday	Two-Day Event, dressage and stadium jumping Immediately after show jumping gallop up hill ¼ mile starting at 550 m/m and finishing as fast as your horse wants to go This "pipe opener" allows the lungs to expand once to their fullest degree
May 1 - 6	Cross-country
May 7 Sunday	Relaxed program
May 11 Thursday	Resume interval training Gallop three 6-minute works at 400 m/m (7,200 meters)
May 15 Monday	Gallop six minutes at 400 m/m, break;
May 17 Wednesday	gallop five minutes at 400 m/m and one minute at 550 m/m, break;
May 18 Thursday	gallop five minutes at 400 m/m and one minute at 640 m/m (7,590 meters)
May 19 Friday	Repeat May 11 program
	Walk
May 20 Saturday	Vet check for three-day event
May 21 Sunday	Three-Day Event, dressage
May 22 Monday	Immediately after your test repeat "pipe opener" of April 29
	Cross-country
	Stadium jumping
	Rest

*Although classified as a one-day event this may spread over two days to accommodate large numbers of entries and provide the horses with an over-night rest before the cross-country.

Above left: Bruce Davidson taking a young horse through his dressage paces, under ideal conditions in a superb sand school. **Above:** A possible itinerary for interval training leading up to a three-day event. This schedule, outlined by Davidson, first appeared in the January 1978 issue of the American magazine *Practical Horseman*. **Left:** An event horse should be well protected for travelling. Here, one of Davidson's eventers wears a poll guard, a padded head collar, thick leg bandages and a tail bandage.

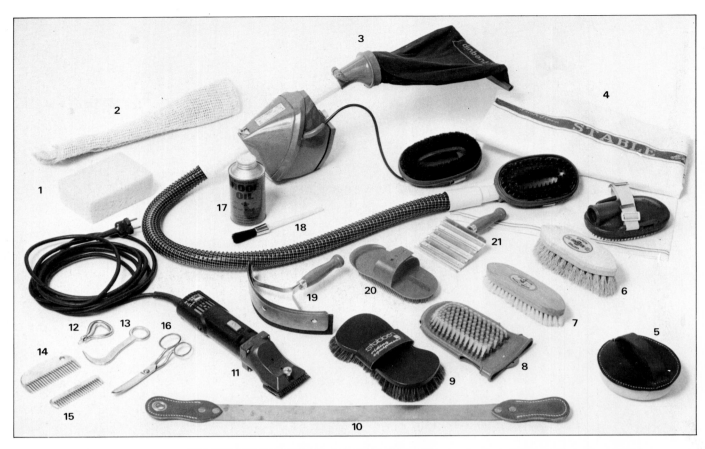

Grooming equipment
1. Sponge, 2. 'Cactus' cloth,
3. Electric brush, 4. Stable
rubber, 5. Wisping pad, 6. Dandy
brush, 7. Water brush, 8. Brush
grooming glove, 9. German
pattern body brush, 10. Brass
double handed sweat scraper,
11. Electric clipping machine,
12/13. Hoof picks, 14/15. Mane
combs, 16. Curved blade
trimming scissors, 17/18. Hoof
oil and brush, 19. Sweat
scraper, 20. Rubber curry comb,
21. Metal curry comb.

Feeding and stable management

There is no extra 'magic' to the feeding and
stable management routines for an event
horse; they follow exactly the patterns of a
working hunter or any other competition horse.
The eventer in hard competition is similar to
the point-to-pointer as regards feeding; that
is, he can have all the protein he will eat – although, of course, you must be sure you are
working him enough for this. As always, build
up the rations gradually, keeping the protein
level comparatively low in relation to the bulk
feed when he first comes up from grass into
work.

You may find that as he gets fitter and is
asked to do harder, faster work, like the point-
to-pointer in training, he tends to go off his
food. Again, you must tempt him with different feedstuffs. A good way of getting the
necessary protein into a fussy feeder is to feed
'milk power pellets'. These give very high protein, yet are contained in very low bulk. Mixed
with a small, appetising feed, most horses will
eat them readily.

A regular stable routine of grooming, feeding
and regular observation of the horse must be
followed. Give four feeds a day when he is
having top rations and remember to feed the
bulk of the hay ration after exercise. Keep the
box clean all the time, removing droppings at
regular intervals – but leave the horse alone
whenever possible. If you constantly fuss
round him he will soon become unsettled.

Try to turn him out for a while each day, but
not into a field where there is lots of lush
grazing. A horse in this sort of hard work and
top condition should not have extra bulk to
eat. The idea of turning him out is to give him
a little freedom, fresh air and a change of environment, rather than to let him have his fill
of rich, green grass.

It is a very good idea, particularly at the
advanced level of eventing, to have the vet
take a blood test six to nine weeks before a
three-day event. Perhaps your horse has been
slightly off-colour and you are not sure why;
it could, for example, be because the haemo-
globin count is low. This, and other similar
irregularities, will show up in the blood test
and you can take steps to correct them.

Preparing for the event

Providing that your horse is completely fit –
if not, withdraw him – have him shod with new
shoes four or five days before the event and
have the farrier make you a spare set at the
same time. Horses competing in events must
wear studs in their shoes to improve their grip
on the ground, whatever its condition. Ask the
farrier to put stud holes in the shoes (the alternative is to have him fit the studs into the shoes
when he makes them). Pack the holes with wads
of cotton wool, soaked in a little hoof oil, when
the studs are not in position, and change this
regularly. Always fit the studs immediately
before riding any particular phase – a horse
should not wear them in the stable or whilst
travelling.

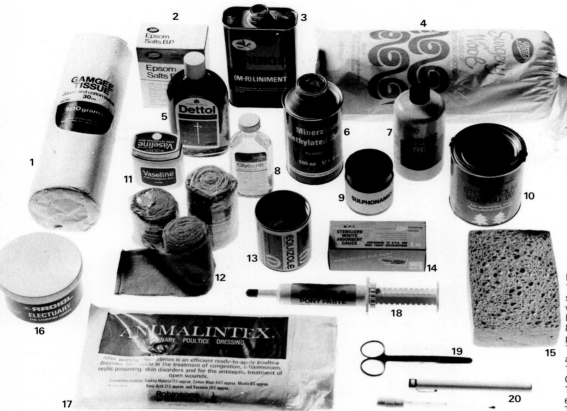

First aid equipment
1. Gamgee tissue, 2. Epsom salts, 3. Liniment, 4. Cotton wool, 5. Antiseptic, 6. Methylated spirit. 7. Specific for colic, 8. Glycerine, 9. Sulphonamide powder, 10. Stockholm tar, 11. Petroleum jelly, 12. Bandages, 13. Worming remedy, 14. Gauze, 15. Sponge, 16. Coughing electuary, 17. Poultice, 18. Worm paste, 19. Round-ended surgical scissors, 20. Thermometer.

You can ease off the ridden work a little in the final week as your horse is already at the peak of his fitness, and there should be nothing left to teach him. Ride him out in this week to keep him interested, and give him one good pipe-opener to make sure his wind stays in good working order. For the rest, try to make him feel on top of the world, so that he goes to the event really feeling contented with himself, ready to take on anything you ask of him.

Other preparation to make sure he looks as good as he feels will be the same as preparing for any competition. Because you may feel a little keyed-up though, there could be a tendency to spend endless hours fussing round the horse, pulling the odd hair out of his mane or generally titivating his appearance in some way. Try to resist this; it will only unsettle him and upset both of you. Devise a routine to cover grooming, shampooing (if necessary), trimming, plaiting and so on – and stick to it.

Clean and check your tack very thoroughly, and remember to take spares to the event. Essentials are spare reins (a complete bridle is better), martingale, stirrup leathers, girths, and any ancillary items, such as brushing boots. Make a list of all the equipment you must take with you; if you are going to a three-day event, which means several nights away from home, there will be a lot of it! Besides the horse's feed and containers, you must take mucking-out tools, grooming kit, first-aid kit (for you, too), rugs, bandages and so on.

You will also need quite a lot of equipment for yourself, as riding in an event entails at least two changes of clothing. The same clothing may be worn in the dressage and show-jumping phase, although many people like to wear the elegant swallow tail coat and silk top hat for the dressage phase. In a three-day event, in particular, it is wise to have a couple of pairs of spare breeches, and perhaps a coat too, in case the weather is very bad or you have a fall that leaves you extremely muddy or wet.

At the event

The procedure at horse trials differs according to whether you are competing at a one, two or three-day event. The procedure at a three-day event can be adapted as necessary.

The day before the dressage phase really marks the official start of the event, as competitors are 'briefed' on the schedule and plan for the days to follow. They will receive their number cloth, a plan of the cross-country course, a riding order and notice of any receptions or parties to be given by the organizers. Most people aim to arrive the day before this in order to give the horses the maximum time to settle into their new surroundings. Try to stick to your horse's regular feeding programme and other routines as far as you can, in order to upset him as little as possible. Again, resist the temptation to fuss round him endlessly.

After competitors have been briefed, it is usual to drive round the roads and tracks that are to be ridden as part of the cross-country phase. A drive around them in a vehicle with a crowd of others is not enough, though. As a competitor, you need to go round them again, planning your route and plotting how long each phase should take you to ensure you ride it in the correct time. This is important – you want to use all the time you are allowed here, so as to save your horse as much as possible for the cross-country jumping, but you do not want to go so slowly that you incur penalty points. Experienced competitors will measure out the distance and plan exact times at which they should reach certain points along the route. Watch an experienced event rider riding the roads and tracks; you will see that he or she frequently consults a stopwatch strapped to his wrist or hand.

Even though you know what type of fences to expect on the steeplechase course, walk the course at least once. Plan the route you will take round the course so that you approach each fence where you want to and plot the times that you must pass certain markers. There is no official break at the end of the steeplechase before going into the next phase of roads and tracks, so try to build in a short period at this point to let your horse get his breath back after the fast pace of the steeplechase course.

The cross-country jumping course should be walked three times. The first time is to get a general impression of the course, to see how the fences look to you when you first see them – which ones appear straightforward, which are partly concealed on approach, which may be in shade or bright sunlight later in the day – and so on. Get a general impression of the state of the going, too.

The second walk is the time for deep analysis; if you can do this with an experienced adviser, so much the better. You should examine each fence in detail, planning exactly where to take off and therefore the line of approach you should be riding. Do not necessarily always plan to take the shortest route; it is usually the hardest. Having planned your route, plan an alternative one in case the state of the ground has altered by the time you ride, making the

take-off to certain jumps very sticky or slippery. Pace out the distances between combinations, so that you know exactly how many strides your horse will need to take and whether any of these must be shortened or lengthened. Plot the times you should pass certain markers round the course to stay within the time allowed and memorize the penalty areas and zones of the course (if you fall off your horse outside these, you do not collect penalty points). Make notes and sketches as you go round the course.

Pay particular attention to the difficult fences on the course – the coffin, for example, or the water jumps, and plan exactly the way to ride them. A thorough knowledge of how your horse reacts to such fences will be needed for this. You should know where you must really push him on so that he has the necessary impulsion to take him over a fence and know, too, where to steady him, so that he does not overjump and land himself in trouble – at a drop fence for example.

Having walked the course this second time, spend time thinking about it, going over and over your planned route in your mind, so that you can be sure you really know it. Walk it again, following the route you intend to take the next day, perhaps after your dressage test.

Ready to ride

Try to watch some other competitors ride their dressage test – it should help to calm your nerves, if nothing else. Give your horse as much exercise as he needs to settle him, keeping this slow and calm and steady. Do not attempt to ride him through the progressive movements of the test; it will take the edge of spontaneity out of them. You will know by knowing your horse how much exercise he will need; your aim is to loosen up his muscles, to make sure he is going forward well, is well-balanced and is thoroughly attentive and responsive. Above all, he should be calm. Run through the test in your mind before going into the arena. Having warmed up your horse, dismount a little before you are due to do the test and make

Below left and right: A horse is led from his box and given a warm-up session on the lunge. Always give a horse time to get used to new surroundings at an event and make sure he is really settled before the start of your competition.

BADMINTON HORSE TRIALS

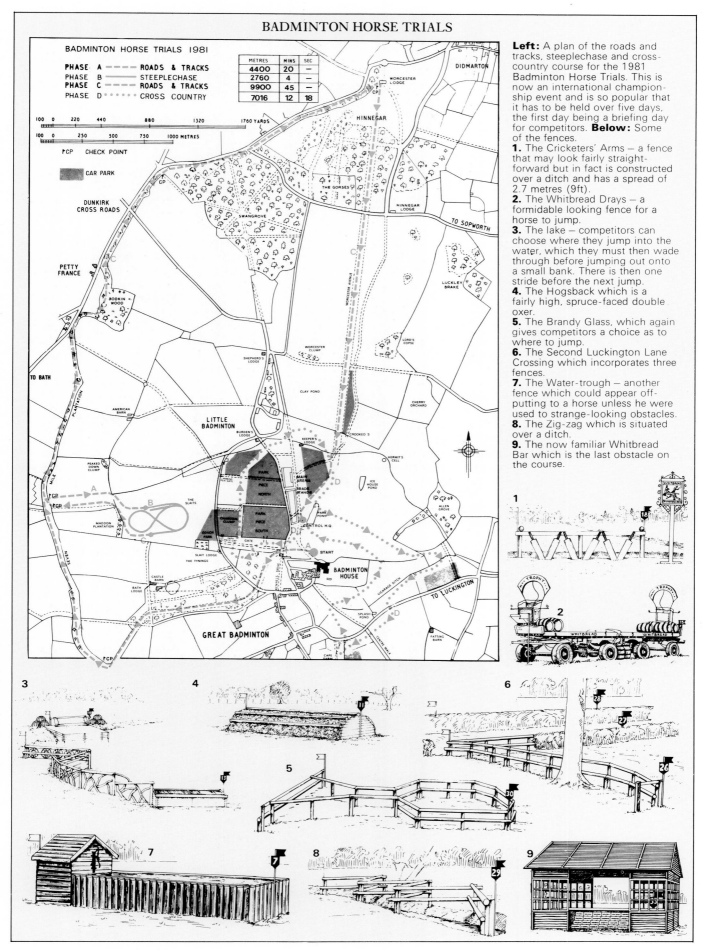

BADMINTON HORSE TRIALS 1981

	METRES	MINS	SEC
PHASE A — — — ROADS & TRACKS	4400	20	—
PHASE B ———— STEEPLECHASE	2760	4	—
PHASE C — — — ROADS & TRACKS	9900	45	—
PHASE D ·········· CROSS COUNTRY	7016	12	18

100 0   220   440   880   1320   1760 YARDS
100 0 250   500   750   1000 METRES

PCP CHECK POINT

CAR PARK

Left: A plan of the roads and tracks, steeplechase and cross-country course for the 1981 Badminton Horse Trials. This is now an international championship event and is so popular that it has to be held over five days, the first day being a briefing day for competitors. **Below:** Some of the fences.

1. The Cricketers' Arms — a fence that may look fairly straightforward but in fact is constructed over a ditch and has a spread of 2.7 metres (9ft).
2. The Whitbread Drays — a formidable looking fence for a horse to jump.
3. The lake — competitors can choose where they jump into the water, which they must then wade through before jumping out onto a small bank. There is then one stride before the next jump.
4. The Hogsback which is a fairly high, spruce-faced double oxer.
5. The Brandy Glass, which again gives competitors a choice as to where to jump.
6. The Second Luckington Lane Crossing which incorporates three fences.
7. The Water-trough — another fence which could appear off-putting to a horse unless he were used to strange-looking obstacles.
8. The Zig-zag which is situated over a ditch.
9. The now familiar Whitbread Bar which is the last obstacle on the course.

THREE SPORTS IN ONE

sure the tack is all properly adjusted. Rub over the saddle to ensure it is looking its best.

Obviously you will ride the test as well as you can, but try to make sure your entry is particularly good, that you are moving in a completely straight line and that your horse is attentive and lively. You want him to catch the judges' eye immediately. Do not try to teach your horse anything new; ride each movement as well as you can without being tempted to ask for anything extra. If you ask too much of your horse now, you may well unsettle him, causing him to break out of the pace at which he is moving. If you do make a mistake, forget it instantly and concentrate on the next part of the test. Remember it is essential for you to give your horse all the help you can by giving clear, concise aids and preparing him when-

Far left: Julian Seaman jumps the Whitbread Drays on The Reverend at the 1980 Badminton Horse Trials. **Left top:** Mark Phillips riding HRH the Queen's horse, Columbus. The royal family's interest and participation in the sport has done much to enhance its overall popularity. **Left:** The French are a force to be reckoned with on the international scene. Jean-Yves Touzaint takes one of the show-jumping fences at the 1980 event at Fontainbleau. **Right:** Also at Fontainbleau, but this time in the dressage arena. The competitor is Nils Haagensen, riding Monaco. **Above:** A quick sponge down with cool water will help to refresh a horse.

Below, right to left: A good breakdown of approach, take-off, suspension and landing over a post and rail fence at Badminton. The rider is Christopher Collins and his horse is Gamble VIII.

ever possible for the next movement.

If you feel your horse is a little full of himself, ask for the movement gradually when coming to a halt. Better this, than to have him stop suddenly with his head in the air. If you have to rein back, do this as quietly as possible; take only the number of steps stipulated.

Dismount after the test and take your horse back to his box, making a fuss of him. Later on

in the day, give him a short pipe-opener to prepare his wind for the cross-country phase.

Aim to begin the first phase of the roads and tracks with your horse settled and attentive, so that he is prepared to go at your pace rather than his! This phase can usually be conducted at a brisk trot and it really serves as a warm-up to the steeplechase. Try to arrive at the beginning of the steeplechase with a couple of minutes to spare to give the horse a breather. Dismount, adjust the saddle and tighten the girths, and take up your stirrup leathers by a couple of holes.

Ideally, you want to pass the start line of the steeplechase at a steady gallop. Ride the course as you planned, letting your horse ease up on any inclines. Push him on the flat or slight downward slopes if you feel you are slipping behind time. Riding in a good forward position, both on the flat and over the jumps, will help to ease your horse, too. If your horse is really pulling against you, full of fitness and freshness, try to steady him down, but do not fight him – that will only upset him.

Some riders like to dismount at the end of the steeplechase course and readjust their tack again, perhaps even arranging for a groom to be there to sponge out the horse's mouth. Your time at this point may be the deciding factor, as you do not want to have to push the horse too much over the second phase of roads and tracks. There is a compulsory 10-minute break at the end of this section before the start of the cross-country jumping, during which the horse must undergo a veterinary examination. Aim to arrive two minutes inside the allotted time for the break at an even, steady trot.

After the veterinary inspection, the horse should be sponged down, excess water removed with a sweat scraper and then towelled dry. Check him over to make sure he has suffered no injury and treat any minor cuts or abrasions. Wash his mouth out with a spongeful of water, but do not let him have a drink. If there is any breeze, stand your horse to face it. Walk him round, with a string rug over his back if necessary, and make sure he is tacked-up again – with girths and stirrup leathers checked thoroughly – three or four minutes before it is time to go.

Again, ride the course as you had planned, making any adjustments that you find necessary, according to the state of the ground. Save your horse as much as you can, letting him ease up when going uphill; better to push him on on the flat, if necessary. Give him every possible assistance at all times, keeping your weight forward as you gallop along to take the strain off his back and adjusting your weight as necessary when he is jumping. If you really feel he is tiring to the point where it would be dangerous to ask more of him – then pull up. There is always another event; there may not be another horse.

When you have finished the cross-country course, dismount immediately, slacken off the girth and walk the horse back to the stable. Have someone meet you at the end of the course with an anti-sweat rug. Make a fuss of the horse and give him a small drink of water which has had the chill taken off, and, ideally, has some glucose added to it. Remove his tack, massage over his back and shoulders with your hands and then sponge him down with lukewarm water. Remove the excess water with a scraper

and towel him dry. Examine him thoroughly for injuries.

Pick out his feet and remove the studs. When he is dry, rug him up warmly and bandage his legs to keep them warm and to help reduce any strain. Hot kaolin poultices applied to the legs help to reduce strain still further. Make sure the horse has a really deep bed of straw and that the windows in the stable are open to give adequate ventilation (but no draughts). When he has settled, give him a longer drink and then a small feed – ideally a hot mash. Leave him for a while, but come back later, walk him out of the stable and look him over again for injuries of any kind. Give him his evening feed and some hay at his usual time.

The next day the horse must go through another veterinary inspection to ensure that he is fit enough to enter the show-jumping. He is almost bound to be stiff after the previous day's exertion, so ride him gently for about half an hour, including some light trotting and cantering to loosen him up. Make sure he is well-groomed, so that he looks smart and arrive in good time at the inspection. You will have to lead the horse in front of the veterinary surgeons, who will inspect him at a halt and also at a walk and trot. Take the horse back to his stable afterwards, and rug him up until it is time for the show-jumping.

Competitors walk the show-jumping course before it is due to start in the usual way. Do not be beguiled by its apparent simplicity and the smallness of the fences; there will be one or two tricky aspects to it, and as your horse is tired, it will be quite a test for him. Check the strides between fences and decide again which route you mean to take.

Your horse will certainly need riding in before the jumping to supple him still further. Again, how long and what sort of exercise will depend on each individual horse, but ride him sufficiently to loosen all his muscles and prepare him for the sort of jumps he is to face. Some simple dressage movements should help to eliminate all the stiffness, but take him over a few practice jumps, too, making him take them on a steady, bouncy stride, rather than the longer, faster stride of the cross-country. When your turn comes to jump, ride him as sympathetically as possible, taking the line you have planned and timing yourself carefully so that you complete just inside the time allowed.

Obviously you will take your horse home as soon as possible after an event of any sort and he will need careful observation for a few days after the event. If he has suffered any injury that did not show up to begin with, it will certainly have done so four or five days later. Give him light exercise in the days that follow; you cannot get a horse to this degree of physical fitness and mental alertness and then just turn him out in the field after the event. If he is to have a rest period soon, keep him stabled by night for at least two or three weeks, turning him out in the field for a few hours each day.

A twelve-month programme for an event horse obviously varies considerably according to circumstance. The principal factor to affect it is which grading the horse has reached and therefore the standard of competition he will be entering in any given year. The programme here is for a six- to seven-year-old novice eventer, the aim being to get sufficient points (six) to qualify for a novice three-day event (his first one).

Spring events generally start in early spring and continue for ten weeks or so. This gives you a maximum of ten weeks to prepare your horse for the first event, so it will be impossible to reach the top level of fitness for the first competition. Indeed, it would be undesirable to keep a horse at tip-top fitness throughout the spring season, so the early events should be looked on as part of the overall training.

In addition to the early events you enter, try to compete in some individual dressage, show jumping and cross-country jumping (hunter trial) competitions. If these have a higher standard of competition than you will meet at your one or two day events, so much the better. Not only will you know that you are up to the required standard, but the actual events will be less daunting for you and your horse. Throughout your eventing career, it pays to enter these individual competitions, rather than just schooling endlessly on your own between events. It keeps both of you sharp and on your toes and gives you a realistic view of your performance and the standard you have acquired. The horse whose year is considered below, for example, should have spent the previous spring, summer and autumn competing in local shows and hunter trials and riding club one-day events.

Another point is that most event riders do not go through a 'running-down' period with their horses at the end of the spring and autumn seasons. There is not time to do so if the horses are to get sufficient time off, and by and large, it is not considered necessary in this sport. Also, it is usual to leave the shoes on whilst the horse is turned out, particularly in the summer when the hard ground could cause the feet to crack. As this is such a short period, it would be silly to take any such risk.

You should plan the calendar of the events you wish to enter very carefully. Individual events vary considerably, even when you are competing at the same level or standard in each one. Some have comparatively easy cross-country courses and difficult show-jumping; in others the situation will be reversed. Very hilly courses will

THE EVENTER'S YEAR

subsequent one-day events) as part of your training routine and to teach your horse what is expected of him.

Fourth month: Aim to ride in a one-day event every fortnight during this period if possible, so that you have ridden in five or six before your first two-day event. Your aim is still to use the events as training rather than riding to win, or even to pick up any points. In between events, school your horse on any weak aspects, giving him one day of rest a week.

Fifth month: Early this month, enter a two-day event. Immediately after this, turn the horse out, cutting down his feed. If the weather is good, he can go out all the time, although initially he will need a New Zealand rug at night. If the weather is cold, you may have to bring him in at night, but avoid doing so if possible; keeping your horse out will reduce the possibility of his legs swelling up overnight.

Sixth month: Bring up from grass at the beginning of the month and follow a conditioning routine for three weeks. It will not take long to get him back into training. After about three weeks begin schooling as well as general exercise.

Seventh and eighth months: Enter local dressage and show-jumping competitions and local hunter trials. Working hunter classes are good competitions for eventers, as they include a fairly demanding jumping course in which style (as well as accuracy) is taken into account. Again, try to enter competitions at a slightly higher level than those you can expect to meet in one- or two-day events and intersperse these competitions with one-day novice events. Aim now to pick up sufficient points to allow you to enter a three-day event; your goal is to win a one-day event during this period. Plan to enter your final one-day event a fortnight before the three-day event, and look for one that is as difficult as possible.

As you may be hoping to upgrade your horse at the end of next year, use this summer period also to bring on his dressage to intermediate level, taking lessons if required.

Ninth month: Enter a three-day novice event. Again, you can turn your horse out to grass as soon as you have finished competing this season.

Tenth and eleventh months: Complete rest for the horse. If you can leave him out all the time, so much the better, but if the weather is very bad you should bring him in at dusk. Before doing this, try putting on two New Zealand rugs at night and give him plenty of good feeds (at least two a day). These will help to keep him warm.

take much more out of a horse and demand a higher level of fitness than those that are held on fairly flat ground. The state of the ground is another consideration. In some of the late spring and autumn events, the ground can be very, very hard. It may be unwise to compete in such conditions unless, that is, you feel you must in order to get the necessary experience. If this is the case, ride very steadily, or you will find yourself with a lame horse.

Last week of mid-winter: Bring up from rest.

First month: Condition horse by following a programme of steady walking and trotting, similar to the hunter's routine. Towards the end of the month, start looking for some local dressage competitions and enter them. Remember your horse does not have to be in peak condition for these, since he will not be asked to work fast or hard.

Second month: Start introducing jumping into the regular exercise routine at the beginning of this month, so that you can enter some hunter trials towards the end of it. If there are no local hunter trials, you must go to a cross-country course to gain experience before your first event.

Third month: Enter a one-day event in mid-month. Your aim is to ride a good dressage test, hopefully go clear round the cross-country and the show-jumping, but without trying to go fast enough to be placed. Use this (and

CHAPTER FIVE

SHOW JUMPING

UNTIL QUITE RECENTLY – just over a generation ago – show jumping was a small minority sport that attracted only a small côterie of enthusiasts and was run on somewhat parochial lines. Today, the sport has a world-wide following of millions. There is a way to the top for real talent, although money is a necessity at the highest levels.

The sport originated about 300 years ago in England, when the open-farming systems were changed by a series of Enclosure Acts. Until the early part of the 18th century, the countryside had been mainly unfenced woodland, field and common land, open and accessible but for an occasional ditch or small bank to define boundaries. Then agriculture changed. England's population was growing and had to be fed. Fences were thrown up around the larger estates and farms so that crops could be grown more scientifically and cattle fattened more efficiently.

The enclosures brought a new set of problems for the hunting horse. Up to that time, he had met few difficulties in the field. Since the land was almost uninterrupted by obstacles of any significance, those who hunted could ride through forest and field intent only on the quarry. The Enclosure Acts, in addition to helping to grow more crops, gave the rider a new thrill and a new skill – jumping his horse over a fence. It was soon apparent that both rider and horse enjoyed this.

The first contests

The first organized jumping contests were mounted in 1866, when a show jumping class was included at a Paris harness show. However, this was more on the lines of eventing than of modern show jumping. Competitors were asked to perform a *concours d'elegance* then ride off into the country to negotiate a series of natural obstacles. Of only marginal interest to spectators, the system was soon modified so that the jumps were brought into the arena for all to see.

Some 15 years later, the new sport arrived in Britain, where it was dubbed 'leaping'. It remained a minority interest for a decade in which a small band of competitors, including a side-saddle class, jumped half-a-dozen flimsy fences as light entertainment for the crowds in between more important events.

Left: Night Mummer ridden by Tim Grubb, photographed during a show jumping competition at the Calgary Horse Show. Notice how Night Mummer has tucked his hind legs right up beneath him; compare this with other show jumping photographs and you will see what an unusual position it is!
Above: Show jumping is a fairly young equestrian sport but nevertheless has its share of legendary figures. Lt. Col. Harry Llewellyn and Foxhunter compete for the Nations' Cup at the International Horse Show at the White City in 1951.

Right: A print dating from the mid-1880s depicting a jumping competition in an elegant indoor arena. There is clearly an element of racing in the competition, and judging by the spectators, this was a very fashionable sport of the time. Show jumping as we know it today, however, did not really begin until the early 20th century.

As early as 1912, however, show jumping, in the form we know it today, was given official recognition when it was included in that year's Olympic Games. Only male riders were permitted to compete, a rule that was relaxed only after 44 years of female lobbying. The first lady to compete in the Olympic Games (1956) was Britain's Pat Smythe, a rider who was in effect the 'First Lady' of show jumping for many years.

The rules for those early show jumping classes were usually compiled by the local Master of Foxhounds – often on the spot at a show – and were vague and sometimes prejudiced. This led to the formation of a governing body, the *Federation Equestre Internationale* (International Equestrian Federation) which today controls the sport throughout the world and compiles the Olympic Games rules. Now, whether a rider jumps in a class in Montreal or Manchester, he or she knows exactly what the penalties are for refusing or running out or demolishing a fence. In earlier days marks had been given – or deducted – for the severity of the jumps or the style of the rider; a common practice had been for the competitor to ride up

to the fence, show it to his horse, then ride back to take the jump. If he refused three times he might be disqualified, or he might be asked to take the following jump. Such rough and ready interpretation has ended.

Show jumping soon became an integral part of every country show and later began to take on an identity of its own (although even today many of the larger agricultural shows hold major show jumping contests as part of their programme). However the fame of the sport ensures that show jumping competitions now draw far larger crowds than ever before in their history, competing with the world's major sports for popularity.

The growth of show jumping

During the past generation the sport has increased in popularity beyond the wildest dreams of its pioneers. Now with television, spectators can be counted in their millions and audiences of up to 10,000 crowd into the world's great stadia. Large permanent halls for the sole purpose of show jumping competition have been erected in many countries, great

schools have been established with successful show jumping as their only goal. A vast new sport has sprung up, and around it a thriving new industry flourishes.

Why has the sport had this meteoric success? Two or three simple facts are important. First and formost is the advent of television. When the first tentative shows were screened in the 1950s, it was immediately obvious that this sport was ideally suited to the medium. The basic rules were simple and subtleties such as refusals and dipping a foot in the water were soon learned by the huge new television audience. They were rivetted to the edge of their chairs at home or, if they were lucky enough to get to a big show, were captivated by the tension, colour and theatre.

Concurrently with the spread of television came increased leisure time and an upsurge of interest in sport generally. More youngsters were given ponies as birthday gifts and new riders soon emerged to challenge the established show jumpers of the day in both Europe and the USA. Thiedemann and Winkler of West Germany, Steinkraus of the USA and the d'Inzeo brothers of Italy, plus d'Oriola of France and David Broome and Harvey Smith of the UK were becoming the new champions of the show jumping arena.

The great growth of show jumping in Europe stemmed from a single show, the Victory Championship, held at White City, London in the late summer of 1945. It was planned and mounted by Colonel Mike Ansell, then recently returned from a prisoner-of-war camp in Germany, and the newly re-organized British Show Jumping Society. The show opened the gates to the sport as we know it today, not least in its general visual appearance. Ansell substituted for the often flimsy (and always dull) jumps of pre-war days a new variety of fences that would need different skills to negotiate, decorating them with 'barber-pole' stripes and placing colourful shrubs, flowers, plants and brush around the obstacles to lend interest to the scene. His imaginative use of nature and colour helped in no small way to bring the sport to the popular attention as a spectacle, a show for the family rather than the knowledgeable few. The International and Olympic contests that were soon to follow brought even greater universal acclaim to the sport.

COMPETITORS AND COURSES

Left: One of the most consistently successful of today's riders, Malcom Pyrah, riding Charles Fox. **Centre left:** Two night-time competitions, one held outdoors under powerful floodlights and the other in an indoor stadium. **Bottom left:** International riders must be prepared to travel. Here, America's Armond Leone is competing in Rotterdam, Holland. **Right:** Another very famous show jumping personality, David Broome, who has been at the top of the sport for many years. Here he rides Queensqay Philco at speed over a fence. **Below:** Christmas trees appear to be growing up through the centre of this fence at Hickstead. However, they pose no problem for Dennis Murphy and Trouble Shooter.

Show jumping today

Traditionally a summer sport, show jumping – in common with many other activities that have caught the public's imagination – has overspread its natural season. Today, jumping competitions can be seen at almost any time of the year, ranging from small local school rings to the sophisticated enclosed riding halls of international competition. And from the early experimental show jumping classes of post-war days there are now a tremendously popular series of contests – the four-yearly Olympics and World Championships, international shows such as the Royal International and Horse of the Year in Britain, plus similar events in all the equestrian countries of the world. These not only provide a year-long season for spectators, but also a hard year-long round for riders and horses. There are now some 70 FEI international dates in the calendar; these range from Dortmund (Germany) in March, to Olympia (London, UK) in December, with venues as far apart as Athens and Puerto Rico in the list. Prizes, once notional, are today very large indeed and have become part of the substantial income that a successful horse can bring its owner (or in certain circumstances, its rider).

With sponsorship swelling its funds, show jumping has become one of the great attractions in the sports world. It is also big business, as top horses command large prices and the owning and training of show jumpers has become a competitive industry. Over 10,000 horses and ponies are registered in Britain alone, competing in more than 2,000 horse shows every year.

The local show

If you have been introduced to show jumping via the television screen, you may find that the lure of the sport will sooner or later take you out to a local show. So how do you watch a small show? Are the regulations the same as the ones the international riders have to follow? Are the rules and penalties similar? Does the small show groom the rider for the top echelon of show jumping? The answer, of course, is yes. The entire sport from grass roots up to international contest is designed to bring young riders (and horses) on until they qualify for the more important classes.

The basic principle is that the horses are judged solely on their performance over the fences; sometimes a time element is marked into the judging, but the style of the rider is never considered; he or she may jump in copybook fashion with not a finger out of place, or may look like a sack of potatoes – if the jump is cleared then no penalties are awarded. Secondly all competitions are judged under the same basic international rules or national rules. In effect, these are identical, so you will have no problems, wherever you are watching show jumping.

Rules and regulations

The most common set of rules in operation is that defined as Table 'A'. There are various sub-divisions and variants, as follows. According to Table 'A1', in the event of equality of faults for first place in the second jump-off the prize money will be divided. This means that the competition may end with several equal winners. A1 is used in competitions where there is no automatic timing and when no other table is indicated. Under Table 'A2', however, the rules state that in the event of equality of faults for first place, the second jump-off will be against the clock. Here, with electronic timers that can gauge a rider's time to a small fraction of a second, it is unlikely that two equal winners would emerge. According to Table 'A3', in the event of equality of faults for first place in the first jump-off, time decides the winner and the place order. If there is an equality of faults-and-time a further jump-off may be held over not more than six obstacles. Finally comes Table 'A4'. Here the first round is jumped against the clock so that the competitor with the least number of time and jumping faults is the winner.

The only types of competition that do not use Table A rules are those in which penalties are connected with time faults. These competitions are governed by Table 'S'. In this six to ten seconds are added to the total time taken to complete the round for each fence knocked down, the winner being the competitor with the shortest time.

Competitions are varied thus so that riders may select the type of contest to which their horses are best suited. The grading of horses and ponies in affiliated competition is based on previous winnings. The lowest is Grade C, the highest Grade A.

Faults and penalties

Assessing faults incurred by knocking down a fence or by refusing or running out and so on is a clear and simple matter, with little room for confusion. This is one of the main reasons for show jumping's universal popularity. With four faults for a knockdown, three faults for a first refusal, six for the second, then elimination for a third and four for putting a foot in the water, every spectator whether at the ringside or in front of the television screen can be judge and jury at any competition.

Demolishing a fence, refusals and falls are naturally not the only faults for which a competitor may be penalised during the time the horse and rider are in the ring. Still further errors lead to elimination. These include starting or jumping before the given signal; failing to pass through the start within a minute of the start signal; refusing a fence for longer than a minute; showing a fence to the horse; leaving the ring; jumping a fence in the wrong order or taking the wrong course;

Above: Show jumping has its hazards, like any sport. Here Koh-I-Noor and Rob Ehrens come to grief over a fence in Rotterdam. The impact with the fence was so great that the pole has actually snapped. Such calamities usually occur if a horse approaches the fence on an incorrect stride.

OFFICIAL FAULT AND TIME PENALTIES

1st disobedience*	3 faults
2nd disobedience*	6 faults
3rd disobedience*	elimination
Fence knocked down	4 faults
1 foot or more in water jump	4 faults
Fall of horse or rider	8 faults
Exceeding the time allowed	1 fault for each second
Exceeding the time allowed in a timed jump-off	1 fault for each second or part of second
Exceeding the time limit (twice the time allowed)	elimination

*Disobedience faults are cumulative throughout the round.

receiving unauthorized assistance; and failing to retake all the obstacles in a combination after a refusal or a fall. There are a number of more obvious faults, such as not crossing the finish line mounted, knocking down the timing apparatus and other little slips that could be guaranteed to earn the censure of the judges.

Although the penalty system is easily understood, the definition of some faults sometimes calls for more knowledge of the sport than at first seems necessary. A refusal, for instance, may be an involuntary circle on approaching a fence, a run-out, or a simple resistance. These terms themselves have to be explained – a resistance, for example, is defined as when a horse or pony either refuses to go forward, stops, runs back or rears. More than 60 seconds of this and horse and rider are eliminated.

The knock-down, too, is not necessarily as simple as it appears. If the top pole of a post-and-rail upright is dislodged there is no doubt about it. But if the pole immediately under the top is dropped, is that penalized? Or if just one end is bounced out of its cup and the other remains in position? Or part of the framework of the fence is kicked away leaving the main structure intact? In the past, these questions often led to controversial decisions by judges whose separate interpretations of the rules differed considerably. Today, happily, the rules are less open to criticism. A fence is deemed to be knocked down when, through the fault of

horse or rider, any portion including a wing, boundary flag, bush, shrub or any part has been lowered or knocked downwards, even when the dislodged part is arrested in its fall by another part of the fence. However, when there are several parts to a fence, only dislodgement of the top pole counts as a fault.

The water jump has its own system of penalties. Knocking over bits of the brush hedge on the approach side of the water is not faulted, but a penalized 'foot in the water' means anything from a thorough dunking to a touch of a hoof on the edge of the tape along the water's edge, even though it may leave the water itself undisturbed. One of the most difficult obstacles to judge, the water jump needs constant vigilance.

Lastly, what is a fall? What may often look like one may not be technically a fall and so escape penalty. A fall occurs when a rider is separated from the horse (which may not have fallen) and has to remount. A horse has fallen when his quarters and shoulders have touched the ground, or the fence and the ground.

Fences and courses

It should be remembered that no horse needs to be taught to jump – it is a natural ability. He may, however, need to be taught how to jump efficiently and cleanly, how to clear an obstacle, how to jump several fences in rapid succession,

SHOW JUMPING FENCES

There are two basic types of fences — spreads and uprights. **1.** A triple bar or staircase type fence constructed of rustic poles. The poles are arranged in ascending height and because a horse's jump follows such an upward progression, this is one of the easiest of all fences to jump. **2.** A five-bar gate is an upright fence, nearly always included in show jumping competitions and far harder to jump than the triple bar. **3.** A Hog's back. A spread fence constructed of parallel poles with a higher pole in between them, not as easy to jump as the triple bar as a horse could be tempted to drop his hind legs after clearing the centre rail, thus catching the far one. **4.** A bank is a relatively recent feature of show jumping courses and can really only be incorporated when the site is permanent. The most famous bank in show jumping competitions is the Derby Bank at Hickstead. Horses may either slide down the bank as shown here or jump straight off it. **5.** The water jump is a feature of most international competitions held in outdoor arenas. A low fence precedes the water and a horse has to be encouraged to spread himself as much as he can. **6.** An upright fence comprising poles arranged directly on top of one another. Uprights will present even greater difficulty if placed on a downhill stretch or so that they are jumped going towards home — both situations which tempt a horse to rush at a fence. **7.** An oxer is a hedge bounded on either side by parallel poles. **8.** A wall is another upright fence, although as far as the horse is concerned its solid appearance will make it a more attractive proposition than some other uprights. Course builders will sometimes incorporate walls into oxers. **9.** Parallel poles are similar in principle to an oxer and as long as they are solidly built in front will be attractive to jump. A true parallel has the top poles the same height as each other.

and how to recognize different signals from his rider: It is also arguable that, though all horses enjoy jumping, this very willingness needs discipline, rather than simple encouragement, as far as competition jumping is concerned.

There are, in fact, only two kinds of fences or obstacles for a horse to jump – a high one and a long one, an upright or a spread. Uprights are more difficult to clear for a number of reasons; although spread fences have their own hazards, they are the more 'natural' of the two.

There are several permutations within these two basic types of fence. Uprights can take the form of five-bar gates, oxers and so on, while spread fences may be a triple bar, rising like a stairway, a water jump, or wall-and-rails, in which the elements are well separated necessitating a longer leap in a shallower arc. Perhaps the most difficult fence of all, however, is a spread which in effect consists of two upright fences a few feet apart, presenting the horse with the hazards of an upright and spread in one fence. An upright or 'straight' fence requires great upward impulsion (spring) from the horse's hocks, while a spread fence needs forward speed and accuracy to negotiate it.

An upright fence – gate, plank wall, sleepers, post-and-rails and so on – is only a single element deep, the thickness of the top bar of a gate, the coping stone of a wall, or, in the case of a brush-and-rail fence, the depth of a small 'box' hedge. Heights vary. Then there are narrow fences, such as a small gate or a stile, which are designed to test the obedience of a horse and the accuracy of the rider. In both upright and spread fences, the wings each side of the jump support the elements of the fence itself in some cases, but their main purpose is to define clearly to the horse the limits of the obstacle and to discourage him from running out.

A spread fence demands jumping length as well as height, though its height is usually less than that of an upright. Spreads include triple bars (a sort of stairway of poles); parallel bars (in effect, two upright post-and-rails fences a few feet apart); a double oxer (two small upright fences with a hedge between them); a reversed oxer (two short hedges on the approach and the landing side of upright fence), and a hogsback, which is similar to a triple bar with an additional bar on the landing side. A water jump is also a spread fence. It is usually the longest jump in the course and thus calls for somewhat more complex judging.

You will notice that a spread fence is usually more easy to jump than an upright fence. The secret lies in the former's ground line, a stout pole at the base of the fence on the approach-side. This is seen by the horse and is used by him to judge the point at which he takes off. The ground line of an upright – the bottom element of the fence – is right under its summit, a tricky line from which to calculate the take-off distance. Horse and rider must approach this type of fence very precisely, as it demands an

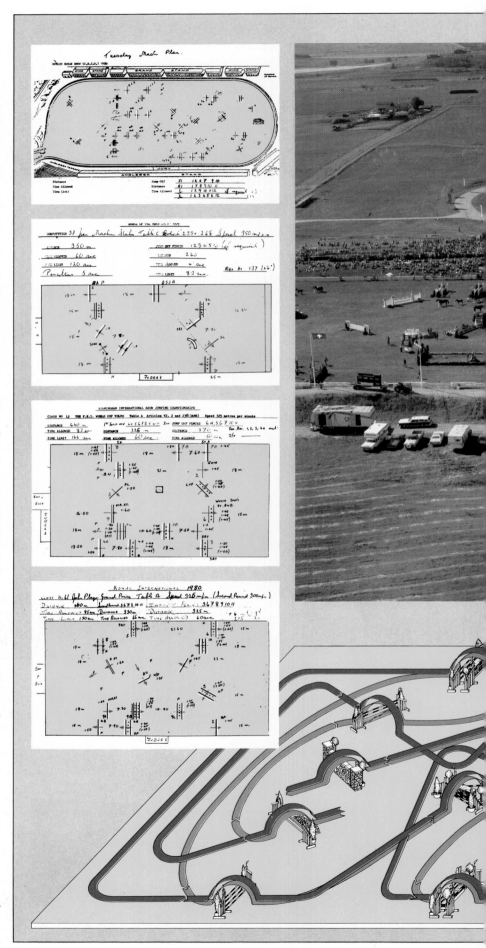

COURSE BUILDING

Competition jumping courses are designed by a course builder, whose aims are to set out the fences in such a way that the course will test the ability of horse and rider to the full, yet will not over-face the competitors and lead to falls and a poor standard of competition. On the other hand, he must ensure that a course is not too simple, or the first jump-off would be crowded with clear-rounders, leading to further time-consuming eliminating rounds. Other problems for the course builder are the size of the arena, which determines the number of jumps he may fit in, and so on. Four examples are shown **opposite**.

Every course builder has to consider these factors when planning a course. They apply just as much to your own practice course in the paddock as they do at an international event. He will plan every obstacle to bring out the various qualities of the horse — fitness, obedience and impulsion. His intentions will be several: to build a course that will produce a competition the audience will be happy to sit through and a course with some imagination and variety. He will also want to build a course that will encourage the horse to show his best ability,

not to trap him into making mistakes. He will also make sure that the fences conform to the regulations and recommendations. Fences should for instance be about 3m (11ft) wide and should have wings that remain upright if an element is knocked down. If a pole is hit it should dislodge fully from its curved holder or cup. Fences should be bright enough to stand out against a colourful background of spectators and ringside vehicles; wings should be placed in such a manner as to encourage the horse to jump the correct part of the fence; height and depth measurements should be accurate.

The easier fences should be situated in the early part so that both rider and horse are helped to gain confidence as they progress. At a small show at least nine fences should be included. Some fences may be jumped twice if the course is small. Distances between jumps will vary with circumstances. Upright fences should alternate with spreads, so that the horse is asked to exercise different jumping qualities and the rider to employ different jumping techniques. Changes of direction should be built into the course. A combination (or two) should be included.

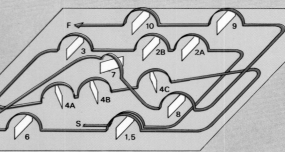

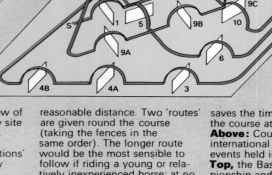

Top: An aerial view of the Spruce Meadow site at Calgary in Canada. It is the only North American venue of the Nations' Cup — an international show jumping team event held at official international horse shows where there are three or more teams participating. **Left:** A not-too-demanding layout for a show jumping course. Although there are a number of changes of direction, it is possible to approach each fence in a straight line from a

reasonable distance. Two 'routes' are given round the course (taking the fences in the same order). The longer route would be the most sensible to follow if riding a young or relatively inexperienced horse; at no time would he be asked to jump a fence awkwardly. The other line would be relevant if the competition were against the clock; in such an event it is cutting corners and making fast turns into and out of jumps that

saves the time, rather than riding the course at break neck speed. **Above:** Course layouts of two international show jumping events held in the U.K. in 1978. **Top,** the Basildon Bond Championship and **bottom,** the Queen Elizabeth II Cup. Nowadays, with so many jumping competitions held round the world and the high standard of horses competing, course building is a great art.

Above: International riders walk a course laid out in the indoor arena before the start of a competition at the Royal International Horse Show, Wembley. This is the only chance they get to examine the fences. In an indoor arena they will pay particular attention to the distances between the jumps as the fences often have to be placed very close together and the striding is therefore very important. They will look, therefore, at the fences in relation to one another as well as assessing them as individual obstacles.

exact point of take-off, using an exact power of impulsion.

A spread fence, on the other hand, usually has its ground line well forward (nearer the approaching horse and rider) so that the two jump the fence in a more natural arc. However, the spread demands more speed in the approach, which, in turn, presents considerably more difficulty for the rider in adjusting the pace of the horse to arrive at the take-off point accurately. If a spread fence has the added complication of an upright element on the approach side in addition to a fair spread, then there can be a real problem.

The more solid the fence, the more prepared the horse will be to jump it. A single rail without a ground line (rarely used in competition) can be very much more difficult to negotiate than a substantial fence, such as a wall or post-and-rails, of the same height. For the unwary the water jump is probably most difficult to clear, if only because it looks simple. There is no height to speak of, while the length of the jump is well within the capacity of the grade of horse for which it is designed. However, you will notice that an over-enthusiastic rider can bring a horse up to the water jump far too quickly, so that the animal may be unbalanced on his arrival at the take-off point. The mark of the

cool experienced rider is a moderate, calm approach, increasing speed only over the last few strides, when the take-off point can be accurately estimated. If the effort is made too early – even though the length of the jump may not demand a great effort – the horse may 'waste' distance on the approach side of the small leading fence and clip the tape at the far end of the water with its hind hoof. This small miscalculation has been the downfall of many a rider.

Fences more than 24m (80ft) apart are held to be unrelated, but if two or three fences are placed so that they follow each other at a distance of less than 12m (39ft) they are designated a combination fence and therefore are numbered as a single obstacle. It is the distance between each part of the combination that presents horse and rider with their main problem; at most shows, combinations will have a mixture of upright and spread fences deliberately chosen to ask the horse to show his qualities in both types of jumping.

Walking the course

About 15 minutes before the first horse is due in the arena the competitors will enter the ring together on foot and carefully walk the course.

This is a vital part of show jumping and is rarely ignored by even the best and most experienced riders. It is the only chance to examine the course in detail, since, once the competition has started, riders are not permitted to inspect jumps or routes except from behind the crowd barriers.

The riders will walk over the precise track they intend to take when mounted (although they will not count paces between unrelated jumps), examining each fence in some detail, checking its height and, if it is a spread fence, its depth. Some riders inspect the fences for solidity too, while others check them for 'bounce' – handling the top bar to see if it is likely to jump out of its cups when rapped by a hoof. If a fence proves particularly solid, some extra risks can be taken in the hope that even if hit, it will remain standing.

Riders will also be deciding the best way to take (or cut) a corner, make a necessary change of direction and how to approach a fence and how to clear it, remembering that spread fences, although generally more inviting than uprights, are progressively more difficult to clear as the angle of approach becomes more acute.

Distances between the elements of combinations are even more important. These distances will be meticulously paced out by the riders to decide on the speed of their approach and the number of non-jumping strides (if any) between the parts of the double or treble. Then the competitor may have to decide whether to take a combination straight or at an angle, if possible. Angling a tight double (one with short distances between elements), perhaps taking the first on the left side and the second on the right increases the effective distance between elements. In addition particular attention will be paid to whatever type of fence this or that rider's horse dislikes the most. The dangerous ones will be approached straight and jumped with care.

Outdoors and indoors

Show jumping courses may be constructed in a closed arena or outdoors, such as at St Gallen (Switzerland) or Hickstead (UK). Circumstances and season generally dictate whether a course should be indoors or out. Obvious advantages of an outdoor course are that there is more space in which to work and an outside venue is more natural for the horse. Grass, rarely used for indoor jumping, is also the best surface when in good condition, while fresh air lessens any respiratory problems the horse might have.

On the other hand, grass tends to get cut up quickly in front of the fences in poor weather and consequently outdoor competitions are usually restricted to daylight. Really foul

Above left: Compare this picture with the one opposite; there is a much greater feeling of space in an outdoor arena. Riders often experience difficulty in controlling their horses in an indoor arena, particularly if they are more used to jumping out of doors. **Above:** You can see the concentration on this rider's face as he counts the strides between fences in a combination. He will know exactly how many of his paces equal one of his horse's strides and will therefore be able to prepare him for the approach to the fence.

weather can cause them to be cancelled. Indoor surfaces also gain points because they can be re-raked after a class and can mount a competition at any time of the year. However, indoor venues necessarily include tight turns, present dust problems and rely on artificial lighting. The last can disturb a horse, as may the noise, and the proximity of the spectators.

On the whole it is advisable, as a young rider intending to start competition jumping, to enter in local outdoor shows and progress to indoors when you are more supple and confident.

Championship course

At the higher levels of show jumping a typical championship course (indoors or out) would consist of perhaps 15 jumps, including a double and a treble combination. Up to eight changes of direction left and right, and complete half-circles are called for and of course a variety of upright and spread fences would be used, plus a bank (sometimes) and a water jump.

A hypothetical course, about 700m (2674ft) long (Time Allowed, say, 2 minutes 5 seconds; time limit 4 minutes 10 seconds) could look like this: Fence No. 1 a small gate, simple and encouraging, is followed by a hogsback, then a triple bar before a 180 degree right turn to swing right round into the middle of the arena facing the opposite direction. A wall-and-rails is the first element of a combination (double) that also includes oildrum and rails. Then the horse inclines right to take a small spread of planks-and-rails followed by another complete change of direction starting with a big red brick wall, then a crossed poles. No. 8 is a double again, walls-and-rail spread, and an ornamental gate.

A wide left turn back into the middle line of the arena takes horse and rider over a tricky triple-bar which can be approached at any angle, followed by a quick canter and another gate and a double oxer. Then the most tricky triple combination and around into the water jump, then on in a straight line to the last jump, an ornamental wall. Such a formidable series

Above left: Pat Smythe on Carousel III at the Horse of the Year Show, Harringay, in 1956. **Above right:** Another famous team, David Broome and Mr Softee. **Below left:** Lt. Col. Harry Llewellyn takes a fence at Badminton on Foxhunter in 1952. **Below right:** Princess Anne presenting a trophy to Hartweg Stenken on Simona.

would normally take a rider just under two minutes to complete. In an indoor arena where space is invariably limited and fences are closer together, the distance and time may be shortened by a fraction.

A good show jumper

What do top riders look for in their never-ending search for the horse with the qualities that will take it over a show jumping course successfully? What is the secret of selecting a horse that may have been a hack or a hunter, or even a youngster's riding pony, for training up to the demanding standards of the show jumping world? Is there any definition of a show jumper? Is there a pony in some quiet meadow, that, once seen, can be recognized as a potential world champion?

If the finding and the making of a show jumper was as simple as this every good rider would have an Olympic horse and every novice a potential champion. In fact there is no simple way to define a potential jumper. There is no

specific type and there is no specific shape. A particular horse's action, for instance, is no real guide. He may be a long-strider or a delicate and dainty stepper – both types are to be seen in the international arena and both have won top honours.

Attempts to breed a jumper, a process that seems logically simple, have had doubtful success. Sire and dam rarely seem to co-operate in getting the right genes together in the correct formula, although some crosses have been successful. For instance, speed crossed with size and strength have produced some fine specimens, but never consistently.

Some of the best show jumpers have been of very humble origin. An early winner, Craven A, was bred out of a draught mare in Ireland; another equally famous jumper, and Olympic winner, was bred out of a shire mare. Character, that unknown quantity in the makeup other horses lack, is undoubtedly the touchstone that separates the great jumper from the rest.

It is clearly reasonable, however, to try to avoid a horse with built-in faults. Size need not be important, though stamina relative to size is of some account. If there is one factor which is vital – it is one that is sometimes difficult to spot on short acquaintance – it is athletic vigour. A show jumper is both a gymnast and a competitive athlete, and an outstanding show jumper is as rare as a top class human athlete.

So a show jumper may come in almost any shape, but the true champion will be courageous although not impetuous, bold but not rash, and should have stamina without stubbornness, perseverance without obstinacy and calmness without lethargy.

This last quality, that of an equable nature, is perhaps the most important of all. Accuracy in jumping time after time over a demanding course is essential. If the horse is tense or highly strung, the rider will have less chance of success in placing him correctly before a fence.

Some experienced riders may opt for a slightly small head – the bigger the head the more the horse has to carry – and shortish front legs. If the legs are too long they are more likely to get in the way over a jump. Similarly the hind legs should not be too long – if a horse can bend his hocks tightly as he takes the fence he is more likely to have a show jumping career ahead of him. Horses who trail hind or forelegs are clearly more likely to hit the top element of a fence.

The first essential physical trait of the show jumper is the bone structure; it should be strong and clean and the pasterns compact and resilient. The well built-up quarters will give the horse a high tail carriage – curiously, a horse with a low tail carriage is seldom an outstanding jumper. But most of all the soundness of the hocks – the means of impulsion and fulcrum of the whole operation – and their link with the quarters, the second thigh, are the focus of the horse's jumping ability.

Earlier we said that all horses can jump. But this does not mean that all are up to competition standard. It would be a cardinal error to expect any horse with little or no experience in jumping to perform efficiently. However, most equines are interested, and will reward the rider with a lot of fun if the business of training is carried out with understanding as well as discipline.

Training and practice

A good age to introduce a horse or pony to jumping is between six and eight years. Never try to work with a very young horse; it needs an experienced horseman to train a complete novice. Rider and pony will hopefully have known each other for about a year. Twelve months hacking and caring for a pony through all the seasons does wonders to increase knowledge and ability on the part of both rider

---

EXERCISES FOR HORSE AND RIDER

During a **horse's** early training, working over cavalletti is vital. Start by walking and trotting over poles on the ground, then over cavalletti at their lowest height, spaced so that your horse can step over them in his natural stride.

Once your horse can trot evenly over a line of cavalletti, turn the end one so it is a little higher and he has to make an actual jump. Gradually replace this with a small jump at the end of a line of three cavalletti. Canter over cavalletti only when you are confident that your horse will still trot if you ask him. Placing cavalletti in a circle will also slow him down.

Long sessions over cavalletti are monotonous and should be interspersed with normal flat work training. Start on a loose rein. Let the pony stretch his neck and balance himself. Gradually take up contact with your hands, using seat and legs to push him into the contact. Progress to circles, serpentines, changes of diagonal across the schooling area. Turning frequently, make him use his hocks and hindquarters generaly (the muscles used most when jumping) by working constantly from behind not from the forehand.

Start including halts (making him stand squarely and collectedly) then half-halts – give aids to halt and as he is halting, ask him to move on (do not practise this if the pony is confused) – and reinbacks. All these exercises make him use his hocks and back end. Always move forward as a reward after these exercises.

Put two or three cavalletti in different places in your schooling area so your horse does not get used to them in one place.

Rider exercises are still necessary in most cases and should include all those shown in manuals – trotting without stirrups, bending to touch toes, touching tail and ears (pony's), opposite toe (yours), hand-on-head, arm-swinging, ankle-rotating and so on. And on the move – trotting over cavalletti and low jumps (bales) without stirrups, without reins (knot them or the pony could trip over them), with hands on head (yours again), with arms folded (**see above**) and with outstretched 'aeroplane' arms. Try one of the toughest exercises – go forward into the jumping position with stirrups a couple of holes shorter than normal, at a trot, and keep it up for five minutes. If your back aches, you are not yet fit enough. Try the same exercise at a canter, but only for about ten strides at a time, alternating with a normal position for ten strides. You'll feel much fitter after a week or two of this, combined with the natural exercise of jumping practice.

and mount, and more importantly, mutual confidence. If hunting has been included, so much the better.

Assume that you have already completed your own and your pony's training on the flat some time ago and have built some simple jumps and taken him around a varied 'miniature' course of your own design. You will have built your own small fences from perhaps a low pole on a couple of oil drums filled in with some other material to give it a solid look; you will have made a forward ground line to encourage the pony to take off at more or less the right distance for the type of jump. You now have some knowledge of the basic practice of jumping; you know something about the correct forward seat, about the use of distance poles on the ground to achieve balance and rhythm, and how to employ cavalletti for the same purpose. In short, you have completed the first stage and are ready for more formal training over genuine fences.

All of the next stages may be done without a trainer; ideally, however, an experienced rider – as often as not an experienced friend – should be present. The trainer can pass on his or her own experience as well as assessing your, and your pony's, progress. He or she will also be able to see immediately if anything is performed incorrectly. Only someone on the ground, i.e. not involved in the actual work,

Above: A saddle specially designed for jumping. The flaps are cut further forward than in a normal saddle and the front part of the flap is more padded than usual. This padding is known as the knee roll and it allows the rider's knees to lie snugly against the saddle, so that when he is riding with the shorter leather needed for jumping he can adopt the forward position more easily.
Left: Most horses show some fear of water the first few times they are asked to jump it, yet it is essential that they get used to it. Dig a ditch in a flat part of the field and fill it with water. Placing a pole either side of the ditch as shown here helps to define the area more clearly, giving the horse a better idea of the width he is to jump. Let him examine it very thoroughly before asking him to jump it.

can do this. And of course the trainer can help to rebuild fences, re-arrange the course and remove debris when fences are knocked down. This may seem a minor point, but schooling becomes very tedious if you have to keep getting on and off!

The first real show fences

Until your first jumping lessons, you will have been advised to sit deep in the saddle, using longish stirrups so that the muscles of the hip, knee and ankle joints are developed. Since the propulsion comes from the hindquarters of the horse and the less riding weight in that region the better, the stirrup leathers should be shortened by two or three holes for jumping. The rider's body should be at a sharper angle to the horse's thighs, an angle which will enable the rider to move the body into the forward position more easily when beginning a jump. This position means that, when jumping, more of the rider's weight will be on the front of the foot in the stirrup, the reins will have shortened, (but the light contact with the mouth will be retained) and the hands will be ready to move forward with the stretching out of the horse's neck.

Although this may have been practised earlier, the forward jumping position should be consolidated by work over trotting poles. Even though your pony may have been taken over poles before, it is sensible to repeat the process now that larger fences are to be met. Six or eight poles are placed in a straight line with room at the approach and at the end for the horse to negotiate them all without starting to turn.

Walk the horse down the length of the lane of poles, allowing him to find his own way over them. He will automatically stretch his neck forward and downward, which will draw the rider's body into the forward position, with the weight slightly out of the saddle.

When the poles can be walked quietly and without fuss, try trotting over them to teach him to balance, to place his feet accurately, and to accept the discipline of the poles without argument. It also helps the rider to develop a rhythm with the movement of the horse and to maintain the correct position whilst performing a rising or sitting trot.

A cavalletto (or a small pyramid of three) may then be placed a short distance from the far end of the poles. If the horse has had some experience of natural obstacles, this may quickly be replaced by a low crossed pole fence supported by small wings. This fence is later augmented by a horizontal top pole. A short course may now be set up immediately following the trotting poles: a cavalletto, then at a reasonable distance, crossed poles, followed by a small spread fence, not necessarily in a line with the earlier fences.

As the rider and mount gain experience more sophisticated fences must be built to a standard

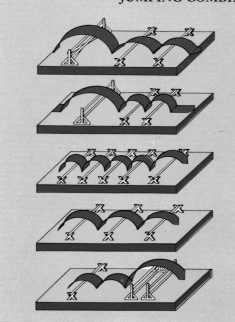

JUMPING COMBINATIONS

Trotting over a line of cavalletti with a small jump at the end is, in effect, an introduction to jumping combinations — two or more fences placed sufficiently close to be 'related' This means they will be separated only by a few strides. Learning to jump a variety of combinations is a vital part of a show jumper's training, for all course builders will include such obstacles. If you know you are going to have to put in two short strides between elements, it is important that you approach the first element on a short stride, otherwise your horse will take too long a jump. If, on the other hand, the second element of the combination is a spread fence after perhaps two or three non-jumping strides, push on at the first element to make sure you have sufficient impulsion to jump the spread.

Above: Jumping on the lunge is an important part of the continued training of a show jumper, although it generally figures most prominently at the beginning of his training. Here, successful international rider Caroline Bradley is training a horse on the lunge and is really asking him to spread himself out and bascule over the fence. Note the pole on the ground in front of the fence, to steady the horse and help him adjust his stride for a correct take-off.

matching those that will be met at a small show. As we have mentioned, the fences to be seen in competition fall into two categories, upright and spread. But now we must look at fences more individually: the 'two-dimensional' up-right with no depth, the parallels, upright with some depth, the staircase type of spread which encourages the horse to jump, the hogsback or pyramid fence, and the water jump which is all length but virtually no height.

The fences a horse will meet at the schooling ground should not be large – overface a horse in his early days and his confidence may be destroyed forever – but will be brightly coloured and varied in preparation for the variety he will encounter in competition. The more varied the fences in the school, the less likely is the horse (or the rider) to be surprised by an unusual fence in the ring. When a small course of school fences has been set, remember that too much jumping for too long over the same course will allow a horse to jump from memory, leading to loss of concentration. He should have to think about each fence as it is faced.

You should change the location of the course fences frequently and also change the route around the course. It is also a good idea as a matter of habit after work on the flat to take the horse over a round or two of the course and conversely to go out for a hack after a few rounds of practice jumping. Too much appli-cation to one subject will wear down the sharp edge of enthusiasm for both horse and rider.

Remember, the current aim is for you and your pony to jump well. Height is as yet im-material. It is preferable to keep lengthening fences (into spreads) rather than raising them to elevate the arc of the leap. Practice over parallels as well as other types of fence although these are not as easy for the novice jumper because they often have no ground line and the horse cannot see the far pole until he is in the air. The pony must judge his take-off distance even more accurately here so that his arc will take him clear of the back pole. Set up your course to include a fence that needs a sharpish turn after jumping it. Use reins, legs and the swing of your body and ensure that the pony is

on the correct leg as he lands and turns. Then try another jump at a different angle so that you both become used to the rapid change of landing and approach that all competition courses include. Practise jumping in a circle too. A pony can do this easily if well balanced and it is useful in indoor competitions where there is less room to turn, or in jump-offs where tighter turns are often necessary.

How long should training for small show fences take? About two weeks should be taken up initially in improving work on the flat. This should be followed by trotting over poles for two or three weeks, with rider exercises, trotting over poles-with-cavalletti-at-the-end, and strawbale jumps, cantering over poles, and poles-and-cavalletti. Continue this routine for a further two weeks, at the same time introducing the pony to various small jumps. Make this part fun for you both, leaving it until the end of a session of more monotonous work. If there is another rider to work with you, so much the better.

Continue all these exercises for another two or three weeks, building-up the programme to include turning after jumps, using a jumping lane and jumping off circles. At the same time slowly increase the spread of the jumps. Then spend two more weeks continuing as before, plus jumping your small course (not more than twice a week at first) gradually building up the course and the jumps. You should now be ready for your first show, the first of as many as

Right above: It is not necessary to have proper show jumps for home schooling, particularly in the early days of training. Here a rider is taking his horse over a really makeshift jump — no more than a pole resting on a barrel at one end and a log at the other. **Right below:** This is a more impressive home-built practice fence. The matting suspended beneath the pole gives the impression of solidity which will encourage the horse to take more care as he jumps. **Below:** As with all aspects of equestrianism, having professional lessons from a qualified instructor is vital to success in show jumping. He will help you to improve your ability and your horse's performance, quite possibly correcting faults of which you were unaware.

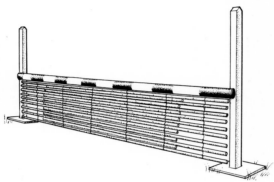

possible during the season to bring your horse into contact with all the noise, company, urgency and bustle that are a part of competition jumping.

Schooling fences will involve you in some cost, since the home-built type of obstacle is not really a satisfactory substitute. A flimsy structure will not encourage your horse to jump. If it has little or no ground line it may be dangerous for him even to try, while it can also be dangerous for the rider. Some variety too, in the look and type of fences make it easier on horse and rider, both of whom can become very tired with repetition.

Up and over

As we have seen earlier each of the two basic types of obstacle has its own characteristics and may have to be approached differently. Assuming the horse's willingness and competence to get over the fence the most important factor in achieving success is the ability of the rider to 'see' a stride.

As the fence is approached at a trot or canter, there is no more than a split second for the rider to judge the rapidly diminishing distance ahead, but at a crucial three strides away from the take-off point it is vital that the horse is able to jump with his stride completed at an almost-precise spot in front of the fence. It is this ability on the part of the rider, and his skill in adjusting the horse's stride that separates the winners from the rest of the field.

The rider's jumping position is also vital. This is something that by this time will have been practised both on the flat, over distance poles or cavalletti and over small jumps. Since the day when in the early part of this century the great rider Caprilli, father of modern equestrian sport, developed the forward seat (finally persuading riders out of the unbalanced 'lean-back' seat that is seen in old hunting pictures) the classic jumping take-off position shows an imaginary straight line following through from the bit to the rider's elbow with the forearm and hand part of that direct line. The rider's weight is removed from the saddle by his forward attitude, lower leg almost vertical, heels down. This puts the rider's weight just forward of the horse's centre of gravity, but does not take it off the quarters as the spring is made. If the rider's weight is left behind the centre of gravity during the first part of the jump, the horse's weight will be thrown to the rear, lessening his impulsion. If the rider's weight is too far forward, however, control and balance are diminished on landing.

The picture of rider and horse when seen from the side should show the rider's knees acting as a pivot at exactly the pivoting point of the horse – that is, a little below and behind the withers and slightly above the heart. The thrust of take-off and the shock of landing are taken by the rider's hip and knee joints. With a shortened stirrup, which makes a V-spring of hip and

knee, the rider can weather the take-off, the bascule itself and the landing on this strong natural suspension unit. The hands are in the lightest possible contact with the horse's mouth, allowing him to stretch his head and neck out for balance when taking the fence. The rider's hands and arms should follow those 'elongating' movements willingly, but the shoulders must remain in the correct firm-backed forward position and should not be allowed to collapse and move forward in front of the knees.

So with that reminder of what every rider will have learned by the time she faces fences that are designed to bring on both horse and riders to show standard, and with some knowledge of show fences from your observations from the ringside, here in front of you is the first fence.

Upright fence

The take-off point for an upright fence is ideally the same distance in front of it as its own height. If an upright – a gate, for instance – is 1.2m (4ft) high then the take-off point is normally the same distance in front of it. The arc jumped by the horse will describe an approximate semi-circle. At three strides away the decision must be made. To arrive at the exact take-off point, you will probably have to adjust stride if the fences are unrelated – if they have not been set up at an exact number of strides apart in other words. If the horse has to take-off too close to the fence, he will jump up into the air 'off all four feet' and could return to ground right in the middle of the fence. He can alternatively come to a 'dirty stop', the sort of thing that can all too easily unseat a rider. If he stands too far back, he will either have to try too big a leap and probably hit the top with a foot, or try to put in an extra small stride to bring him closer which will throw him off balance, causing him to plunge right through the fence.

A spread

Any form of spread is easier to clear than an equally high upright. The most inviting spread is the sort that rises in stages, the 'staircase' fence. It needs a fairly close take-off point, a spot that is not difficult for the horse to judge, as the fence provides a good ground line that is normally quite visible. As with an upright fence a stand-off that is too far from the fence can land rider and horse in the middle of the wood-work usually as a result of the animal catching a hind leg in one of the back poles. Too close and you will be right into the bottom of the leading edge, or alternatively the horse will stop.

This fence needs speed. The horse has to go forward as well as high so on the crucial three strides away (when all jumping decisions have to be made) sit right down in the saddle and really push, using your seat and your legs (but avoiding throwing your hands about, a fault too often seen in the ring) to ask for a burst of speed. Watch the top of the fence, not the bottom. When he stretches his neck to jump, be ready for it – ready to let your arms move forward, keeping only a light contact with the horse's mouth, and moving into the forward seat as the hocks begin to impel you both upwards.

Water jump

Many young riders imagine, perhaps from techniques they see at show jumping competitions, that water, once sighted, is galloped at as if it were an oasis in the Sahara – and it must be admitted that it often looks as though some expert riders do precisely this. Do not copy this technique, however, if you want to clear the water accurately.

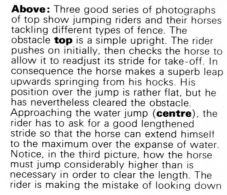

Above: Three good series of photographs of top show jumping riders and their horses tackling different types of fence. The obstacle **top** is a simple upright. The rider pushes on initially, then checks the horse to allow it to readjust its stride for take-off. In consequence the horse makes a superb leap upwards springing from his hocks. His position over the jump is rather flat, but he has nevertheless cleared the obstacle. Approaching the water jump (**centre**), the rider has to ask for a good lengthened stride so that the horse can extend himself to the maximum over the expanse of water. Notice, in the third picture, how the horse must jump considerably higher than is necessary in order to clear the length. The rider is making the mistake of looking down at the obstacle, although she is well balanced on landing and ready to turn the horse towards the next fence.

At the **bottom**, Ireland's Eddie Machen tackles the famous Derby Bank at Hickstead. He has chosen to slither halfway down before making a leap off. Notice how the rider is beautifully poised over his horse's centre of gravity, never leaning back and putting too much weight on the horse's back legs. In the fourth picture he is leaning well forward, anticipating the horse's jump off the bank. **Right:** The horse's stride between fences placed close together in a combination. On landing, the hind legs come to the ground and immediately have to provide the impulsion for the spring up and forward to clear the second element.

HOW TO TAKE FENCES

Above: Life for a top show jumping rider is not all glamour. Here David Broome helps to load hay into the horse box to make sure his horses will be well supplied throughout a show away from home.

Again, you must look for the last three strides, and have the horse 'on his hocks' before you let him go with a last burst of speed. Any other method means that the horse will arrive at the jump with his forehand unbalanced.

For those vital last three strides, therefore, you 'push' hard with a lengthened stride and increased speed, getting him as close to the small leading water jump fence for take-off as possible. A common error is to take off much too far back thus wasting space and effort.

The very fact that the water jump has no really challenging fence at its leading edge is one of its less obvious hazards. There is very little apparent incentive for the horse to make a real effort. In schooling, this can be overcome by placing a distance pole three or four strides back from a fence built to represent a water jump and practising the last phase of the approach or building the fence up into a spread with height in the last part to encourage the horse to jump up and out.

Bank

A plain bank without a fence at its top needs a lot of impulsion as you approach the leading side. Arrival at the summit is the time to start collecting the horse again. If the bank is fairly small, then a spring straight off the top is normal. If it is a high bank that needs riding down on the reverse side, then take the horse down gently at a walk, leaning forward not back. It is important here to keep your hands in light contact. 'Throwing' hands will unbalance the horse very easily.

A combination

Combinations (a double or treble) cause most of the trouble in the ring. They may be made easier or more difficult by varying the type of fence and the distances between fences. In the earlier stages of schooling over fences of the show type, it is obviously sensible to make the distance between combination fences match the horse's stride as closely as possible, introducing no artificial distance difficulties between elements.

A school combination could be made of, say, a simple three-pole upright followed by a spread of about the same height and depth. Make the distance between elements enough to allow one non-jumping stride between fences. This distance will have to be checked and adjusted to your own horse's stride. Later the distance between jumps may be lengthened or shortened to introduce flexibility into the horse's performance. Alter the measurements by degrees and do not expect instant accuracy.

Misjudging the first fence of a double or treble combination is one of the common difficulties. If you do not ride fast enough to take the first part (a spread perhaps) properly, then the horse will end up too near the back of the first jump to take just the single non-jumping stride that the distance requires before jumping the next fence. With the approach then one-and-a-half strides away the stride will have to be shortened to make two smaller strides before negotiating the next fence. The answer is to get the first fence right, in anticipation of taking the second clear. In a treble it is even more complex, as the horse has to make two first-class jumps to approach the final part of the combination correctly. Distances between the elements of a combination will be increased for competitions where the horse is required to go round the course at speed.

As the fences get larger the take-off zone becomes narrower and stride adjustment increases in importance. The rider must continue to develop the ability to make a fast and accurate calculation of those three last strides before the point of take-off.

Practice this calculation by erecting a good-size upright and place a cavalletto 'distance rail' in front of it in the same riding line. At a steady canter the distance should give three strides from landing after the small cavalletto

jump, to the take-off zone in front of the upright fence. When jumping the cavalletto watch the following fence and count off the strides to the take-off point. Determined practice at this trains the eye to see the three-stride distance. Indeed you may find yourself one of the lucky riders: some people have a flair for 'seeing' a stride at a glance and need little training. Most of us, with a less accurate sense of distance, will need a lot of practice. Later remove the cavalletto and carry out the same exercise without it. Then place the cavalletto at four strides from the fence and try this distance. Now the length of stride may vary a little and will have to be adjusted to end up in the take-off zone.

To adjust the stride, you must adjust the length of the horse. The stride may be lengthened by a lightening of the hands alone, or sometimes by the use of seat and legs in rhythmic combination with the stride, although heavy use of the leg on the approach should never be necessary if the horse is being trained correctly. Shortening of the stride may be accomplished by holding the horse firmly with the legs to maintain impulsion, with the actual adjustment done by the resistance of one hand slightly more than the other. Obviously few riders can adjust stride to arrive absolutely accurately every time so when it goes wrong –

Above: A good groom can make all the difference to the success of a horse and rider team. How the horse is cared for on a regular daily basis will greatly affect his overall performance and a responsible groom can relieve an owner-rider of a lot of worries and headaches. Here a groom plaits one of her charges ready for a class at the horse show in Rotterdam, Holland. The 1980 Rotterdam Show was of particular significance to show jumping riders. The FEI designated it a 'Mini Olympics' to compensate for the poor attendance at the Olympic Games that year owing to the boycott.

SHOW JUMPING TODAY

Above: A groom removes protective travelling clothing from a horse and saddles it ready for the competition.
Top right: Paul Schockemöhle (younger brother of Alwin) rides El Paso at Rotterdam. **Centre, left:** Show jumping riders are a friendly crowd. Here several walk the course at Windsor together. **Middle:** Even top riders let their hair down on occasions. David Broome and Harvey Smith ride side-by-side in a fancy dress parade at Olympia. **Right:** The autograph hunters are never far away; David Broome and Robert Smith oblige. **Below and below right:** Those two famous names again. Harvey Smith and David Broome on Sanyo Cadmica and Harris Home Care respectively. The first names of the horses indicate the firms that sponsor these two riders. Few top riders could afford to compete regularly throughout the show jumping season without the backing of a sponsor.

and it will – just sit still and let the horse sort it out. Remember, his ability has been improving during practice in common with yours and, though he may be the junior partner of the team, there are occasionally times when the rider is just something to keep the saddle warm.

Show preparations

Physical preparations for your first show will be made in the main by your trainer, but it is up to you to plan factors such as transport, tack, feeding necessities and so on some time ahead.

The correct dress is stipulated in the rules available in the BSJA Handbook; it obviously includes a hard hat, jodhpurs or breeches, and footwear (juniors may wear jodhpur boots, seniors top boots of rubber or leather). Spurs and sticks are allowed. The type of tack to be used is strictly regulated by the governing bodies of show jumping, although the rules often change with the style and fashion of tack.

You will have to decide when you arrive, after you have found out the time you are due in the ring, whether your horse needs time to settle down after travelling, or whether he needs half an hour of practice jumping, or walking round, before competing. Some horses, for instance, need some jumping practice then need another half an hour to calm down. This you will gradually learn as the season progresses. But one fact of life is useful to learn as soon as possible – to recognise the value of a good groom.

Remember, even if you normally look after your horse completely during the week, you are going to need someone else who is just as competent on the day of a show. As the rider, you will be busy from the time you arrive – registering with the show secretary, collecting your number, getting changed and so on – and will need someone to whom you can delegate responsibility.

Your groom must be totally reliable. A groom is unflappable under pressure, experienced in handling horses under all circumstances and able to endure excitable humans. He or she should ideally be able to stay with one horse/rider team on a long-term basis and be unambitious in the competition world. The groom's job is out of the spotlight – taking care of the animal, feeding, grooming, putting in studs (they must never be worn when travelling), exercising, being an expert at travelling matters, knowledgeable of ailments, stable management, tack and all aspects. Part of the groom's job is to encourage and help the rider to practice, to be on hand before, during and after the competition round, to have the horse ready before time, to be ready to catch it if the rider falls off in the ring, to have rugs ready for the horse's welfare immediately after the jumping round, to walk it about for cooling off, or to keep it warmed up if there is to be a jump-off. A good groom is worth almost as much as a horse. Reward her properly.

THE SHOW JUMPER'S YEAR

It is extremely difficult to give even an outline twelve-month programme for a show jumper as so much will depend on the age and ability of the horse, and on how much of the year you wish to compete. Unlike most other equestrian sports, the show jumping season now extends throughout the twelve months of the year, with indoor shows in the autumn and winter and outdoor shows through the spring and summer. You therefore have to make a decision on whether you are going to compete for the greater part of the year taking it comparatively easy and giving your horse the odd week off jumping when necessary, or if you are going to compete hard for a shorter time and give him a prolonged rest. In fact, most people would elect to compete for at least eight months of the year taking it fairly easily, particularly if they owned a novice horse. If you were to compete with a novice for just a few months of the year, then give it a couple of months rest (after which you would have a good three months bringing it back into form), you would not be much further up the jumping scale the following year.

An outline is given below for a novice show jumper of four to five years old. By the end of its first season, you would hope to have come out of Newcomer classes into Foxhunter classes and be in a position to come out of Foxhunter and start jumping in Grade C classes comparatively early the following year. The routine given is not going to be ideal for every horse and rider by any means; adapt it to suit your horse and your circumstances and, if at all possible, take advice about your specific programme from someone with professional show-jumping knowledge.

Mid-winter-early spring: Enter some indoor shows, but no more than one a fortnight, and then only in one or two classes per show. You should not expect your horse to jump more than two or three rounds per show initially; overface or overwork him now and he will be out for the season. Entering indoor shows at this time is a good idea, however; it will get him going and show him what he can look forward to in the months ahead! Providing he is not a big-striding horse (in which case indoor shows will not really suit him) jumping in the restricted area should make concentration a little easier than in a big outdoor arena where there are lots of distractions round the ring. Also, the ground at indoor shows is prepared to give ideal jumping conditions, so the horse gets his first taste of jumping on good, soft going that will not hurt his feet. In spite of all this, you should not expect too much of him at this stage. Not only has he got to find his form; remember that he is still fairly new to the game and also that he is in no way at the peak of his fitness.

On the days you are not competing follow a sensible routine to get him to the peak of his fitness by the late spring. Besides schooling and some jumping practice, give him lots of interesting hacks to keep him alert and on his toes.

Spring-early autumn: The outdoor show season. By now your horse should be very fit, but again, be sensible about how many shows you enter. One a week now is quite enough, and only enter in one or two classes each time. Take careful note of how your horse goes and his general reaction to jumping; this is particularly important with a novice horse, for if you spoil him at this stage through asking too much, he will be spoilt for life. A wise rider would probably enter for three or four shows over a similar period of weeks and then miss a show for one week. Do not run the horse down during this 'mini-rest' period though; keep him fit by hacking and giving him the occasional schooling session, but give him a break from jumping.

You should in any case be prepared for some time off jumping during this period and your horse will generally see to this by going sour, or perhaps going lame if he has been jumping on hard ground. If he starts to shorten his stride during a course and begins to jump awkwardly or even stop, it is undoubtedly because he is feeling uncomfortable, if not actually in pain. Besides the inevitable leg problems, show jumpers often suffer from painful backs, both from the jarring as they land and also perhaps because they have had to twist themselves every now and again to clear a jump which they met off an awkward stride. Providing you notice minor ailments as they occur, you should not have to lay off competition for more than two or three weeks.

On non-jumping days, treat your horse as you would any competition horse. On the day following the show, give him a rest, turning him out in the paddock for a few hours, providing the grass is not lush. Lead him out for half an hour or so. For the rest of the time, keep him fit by sensible exercise and school him over fences perhaps a couple of times a week.

Throughout early autumn, start to let the horse down a little, entering only a couple of shows and riding a little less diligently during non-competition days toward the end of the month.

End of outdoor season: Turn your horse out for a couple of weeks, bringing him in at night. As he has been stabled throughout the summer he would feel the cold too much to be out at night.

Mid-autumn-early winter: Bring him in and start to get him fit. His short rest should have been sufficient to re-vitalise him, on the basis that you have not worked him too hard throughout the season. If you give him much longer, you will have a major job on your hands. Ride him sensibly and steadily to begin with; even two weeks is enough for him to get a bit soft. Aim to get him sufficiently fit to have a couple of days' hunting towards the end of December. This gives most show jumpers a new lease of life and restores their zest. They seem to enjoy the comparative freedom, coupled with the company of others experienced in the hunting field; they can jump freely without being put on the spot and asked for the precision necessary in the show jumping ring, and most important of all, it brings a bit of variety into their lives. Just be prepared to hold them a little in check at the first indoor show!

CHAPTER SIX

DRESSAGE

THE OBJECTIVE OF dressage, or training on progressive lines, is to produce a strong, well-developed and supple horse that is obedient to the wishes of his rider and is comfortable, safe and a pleasure to ride. These are qualities desirable in any young horse, whether or not he is destined for a full-time dressage career, but it must be emphasized that they cannot be instilled by any novice rider. A training programme for a young horse is outlined on pages 142–158, but it presupposes that the rider is skilled and that advice will be sought from a knowledgeable trainer.

Dressage may be said to have begun when the early horse peoples of over 2000 years ago first rode horses and produced the required responses from them in answer to the application of hands, legs and switches – for dressage means no more than training. The word, like so many school riding terms, is French, for this has been the language of the equestrian vocabulary ever since the French took over the international equestrian role which the Italians held until the latter part of the 16th century. Whereas dressage (the verb is *dresser*) describes the training of a riding horse, or even a harness horse,

the word entrainment (from the verb *entrainer*) is reserved for the very different practice of training a racehorse.

The two terms, to train a racehorse and to dress a riding horse, persisted in common English usage up to the end of the 18th century and into the early part of the 19th century, but thereafter the word dressage went out of fashion and use. This was a pity, because all sorts of misconceptions arose and lingered in the Anglo-Saxon world right up to the mid-20th century. The word was foreign and the practice (a misunderstood one, if indeed any effort was made to understand it) was correspondingly foreign and therefore something to be suspected and even derided by the more dyed-in-the-wool hunting man.

The first evidence we have of progressive schooling systems designed to strengthen and supple the horse as well as making him obedient to the wishes of his rider is provided by the Greek general, agriculturalist, writer and philosopher Xenophon (*c.* 430–350 BC). In his books *Hipparchikos*, a training manual for cavalry officers, and *Peri Hippikes*, riding is discussed as a science and art.

Opposite: Jeannie Sinclair on Diorella competing in a dressage competition at Goodwood, England in 1981. Since the Second World War dressage has become increasingly popular as a competitive sport. **Above:** 18th-century dressage; this print shows a riding horse being trained, or 'dressed'.

Above: Louis XIII and his horse receive a lesson, possibly from Antoine de Pluvinel, the first of the French riding Masters.

Indeed, it was to Xenophon that the riders of the Renaissance period turned, at the beginning of the 'classical' riding which was to form the basis for modern dressage. As with most equestrian pursuits dressage has its roots in the practices of war, and the noble riders of the Renaissance were simulating in the quiet of their often sumptuous riding halls the movements which were considered necessary in the schooled war-horse of the armoured Knight.

The Knight's charger had to be handy (so far as the word could be applied to such heavy horses) and obedient. This was particularly so when the Knight and his horse were in actual physical contact with bodies of infantry intent on dragging the rider from his horse or maiming, or killing the latter. Many of the movements taught to the war horse were designed, therefore, to discourage the close proximity of foot soldiers, and it is these movements which provide the basis for the much-photographed 'airs above the ground' (opposite) practised at both the Spanish Riding School in Vienna and the French School at Saumur. These airs, ranging from the *levade* (relatively mild but menacing if one happens to be on foot and in an uncomfortably close position) to the great, soaring leap of the *capriole*, remain a part of the programme of both schools, although they are performed only by selected horses which are found to have a particular talent for them. The 'airs above the ground' do not form any part of modern, competitive dressage riding; they

may, however, be the ultimate extension of a highly collected movement on the flat such as the *piaffe* which is called for in modern dressage competitions.

The sort of leap to which the horse is best suited is governed largely by the conformation and can be gauged, by an experienced trainer, by the way in which the horse rises from the *levade*. In all instances the leaps, a collective word for the High School airs above the ground, include the *levade*, even though this is not technically a movement 'above the ground'. They are first perfected without the restriction of the rider's weight. Only when the horse is confident and assured in his leaps and executes them with his full physical strength is he asked to perform them not only in hand but also with the rider in the saddle.

Initially the rider remains passive, taking care to position his body so that his weight will not upset the horse's balance and prevent the leap being executed correctly. In this stage the movement is initiated by the assistants on the ground and only when the horse is entirely established in the work does the rider give aids for the movement with legs, whip and possibly a click of the tongue. These aids have to be applied at the exact moment in which the posture and balance of the horse is such that the leap can be made with the greatest ease and effect. However skilful the rider, he will always be helped by an assistant encouraging the horse from the ground.

AIRS ABOVE THE GROUND

These were regarded as the highest point in the classical art by the greatest of the classical Masters, Francois Robichon, Sieur de la Guérinière, often termed the 'Father of classical equitation' (see p.135). They can be divided into those in which the horse raises the forehand alone and those in which both forehand and quarters leave the ground. Guérinière defined the 'school jumps' as being seven in number; the *pesade, half-courbette, courbette, croupade, ballotade, half-capriole* and *capriole*. In fact, some of these were variations on or preliminary movements leading to the three classical leaps still practised at the Spanish School today: *levade, courbette* and *capriole*.

Levade is the 19th-century successor to the *pesade*, in which the body was held at some 45° to the ground. The *levade* is a lower elevation of the forehand but one which requires a deeper bend in the hindlegs, the hocks being lowered to some 8–10 inches above the ground, not so much the case with *pesade*. Additionally in *levade*, which is the more difficult of the two movements, the position is maintained for a greater length of time. *Levade* represents the

dividing line between the advanced movements on the flat and movements carried out above the ground belonging to the High School of riding. The advanced stages of collection concerned with the former are the preparatory exercises for the latter. Similarly, it is from the *levade*, the movement which is half on and half off the ground, that the subsequent *courbette* and *capriole* are obtained.

Courbette was developed in the 19th century from the movement called *mézair*. This movement, which would have been understood in its essentials by Guérinière and practised in that period, consisted of a series of brief *levades*, in which the forelegs struck the ground whilst the hindlegs performed a small jump to land behind them. The 'modern' *courbette* calls for the horse to make a number of equal forward bounds on the hindlegs whilst maintaining the bent foreleg position, the latter being high off the ground throughout. Guérinière's *half-courbette* was exactly a half of that, the movement having far less height and the bounds being similarly reduced.

In the *capriole*, the most spectacular of the High School leaps, the word *capriole* being taken from the Italian *capra*, meaning 'goat', the horse leaps from all four legs simultaneously, striking out with the hindlegs whilst the body is virtually suspended horizontally in mid-air. The *capriole* is the extension of *croupade*, in which the horse jumps out of the *levade*, increasing the angle between the body and the ground whilst drawing the hind legs up to the belly. Courbette may also be regarded as leading to the soaring attitude of the *capriole*. *Ballotade* differs from *croupade* in that whilst the forelegs are still folded the shoes of the hind feet are visible from the rear. Guérinière's *half-capriole* was no more than an incomplete *capriole*. Indeed, the exclusion of the intermediate movements, which may in fact still occur when a leap is not absolutely correct in its execution, is a manifestation of the greater precision demanded by the Spanish School.

The growth of classical riding

To what extent the medieval Knight employed these leaps, and with what precision and expertise, is perhaps uncertain, but Xenophon, their predecessor, was certainly familiar with the *piaffe* and *passage* as the parade paces employed by triumphant generals and by the young nobles, including himself, who rode in the Panathenaea, the great processions which were held in honour of the goddess Athena. He also describes the *levade*, and depictions of the movement are to be seen on all types of Greek artefacts. Pirouettes and the correct riding of voltes and serpentines are also discussed in his books.

Federico Grisone, the Neapolitan nobleman who was the first to found a riding school that might be termed modern at Naples in 1532, was also the first of the classical Masters from whose teaching modern dressage derives. He based his training on the recently unearthed books by Xenophon with the advantage of a saddle and stirrups (not invented in Xenophon's day) and a collection of fearsome curb bits which had been developed over the centuries and were severe enough to elicit a response from the most insensitive of heavy war horses. He was also a great inventor of bits, many of which he described in his book *Ordini de Cavalcare* published in 1550. The horses he used, mostly Neapolitan and Spanish, were probably heavy and correspondingly slow

in their reactions, able to carry a suit of armour, as well as a man similarly encased in steel.

The most famous of Grisone's pupils was Giovanni Baptista Pignatelli who also taught at the Academy of Naples. Pignatelli was much influenced by the circus and he discarded many of Grisone's forceful methods in favour of a lighter form of riding with less reliance on purely mechanical aids. In fairness to Grisone, whose use of severe bits was inherent in his system, he did insist upon preserving the mouth, achieving this laudable aim by the use of a spiked cavesson!

The Spanish Riding School was founded in 1572, but almost to the end of the 16th century the Italian masters dominated equestrian thought. A common aid in teaching the school figures was the 'ring', a dug-out track in which the horse was both lunged and ridden, often being pursued by footmen to encourage, or ensure, continuous forward movement. By the end of the century, however, the Italian schools had given way to those established in France, which culminated in the Ecole de Versailles and the Ecole de Saumur.

Antoine de Pluvinel, tutor to King Louis XIII and author of *L'Instruction du Roy*, which he published in 1623, was the first of the French Masters. He introduced a far more humane system, incorporating gymnastic suppling exercises in order to prepare horses for the more advanced movements and he insisted upon the use of light aids which were to be

Above: A pair of Lipizzaner horses give a display of Haute-Ecole dressage. The 'airs above the ground' are not a part of competitive dressage but are nonetheless of great interest to the horseman of today. **Left:** Sophisticated training in progress in the 18th century; these three prints by Ridinger date from 1760.

almost unnoticeable in their application. He was the inventor of the pillars, still in use at the classical schools, and taught both horses and riders using this aid. Work on two tracks was included in his system and he stressed the importance of riding the various gaits, in varying tempi, making use of large circles. This was a new and enlightened approach to school riding which was extended further by de la Guérinière upon whose teachings the greater part of modern dressage riding is founded.

Guérinière operated the school at the Tuileries which was founded by Louis XIV and it was from there that his theories and methods of schooling spread over Europe, influencing for ever both the subsequent French schools of equitation and the Spanish School at Vienna. Guérinère used a more active, better-bred and more highly-couraged horse and perfected a system of gymnastic exercises designed to enhance the natural paces of his equine pupils. It was he who invented the supreme suppling and straightening exercise, the shoulder-in (*l'épaule en dedans*, see p. 152), arguably the most important lateral exercise and one which is given great prominence to this day in the Spanish School as well as elsewhere. He extended the work on two tracks and defined as never before the inconspicuous use of the aids in combination, initiating the principles involved in the five-fold use of the rein aids. It was Guérinière, too, who made the final adjustments to the classical saddle, which survives today as the *selle royale* at both Saumur and Vienna. He did away with the high pommel and cantle and incorporated with the still relatively deep seat knee and thigh rolls to give additional but not excessive support. To Guérinière, also, credit is due for the perfection of the suppling exercises which we know as 'head to the wall' and 'tail to the wall', (*travers* and *renvers*) and also for many of our schooling figures. They are little different, if at all, from those used today.

Another Master of some note, and the only English one, was William Cavendish, Duke of Newcastle (1592–1676). A Royalist, Newcastle was forced to flee abroad after the Civil War, setting up a riding arena in Antwerp. He wrote *A General System of Horsemanship in all its Branches* in 1658, returning to England in 1660 on the Stuart Restoration. He has the dubious honour of having invented the draw rein but his system otherwise eschewed punishment and force. France, through the schools of Versailles and subsequently those at Saumur, and Austria through its Spanish School, continued to pursue perfection in the classical art, if with somewhat different accents.

From art to sport

During the 19th century the cavalry schools of Europe, basing their instruction on the classical schools, were responsible for the maintenance and even the extension of riding knowledge. The military 'best trained charger' tests were, indeed, the forerunners of competitive dressage, which has now become an important leisure sport.

It was not, however, until 1912 that dressage was included as a major equestrian discipline in the Olympic Games held at Stockholm. It was staged in an arena measuring 20 × 40m (22 × 66 yds) and was of what would now be considered as elementary standard. No lateral movements were included, neither were competitors required to produce *passage* or *piaffe*, nor demonstrate the changes of leg in sequence. A jumping test, over five fences, was a part of the competition. The result was a virtual clean sweep for the Swedes who took first, second, third, fifth, sixth and eighth places.

Eight years later at Antwerp a more difficult competition was staged which included counter changes-of-hand at trot and canter, and sequence changes of leg in four-, three-, two- and one-time. Coefficients were also introduced for the most important movements. Thirty was the coefficient for the canter circles incorporating changes of rein and without changes of leg and 20 was the coefficient placed upon the counter change-of-hand in trot and canter, the canter serpentine and the sequence changes of leg in two- and one-time. *Piaffe* and *passage* were not included until the 1932 Olympics at Los Angeles, USA, and canter pirouettes were not asked for until 1936 at Berlin.

As the cavalry schools closed and armies turned to mechanisation, so military participation in competitive dressage declined in favour of the civilian riders. At the end of the Second World War the influence in competitive dressage had passed entirely to the civilian competitors. Competitive dressage based itself on the classical precepts still practised at Vienna. But there was a difference. Dressage moved more towards a sport discipline in which the necessity to score points led sometimes to a sacrificing of the artistic element and even to short cuts in the training programmes. At its best competition dressage was an art-sport but it lacked the purity of approach and execution which was hallowed and preserved inviolably within the classical precepts followed so single-mindedly at Vienna. On the other hand, dressage became the sport and recreation of thousands of riders and increased the knowledge and understanding of the skills and science involved in educated horsemanship.

The sport developed more quickly in some countries than others, largely as a result of climatic conditions, accepted practice and traditional outlooks towards riding. Continental Europe, often from necessity, particularly in the winter months, had a tradition of indoor riding which encouraged the practice of dressage. Britain, on the other hand, had no such tradition, British riders usually keeping horses for hunting during the winter then following easily into the allied sports of eventing

THE DRESSAGE ARENA

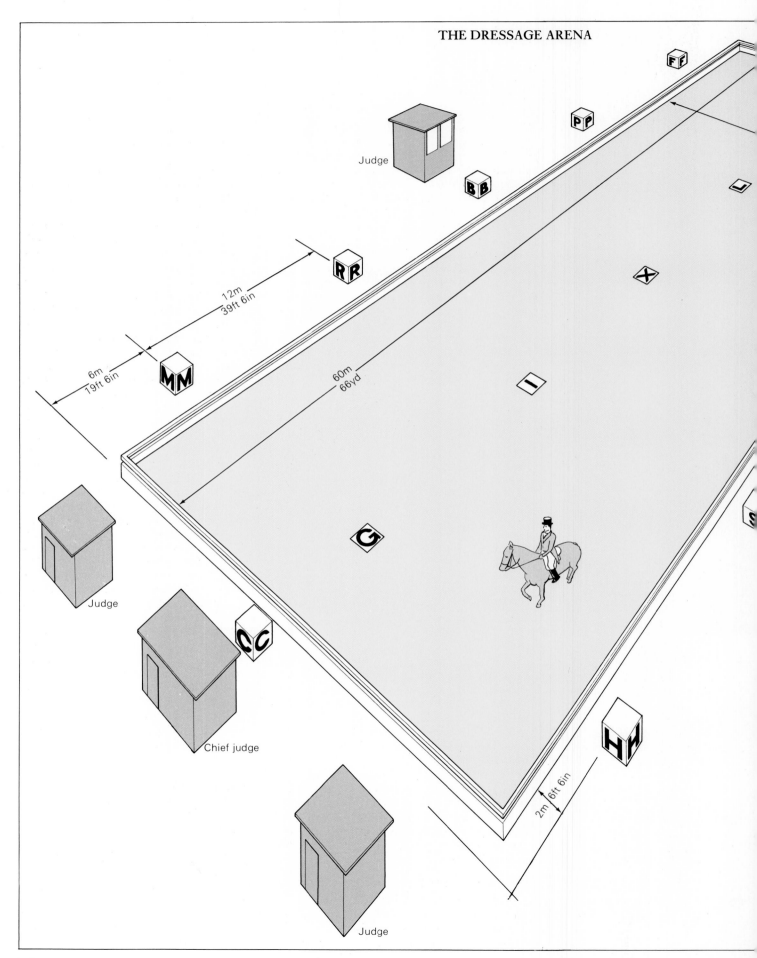

Judge

Judge

Chief judge

Judge

12m
39ft 6in

6m
19ft 6in

60m
66yd

2m 6ft 6in

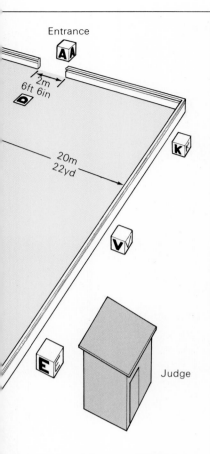

Entrance

2m
6ft 6in

20m
22yd

Judge

Dressage competitions are always ridden in rectangular, boarded arenas either on grass or on a prepared sand surface. There are disadvantages with both surfaces, particularly grass on which the going can be affected by heavy rain or very dry conditions. Sand arenas where the surface material is mixed with bark and is laid over a properly drained sub-soil can give an all-weather surface which will be unaffected by the weather and will give consistently good going. The standard size for arenas up to the Medium level is 20×40m (65×131ft). For international events a bigger arena, 20×60m (65×197ft), is used.

Arenas are marked with letters which indicate to riders and judges where the various movements begin and end. The larger arena has additional markers because of the length involved. These are the letters R, S, V, P, L and I, and are not used in the smaller arena. Arenas are all lettered in exactly the same way in whatever part of the world the competition takes place, but the origin of the letters is one of the equestrian mysteries. The ends of the arenas are marked A and C, the judge or judges sitting at C and riders always making their entrance at A, advancing-down the marked centre line to salute at the opening of the test. Riders make their exit at the same point.

and show jumping. It therefore took much longer for the British to become involved in dressage at either national or international levels.

Modern competitive dressage

The sport covers a range of varying standards, starting with Pony Club tests of the simplest type and culminating in the complexity of the Grand Prix at international and Olympic events. It is controlled by the Dressage Bureau of the International Equestrian Federation (Fédération Equestre Internationale – FEI), a body which was founded in 1921 and has its offices in Brussels.

The Bureau is responsible for the rules, for providing guidelines for organisers, for setting the qualifications required in judges and other officials and for all other matters connected with providing a central secretariat, as well as for ensuring that the standards are maintained. Each nation participating in the sport is affiliated to the Federation and maintains its own dressage bureau to deal with its national affairs and to liaise with the international body.

Each national bureau produces sets of tests for the various grades into which the sport is divided. In Britain these grades are Preliminary, Novice, Elementary, Medium and Advanced. There may be a number of tests applicable to a grade, and each grade may thus be further sub-divided to give more than one degree of difficulty.

The International Federation is responsible for the four tests ridden at international competitions – though they may, of course, also be used at advanced level in national meetings. These are the Prix St George, the lowest international test, the Intermediate I and II and then the most difficult tast, the Grand Prix. At major international shows the first 12 riders in the Grand Prix qualify to ride in a further test, the Grand Prix Special, a shorter test involving more concentrated work and the execution of movements in difficult areas of the arena. At the great majority of international meetings a Kur, or Free-Style, test is also included in which competitors devise a display of their own which has to include certain prescribed movements. Recently, it has become more usual for the Kur to be ridden to music of the rider's choice and for an additional judge, not necessarily a horseman but perhaps a dancer or ice-skater, to award the marks for artistic impression. This type of competition adds another dimension to the sport and gives emphasis to its art content, a quality which is sometimes lost in the search for complete accuracy.

Judging and scoring

In national competitions one, two or three judges are required, whereas in international events five are employed, three sitting at the

end of the arena in separate boxes and the other two stationed one on each of the long sides at the central point. Judges are accompanied by a writer who records the mark given for each movement and any remarks the judge may wish to make in explanation of the score he has given. These are recorded on the test sheet, which is later made available to the rider. The judge may award up to 10 marks for each movement. To help to standardize judging (probably impossible to accomplish entirely) the Federation lays down that marks should be awarded as follows: 0 – Movement not performed; 1 – Very bad; 2 – Bad; 3 – Fairly bad; 4 – Insufficient; 5 – Sufficient; 6 – Satisfactory; 7 – Fairly good; 8 – Good; 9 – Very good; 10 – Excellent. Tests are executed from memory and any errors are penalised.

The problem is to try to obtain overall agreement as to what constitutes a 'sufficient' or a 'satisfactory' movement and since the judges will hold their own opinions, within the framework provided by the Federation, and are like the rast of us human, it would be impossible to obtain complete agreement from five or even three persons judging independently. Occasionally judges appear by their markings to be at odds with each other, but for the most part the ups and downs of individual markings average out pretty well when the marks are totalled. It is of course quite reasonable for one judge to mark *fairly* high and another *fairly* low, so long as he remains consistent throughout the competition.

Obviously judges must understand thoroughly the principles involved and it is desirable that they should have had experience of riding and training horses, preferably, except in the case of the Grand Prix, at a level at least one in advance of the grade they are judging. Equally, they must be very familiar with the individual tests, knowing the movements by heart. A panel of international judges is maintained by the Federation, whilst each national body keeps a list of judges who are graded according to the standard at which they are considered capable of officiating.

Each of the standard international tests is revised every four years so that horses and riders should not become over-confined in their approach to the tests. National competitions are also altered from time to time to broaden the competitors' experience.

In both national and international competitions collective marks are given in addition to those awarded for the actual movements. In the British Horse Society Novice test, for instance, 10 marks are given for 'general impression, obedience, calmness'; 10 for 'paces and impulsion'; 10 for 'position and seat of rider and correct application of the aids'. This amounts to 30 out of the available 140 marks in one test whilst in others the percentage in relation to the movement marks may be more or less. In a BHS Preliminary test 20 collective

THE HORSE AND RIDER

The Horse

The ideal horse for dressage would be one of perfect proportions, with great strength in the back, loins and quarters and particularly strong and well-formed hocks. It would be sound in every way. The joints would be well-formed; the feet open, with a prominent frog, concave sole and hard horn; the limbs strong, the cannons short and the second thigh very well-developed. A sloping riding shoulder is better than an upright one of harness type. The neck would need to be fairly long and to run into well-defined withers, the head in proportion with a big generous eye. Temperamentally, courage is needed but the disposition must be equable.

Thoroughbred horses, built with long limbs and muscles which provide speed, are beautiful but not really suited to dressage where speed is of no account. Only very rarely would they have the temperament which would enable them to submit willingly to the discipline involved. A dressage horse is more likely to be half- or three-qurter-bred, and strength in the structure, so long as the athleticism can be retained, is more important than the conformation connected with galloping ability. Perfect horses are never found but we should always continue to look for them.

The Rider

It is not possible for a rider to train a horse successfully unless he has first taken the time to learn the theory and practice of riding (you cannot teach unless you have first learnt). It is necessary that the rider should have been taught on a progressive system, beginning with the establishment of his seat by regular work on the lunge, riding without stirrups. Unless the seat is correct, the rider is not supple, his aids will become ineffective and, as a result, he will fail to obtain a response from his horse.

For the exceptionally gifted, the genius, it may be possible to be a self-taught rider and compete at advanced levels, but for those outside this category proper instruction of the highest quality is the only solution. Riding, like playing the piano, acquiring different languages or even flying an

aeroplane, has to be taught, learnt and practised — the more so because our partner is a living being.

Below: Christine Stückelberger on Granat.

marks are given and in the Advanced National tests 70, although in this last instance the test may have as many as 25 movements. In the Grand Prix test collective marks are awarded for general impression, impulsion and submission and 20 marks (4% of the total) are given for the rider. Additional emphasis is also given to the more difficult movements by the application of a coefficient. The canter pirouettes, for instance, have a coefficient of 2 so that 40 of the 420 marks are allotted to them. The most difficult of the movements included in the dressage competition are *piaffe* and *passage*, so the work is divided into 12 short sections so that a total of 120 marks can be obtained, i.e. 35% of the total.

Objectives

The objective of dressage, or training on progressive lines, has already been stated. It is to produce a strong, well-developed and supple horse that is obedient to the wishes of his rider and is comfortable, safe and a pleasure to ride. This should be the aim for the owner of any young horse whether or not it is intended to put him to advanced dressage at a later stage in his education. Every horse should, indeed, be educated up to what may be considered secondary school standard, from which point he is fitted to enter higher education in whatever specialist field he seems best suited, whether it be jumping, eventing or dressage.

The official definition, which appears in the International Equestrian Federation's rules, is as follows. 'The object of dressage is the harmonious development of the physique and ability of the horse. As a result it makes the horse calm, supple, loose and flexible, but also confident, attentive and keen, thus achieving perfect understanding with his rider. These qualities are revealed by: the freedom and ragularity of the paces; the harmony, lightness and ease of the movements; the lightness of the forehand and the engagement of the hindquarters, originating in a lively impulsion; the acceptance of the bridle, with submissiveness throughout and without any tenseness or resistance. The horse thus gives the impression of doing of his own accord what is required of him. Confident and attentive, he submits generously to the Control of the rider.'

To reach this stage, at which point the horse would be ready for Grand Prix tests, involves batween four and five years training, the horse being brought on progressively from the Preliminary test (after perhaps the first year of training) through the Novice, Elementary, Medium and Advanced tests until the peak of the Grand Prix is reached. Obviously much will depend on the conformation, temperament and natural ability of the individual as to how far he can progress and how quickly. In general terms, however, a well-grown young horse of between three to four years of age, who has been sensibly handled from birth but

not backed, should be able to compete at Medium level within two years if a programme similar to that outlined later in this chapter can be followed without interruption.

The Medium level of dressage represents the watershed between the lower or Campaign school, called in French *Basse-école*, which has been referred to as the secondary education standard, and the High School, the *Haute-école*. Any riding horse should be able to complete the *basse-école* and any competent and reasonably educated horseman should have the ability to train to this standard. The FEI test for the Three-Day event – surely the testing ground for the all-round horse – is, in fact, at Medium level, although it excludes collection as being unnecessary in the event horse and is content to use the 'working' pace. Whether a horse is able to go further than Medium competition dressage depends largely upon the natural talent he possesses for the advanced work and also, of course, on the talent of his rider both as a rider and a trainer. There will never be many horses able to take on advanced dressage up to and including Grand Prix with any degree of success – it is only the exceptionally talented (with exceptionally talented riders and trainers) who are able to reach those heights.

The purpose of the dressage tests up to the half-way point represented by the Medium competition, and then between the Advanced classes and the ultimate Grand Prix are to help the rider to achieve the defined objectives of dressage. They provide a means of assessing the progress made by evaluating the level and quality of the horse's training at given points. Additionally, of course, they give pleasure and fulfilment to the rider in the sport he has chosen.

Three paces – walk, trot and canter

The walk is a pace of four-time, marked by four distinct hoof beats caused by the successive placing of each lateral pair of feet. The sequence of the footfalls is as follows when the walk is commenced on the left hindleg: 1. left hind; 2. left fore; 3. right hind; 4. right fore. The walk in all its divisions is free, energetic and with the footfalls clearly defined, never hurried or irregular. The four sub-divisions are medium, collected, extended and free.

The medium walk is a free, unconstrained swinging movement of moderate extension. The steps are even and distinctly marked with the hind feet touching the ground in front of the prints made by the forefeet. In collected walk the horse marches forward resolutely with neck raised and arched and with the head approaching the vertical position. The hindlegs are engaged energetically under the body with good hock action. The steps, clearly defined, are shorter and more elevated than in medium walk because of the increased flexion of the joints. The hindfeet touch the ground

THE TESTS

Grade	Requirement	Summary
BASSE-ECOLE		
Preliminary	May ask for only nine movements. Essentially, a couple of stops and starts; for the horse to walk, trot and canter to either hand within the arena; no variation in the paces required.	Up to the Medium level, the tests ask for a progressive improvement in the *freedom, correctness* and *rhythm* of the paces. The horse should become increasingly on the bit: this is the case when the head is held in the vertical plane, or a shade in front of it, and is flexing at the poll (the highest point of the head and neck) and in the lower jaw, whilst the horse moves freely forward from the leg into the hands with a steady, even contact with his bit. There should be a gradual improvement in the outline until the horse is able to shorten his base in the collected movements.
Novice	As for the preliminary test, but 'a few lengthened strides' are asked for.	
Elementary	A greater number of movements is required: more changes of rein; a variation in pace between working and medium; a simple change of leg in some tests; in more difficult tests, a canter departure from walk; in the last of the tests, the shoulder- in.	
Medium	Requires that the horse should go calmly forward in contact with his bit at all three paces, . . . maintaining an even rhythm, changing direction as indicated without resisting, moving sideways and executing a straightforward rein back. He should show some engagement of the quarters so as to produce a degree of lightness on the forehand. Half-pirouette at walk (turn on the quarters) is required, and variation on the individual paces between the points of collection and extension.	
HAUTE-ECOLE		
Prix St George	Medium, collected and extended paces are required, as well as flying changes at every third stride and the first of the High-School movements, the half- pirouettes at canter to either hand.	From the Medium test onwards increased emphasis is given to: *Collection*, in other words a shortening of the outline or posture by reason of the lowered croup, increased engagement of the hindlegs (involving increased flexion of the hocks) and concentration, or compression, of the body forces. The forehand is raised and lightened, the head is held in the vertical plane and the paces become shorter and more elevated: *Paces*, which must be light and springy; *Impulsion*, that state in which the horse builds up a store of energy in the quarters which is controlled, either contained or released, by the rider's hands; *Submission* to the rider, or willingness to be controlled and to respond to aids.
1st Intermediate	Two full pirouettes at canter are required as well as flying changes of leg at every second stride.	
2nd Intermediate	Flying changes at every stride are introduced; also some steps at piaffe. Both Inter-mediate stages are designed as a bridge between the Prix St. George and the Grand Prix.	
Grand Prix	Passage as well as piaffe is asked for, and flying changes up to every stride, pirouettes at canter and all the school paces.	

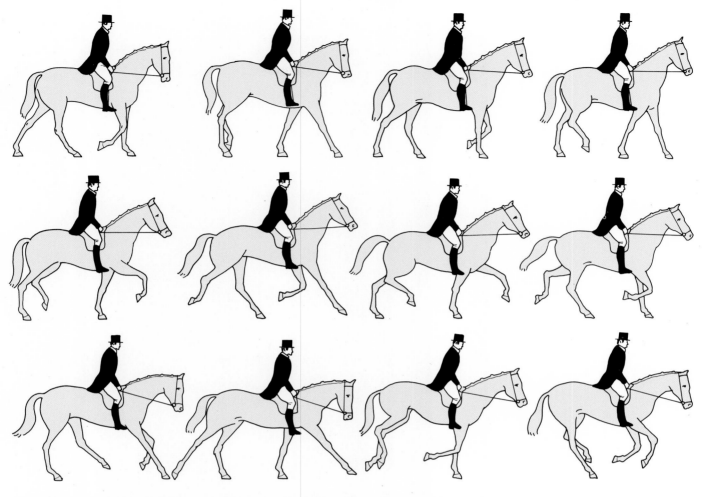

behind the prints of the forefeet. The extended walk demands that the horse move forward energetically, but calmly and without haste, covering as much ground as possible without losing the regularity and definition of the four-beat pace. The head and neck should be allowed to extend but without the rider losing the bit contact. The hindfeet touch the ground clearly in front of the prints of the forefeet. The free walk is a pace of rest in which the horse swings forward in an extended outline with absolute freedom of head and neck. Even so, it remains a pace of four distinct beats which must not become slurred or hurried.

The trot is a pace of two-time, in which the horse places one pair of diagonal legs to the ground simultaneously and then, following a moment of suspension, springs onto the opposite diagonal. The two beats are quite distinct and should not become blurred in execution. The first beat is heard as the left diagonal (the left fore and the right hind) touches the ground, and the second, after the briefest interval, when the right diagonal comes to earth. As with walk there are four sub-divisions of trot, working, medium, collected and extended.

Working trot is the pace between medium and collected, being inclined more towards the latter. It is used up to the Medium tests as a preparation for the full collected trot, horses in the lower grades not being considered ready to attempt the fully collected pace. The hind feet touch the ground just a little behind the prints of the forefeet. Medium trot is between extension and collection, inclining towards the former, and is a preparatory pace to full extension. It is rounder in action than the extended trot but energetic and it should show suppleness, balance and good engagement of the hocks. The hindfeet touch the ground in the prints of the forefeet. Collected trot sees the horse advancing energetically in perfect balance with raised head and neck, the former in the vertical position. The hocks, flexing vigorously, are carried well beneath the horse to give maximum thrust to the movement and the steps become elevated and shorter. Although the pace is slower the impulsion is very evident and the horse becomes increasingly light and mobile. The hindfeet touch the ground behind the print of the forefeet. In extended trot the horse covers as much ground as possible with a lengthened stride. The neck is extended and as a result of the impulsion from the quarters the shoulders are used to cover more ground but without elevating the action.

The two extremes in the trot pace spectrum are collection and extension, working trot being positioned slightly to the collection side of the centre line and medium trot fairly close to the extended pace.

The canter is a pace of three-time in which

Above: In every level of dressage, from Novice to the Advanced tests of Haute-école, the horse is required to walk, trot and canter, three seemingly straightforward paces but with increasingly demanding variations (see left).

MOVEMENTS FOR ADVANCED TESTS

Flying changes
These are normally executed at a collected canter but when performed as a series (every fourth, third, second or single stride) it is advisable to allow the horse to move with somewhat less collection, although he must of course be balanced, light, straight and calm, with sufficient impulsion. When executing the change, the

horse has to hop up and down on the inside legs so that the outside ones can pass by and take the place of the former. A slightly less collected attitude assists in this movement but it is absolutely essential that the rider gives the aid at the precise moment, in other words immediately before the inside foreleg touches the ground.

Half-pass
At half-pass the horse moves diagonally with the legs crossing over each other, neck bent slightly in the direction of the movement and the horse looking the same way. The forehand, not the quarters, must lead the movement.

Pirouette at canter
The forelegs and outside hind

leg have to move round the pivot made by the inside hind foot, the former returning almost to the same spot, or slightly in front of it, each time it leaves the ground. The horse is bent in the direction of the movement and is well on the bit. He should have fully engaged quarters and maintain the exact cadence and sequence of footfalls, the full

the horse leads with the left fore when circling correctly to the left and with the right foreleg when circling to the right. It is a 'false' lead when the horse attempts to canter a left-handed circle with the right foreleg leading or vice-versa. A 'false' lead is, however, permitted in the balancing exercises and in the dressage movement known as 'counter' canter. The sequence of footfalls in the canter is, on the right lead: 1. left hind; 2. left diagonal, in which the left fore and right hind touch the ground simultaneously; 3. right fore, the leading foreleg which completes the three beats. The canter pace has similar sub-divisions to the trot (collected, working, medium and extended) and what has been said of the trot in these respects applies also to the canter.

Training the young horse

Individual trainers obviously employ methods which may differ in detail, and in some

countries a horse's education begins earlier or later than in others. In general, though, a horse may begin working when he is between three and four years old, so long as he has been reared well and is sufficiently developed for his age.

The object should be to take the young horse to a point where he can take part with some credit in a Medium test at the end of a two-year period of training. In practice it may take a little longer, for young horses do not always develop as we intend, however scientific our approach. But it is good to set targets, as long as we do not skimp the work or confuse the horse by asking too much of him.

The rest of this chapter sets out a suitable two-year programme, divided into eight separate phases. The first two phases, or first six months of training, are extremely important and are covered in the most detail (see ps. 142– 150). During this early stage the trainer will be concerned with lungeing the horse and backing pirouette being completed in six or seven strides. The pirouette is a difficult movement and one in which faults are easily incurred. Sometimes because of insufficient collection there will not be enough elevation and the movement will become hurried and unbalanced, being executed perhaps in only four strides. Other faults caused by a loss of balance, usually towards the end of the movement, are when the horse is forced to move sidewyas or backwards with irregular steps. The pirouette has to be performed almost on the spot, not on a circle.

Passage
This is the highly collected, lofty, cadenced trot executed with prolonged suspension while the horse advances majestically, springing from one diagonal to another. The horse remains lightly on the bit throughout with the neck raised and arched and with pronounced engagement of the quarters. There is accentuated flexion of the knees and hocks, the toe of the raised foreleg being level with the centre of the cannon bone of the opposite leg. The toe of the raised hindleg is lifted slightly above the fetlock joint of the other leg. In *piaffe* when the passage slows to the point where there is only a minimal gain of ground to the front, the quarters are lowered a little further and the engagement of the hindlegs becomes even more pronounced.

Training for these movements may be started towards the end of the two-year period aiming at bringing a horse up to the Medium level of tests (see pages 142–158) but they are not required in competitions until the Advanced tests. It would take at least another two years of training, with professional help and the necessary talent, to achieve anything like the standard of these horses and riders. **Far left:** Manfred Schmidtke on Romeo performing a pirouette at canter. **Left:** Passage; Christine Stückelberger at Rotterdam in 1980. **Right:** Mrs J. Loriston-Clarke and Dutch Courage execute a flying change.

him, which involves teaching him the aids, ensuring that he remains balanced while carrying weight and confirming forward movement from the action of the rider's legs.

A workman, it is said, is as good as his tools, and in the case of the horse trainer these may be taken to be a training area with a surface which allows work to continue whatever the weather and also the equipment required to work the horse on the lunge and under saddle. It must be taken for granted that there is proper accommodation for the horse and somewhere, however small, for him to run out for an hour or two each day when his work is over. This is an excellent way for the horse to relax and unwind.

Lungeing

The first stage in the training of the young horse is the regular working on the lunge which will occupy a full three months of the time allocated for training. It is a stage of enormous importance and upon it depends the success of much which follows.

There are objects to be achieved by a systematic programme of lungeing, paying particular attention to working the horse on his stiff side. It will promote the build-up of muscles without their being formed in opposition to the rider's weight. It will also, if carried out properly, paying attention to the stiffer side, develop the muscles equally on either side of the body. It will supple the horse laterally by the equal stretching of the dorsal, neck and abdominal muscles on each side of the body. It will induce an essential tensioning of the spine by the encouragement of a rounded outline brought about by a lowered carriage of the head and neck, accompanied by the engagement of the hindlegs under the body. This last is always easier to achieve on a circle, since the inside leg is bound to be more actively engaged and placed further under the body. Systematic

Above: During the early stages of backing, it is essential that the rider uses clear and correct aids in order that the horse understands exactly what he is being asked to do. For the first two weeks or so, the horse is worked on the lunge, with the rider in the saddle. Gradually the horse associates the rider's aids with the trainer's vocal commands and it is possible to dispense with the lunge rein as control passes from the ground to the saddle.

lungeing will therefore serve to strengthen each hind leg and to increase the flexion of the joints.

Lungeing will induce an increased flexion in all joints as a result of greater and more supple muscular development. So far as it is possible, and there is indeed very little spinal flexion, it will encourage the spine to flex in the lumbar area and thus contribute to correcting the natural curvature, which in turn, and in conjunction with the equal development of the muscle, will assist in the efforts made to produce a straight horse. (A straight horse is one whose hind feet follow directly the line taken by the forefeet and thus ensure that the propulsive thrust from the quarters is channelled directly to the front and not to one side or the other, as would be the case if the track of the hindfeet was to one side of that made by the forefeet.)

Lungeing is a very good exercise for improving the balance and teaching the horse to carry himself – an object best achieved on the circle because of the need for the horse to engage his hocks beneath him. It will also improve the regularity and rhythm of the pace. Apart from the physical benefits, lungeing inculcates the habit of discipline and obedience, since the horse learns to obey the vocal demands of the trainer. The voice has a calming effect on all horses and it provides an opportunity for the trainer to establish a good relationship with his pupil. Most importantly, it teaches the horse to go forward freely.

The exercise is, however, a demanding one for the young horse and the initial periods should not exceed 10–15 minutes each day. As the horse becomes stronger and learns to concentrate for longer periods, the exercises can be increased to last for 30–40 minutes. At the start, the horse should be worked consistently at a walk and only when he begins to take on an improved outline should he be put to a little trotting work each day. Cantering on the lunge should be delayed until well towards the end of the training period and then practised sparingly. It is, however, sensible to vary the work by lungeing over poles on the ground and then over a cavalletti grid. These are excellent strengthening exercises and assist the flexing of the joints as well. They also give the horse confidence, and once he is confirmed in the grid work there is no harm in letting him jump a few cavalletti. It all adds up to relaxing the horse and preventing him from becoming bored.

Backing – the second phase

The lunge work, by strengthening the horse, increasing his confidence in the trainer and accustoming him to work and discipline is the physical and mental preparation to carrying weight on his back. Backing occupies the next three months of training. When this stage is reached, there are three immediate objectives.

LUNGEING EQUIPMENT

A set of boots is needed to protect all four legs (**below right**), for young horses, not yet co-ordinated in their movements, are very prone to strike into themselves. The horse should wear a light lunge cavesson (**below left**) and a snaffle bridle fitted with a thick jointed snaffle bit. The lunge rein should be of tubular web, about 3mm (1⅛in) wide, with the fastening, either a

buckle and chape or the more convenient snap hook, set on a swivel which will prevent the rein becoming twisted. A long lunge whip (**centre**) with a thong of sufficient length should be light enough to be handled without effort. A proper roller fitted with side rings is required, and a crupper will prevent it being pulled forward when side-reins are fitted. Side reins fitted fitted

with rubber rings or inset with elastic are no more than a snare and a delusion. Horses learn to play with them, stretching the elastic and tossing their heads about to do so. They tend to cause problems rather than anything else. A pair of plain leather side reins (**bottom**) are more suitable.

Side-reins can be employed as soon as the horse has learnt

the rudiments of the lunge exercise and will circle to either hand and obey the elementary words of command. they can be tightened gradually over a matter of weeks, first being used from the cavesson and then directly from the snaffle bit. By employing the reins sensibly it is possible to improve the carriage within the framework of which the muscle structure will be developed.

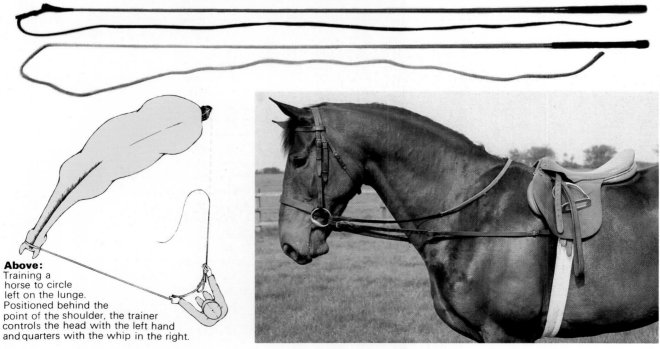

Above:
Training a horse to circle left on the lunge. Positioned behind the point of the shoulder, the trainer controls the head with the left hand and quarters with the whip in the right.

The horse, having accepted the weight on his back, must be taught how to carry it, which will involve his making adjustments to his natural balance. He must learn the rudiments of control through the rider's simple aids. Finally, it must be ensured, as quickly as possible, that the horse, having been given time to adjust to his new circumstances continues to go forward, and does so from the rider's legs.

Backing should present no problem if the horse is first accustomed to wearing a saddle during his lunge lessons and is then further prepared to carry a rider on his back by the latter leaning over him in the stable and per-haps, also, while he is being led round the yard or is returning to his stable after work. There-after, for a matter of a week or ten days, the horse is worked quietly on the lunge, with the rider in the saddle and, gradually, control passes from the trainer with his lunge line and whip to the rider with his hands, legs and body weight.

Teaching the aids

Elementary aids to stop and start are easily enough taught, since the horse has already been made obedient to the voice which supplements the rider's actions. The trainer gives the vocal command, 'walk-on' whilst the rider applies the legs simultaneously, if necessary support-ing the action with a touch from his whip delivered behind the girth, for which reason the whip must be of sufficient length for the tap to be applied without the rider taking his hand from the rein. Quite quickly the horse begins to associate the pressure of the legs with the vocal command to walk forward and in a very short time it is possible to dispense with the voice. The same is true of the aids given to slow the horse down or to halt, and it is similarly quite easy to teach the horse to go into a trot.

Within a fortnight or so it should be possible for the horse to be ridden off the lunge but as he is still learning to carry the weight on his back it is advisable to return to lunge lessons (without a rider in the saddle) at least once or twice a week throughout this second phase of training, which will last for a full three months.

These early lessons under saddle are im-mensely important since they set the pattern for future work and are at the base of the horse's understanding of what is required of him. The rider's responsibility is therefore very great because it will be largely upon him and his actions that the horse's future development rests. Mistakes made now, out of ignorance or ineptitude, will be enormously difficult to eradicate. It is, therefore, of enormous import-ance that the rider should be skilled, experi-enced and educated if the transfer from trainer to rider is to be made satisfactorily and future progress is to be ensured.

The meaning of aids given by the rider must be made absolutely clear to the horse otherwise he will become confused, and confusion can

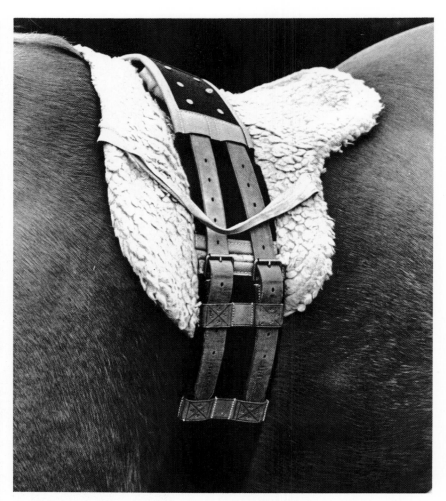

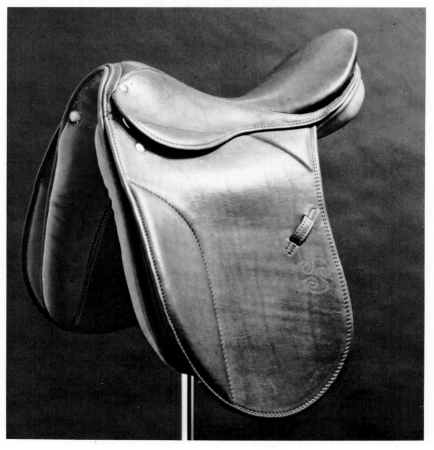

Opposite above: A breaking roller worn during lunge lessons accustoms a horse to having something tightened over its back and under its belly and means that backing comes as less of a shock. It should be supple and well padded.
Opposite below: A Stubben dressage saddle, so shaped that the rider is encouraged to sit in the central, lowest part. **Right:** The German rider Uwe Sauer on Hirtentraum. It is essential that the rider adopts a correct seat, erect but relaxed and with a depth that ensures close contact with the horse. The legs in particular must be used correctly in the early stages of training in order that the horse learns to understand the subtle variations in the aids.

lead both to resentment and rebellion. The aids to go forward from a halt provide a good example of potential confusion. Although it is quite illogical, many riders push the legs backwards in order to make the horse go forwards. Some are even guilty of giving the horse a thump with the heels, which from that moment on precludes the possibility of creating with the horse anything more than a dialogue consisting of rough imperatives. The aids to go forward from halt are as follows. At a signal from the trainer, the rider, whose legs are already in light contact with the horse, closes the legs a little more, in a slight rolling action from rear to front amounting to no more than a nudge; at the same time he closes his fingers on the rein. This is the preparatory command to obtain the horse's attention and warn him that an order (or executive command) is imminent.

A second or two later the rider's legs squeeze gently, but quite decisively, in the same rolling movement from rear to front. This time, however, the legs 'push' rather than nudge. Simultaneously with the action of the legs, the

fingers open a little on the rein so that the horse can move forward from the leg without there being any opposition to the movement at his mouth – which would once more be supremely illogical. As the rider gives the aids to advance, the trainer can help in the initial stages by reinforcing the aids with his own vocal command.

The practice of preparing the horse before an actual order is given persists right through the horse's schooling and beyond. Indeed, it is this preparatory aid which in time, suitably strengthened according to the circumstance, is translated into the half-halt, that invaluable momentary check which acts to reimpose or to correct the balance.

The importance of the legs being applied in the correct manner cannot be over-emphasized. In the later stages of training there are movements which require the leg to be moved from front to rear. This is the case when one leg acts to ask the horse to move sideways or to make a shift with his quarters. The legs are also drawn a little back when the position of the quarters

THE FIVE REIN EFFECTS

1. The simple **Direct** rein turns the horse by moving the shoulders. The inside hand is carried out to the side, pulling the horse's nose in the required direction. **2.** The simple **Indirect** rein is used when making a turn with one hand. With the reins in the outside hand, raise the hand and carry it to the inside, laying the outside rein on the neck. **3.** The **Direct rein of opposition** shifts the horse's quarters. The inside hand acts in momentary squeezes without being carried outwards,

the opposite hand yielding slightly to allow the neck to bend but remaining in supporting contact. Forward movement is 'opposed', or blocked, and rechannelled so that the quarters move outwards. **4.** The **Indirect rein of opposition in front of the withers** causes the forehand to move to the left, or away from the acting hand. The right hand acts strongly in front of the withers in the direction of the left shoulder. The left hand first yields then supports in a direction

parallel to the horse's spine. Both legs act equally to maintain impulsion. The nose is turned a little to the right, causing the weight to fall on the left shoulder, so that the forehand has to move to the left in order for the horse to maintain balance. **5.** The **Indirect rein of opposition behind the withers** has the effect of moving the whole horse sideways. The right hand acts behind the withers, without crossing them, in the direction of the left hip. The left rein yields, then supports

parallel to the neck. Both legs maintain impulsion whilst the weight is put first on the right seatbone, to start the movement, and then onto the left one. The horse moves forward and to the left on parallel tracks crossing his right legs over his left. This rein aid is an essential ingredient of lateral work.

The solid arrows indicate the primary movement of the horse, the outline arrows the direction in which the hand is acting.

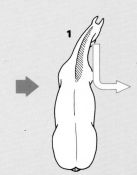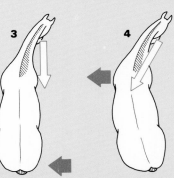

must be held in making a turn on the haunches (ultimately the pirouette). If the horse has been trained to move forward from legs applied in this way it will be only too easy for him to become confused when the legs are applied in the same way to obtain quite a different movement. The spectrum of the aids and their effectiveness is at once reduced. The aid to halt is just as easily taught but once again it must be the correct one.

To teach the aids for a halt from a walk the rider prepares the horse on a signal from the trainer in just the same way as for giving the instruction to move off. The rider, just as before, then puts on his legs in the firmer rolling push from rear to front, stretching his back and bringing his shoulders slightly to the rear at the same time. The effect of the closed legs is to send the horse forward, something which he has already learnt. Just as the push begins, the rider closes his fingers. He has then pushed the horse into the closing hand, which will continue acting in momentary squeezes on the rein whilst the legs are held in contact until the horse stops – a movement which will, of course, again be assisted by the trainer's vocal command.

Teaching the horse to make changes of direction has to begin in the school, with no help from the trainer's voice and by the rider using a simple and perhaps exaggerated opening rein. Working in the school makes it easy for the horse to understand what is wanted and to obey the aids, because as he approaches the corner he is already prepared by continual usage to turn in the appropriate direction. There is, indeed, no other course open to him. Nonetheless, it is helpful if the trainer stands in the corner so that the horse has to turn

outside him and is thus prevented from cutting too far inwards, evading making a reasonable turn. After the preparatory aid (almost a minor half-halt in this instance) given as the horse approaches the turn the rider carries the leading hand outwards, pulling, in effect, the horse's nose in the required direction. His inside leg acts on the girth in firm nudges, whilst the outside leg is held in contact a hand's breadth or so behind the girth. If the rider pushes down a little on his inside stirrup at the same time, his weight will be placed more onto his inside seat bone and this alteration in the weight distribution will result in the turn being made more easily.

The transition from walk to trot, and the return from trot to walk, are just as easily accomplished as the move off from a halt described on page 146, following the same sequence of aid application while in the first instances relying on the trainer's vocal assistance. As before, the aids prepare, then act and, having obtained a result, yield. The sequence and the principle involved does not alter from the earliest lessons to the most advanced. The only other function of the aids is to resist, which they may do in order to check an unwanted movement. Having learnt the elementary aids for stopping, starting and turning, the horse can be exercised in the open under saddle.

Improving balance

In the first two months of this second three-month period the horse works at the walk, with some trotting, on straight lines or very large and gentle curves, since he is still learning how to carry weight on his back.

Opposite: During the three-month 'backing' phase much of the work is carried out at the walk (top) and the rising trot (centre). Short bursts of cantering (bottom) should also be included. Here the horse is about to turn the corner, a manoeuvre best taught in the school where he has little option but to follow the curve of the fencing.

At the walk he must be allowed a long or even a loose rein but with a light contact maintained so that he can use his shoulders to obtain a long, free-swinging walk. He may lower his head and neck without the contact being lost, but he must not be allowed to lean on the hand. If he is kept moving forward actively his balance will improve of its own accord and there will be no need for him to place any reliance on the rider's hand.

Trotting must always be done with the rider rising. Occasionally, towards the end of the period, it is permissible for the rider to sit for a few strides. The sitting trot must not, however, be continued to the point at which the horse hollows his back or becomes unbalanced by the unbroken contact of the rider with the saddle. Once more, the skill of the rider is a critical factor. An insufficiently expert horseman can at this stage ruin the prospect of the horse making significant advances in his training.

Advantage should be taken of gradients, and of undulating or broken ground. These provide natural aids to improving the balance, since the horse is compelled to make constant adjustments, and they also serve to strengthen the muscles and joints.

The canter, potentially an exciting pace, can be introduced on slightly uphill slopes, or the horse can be asked to slip into cater from a trot for a few strides and then be brought back to trot before he has a chance to become unsettled. Practised frequently, the horse will soon cater as calmly as he walks or trots.

The turn on the forehand

In the final month of the section, the sixth in the complete training programme, it should be possible to begin teaching the simple exercises which will form the foundation for more difficult movements. Before this the horse should have become accustomed to turning in response to the conventional direct rein of opposition (see opposite). The transfer from the simple opening rein to the rein of opposition can be made gradually, but it is necessary to take care that the action of the opposing rein making the turn does nothing to inhibit the active forward movement, and no tight turns should be attempted. The simple direct rein turned the horse by moving the shoulders; the direct rein of opposition allows the turn to be made in better balance by shifting the quarters. The rein is applied by the hand acting, on the side to which the turn is to be made, in momentary squeezes without being carried outwards. The opposite hand must yield slightly to allow the neck to bend but it must remain in supporting contact. As long as the legs continue to push the horse forward actively, the forward momentum, the result of maintained propulsion from the quarters, is blocked, or 'opposed', on the side on which the rein is acting. The movement, therefore, has to be re-channelled, and as a result the quarters will move outwards, i.e. in the right hand turn they will be pushed to the left and in a left hand turn, pushed to the right. The extent of the shift is, of course, controlled by the presence of the outside leg behind the girth, the propulsion being maintained by the action of the inside leg.

The first exercise to be taught is that which leads to mobility in the quarters and allows the rider to move them, or to prevent their unwanted movement. It is the comparatively simple turn on the forehand. The horse will already have learnt the rudiments of the turn when being asked to move over in his box. To be certain he understands what is wanted it is usual to hold his head, or to secure it to the wall by the head collar rope, and then to prod him with the butt end of a whip so that he moves his quarters round his forehand.

From the saddle, it is easier if the horse's head is slightly inclined from the poll in the direction in which it is going, i.e. left if the quarters are going to the right. The legs then act as did the prodding whip in the stable, the acting leg placed well behind the girth whilst the other governs the extent of the movement.

The rein effect employed is the indirect rein of opposition behind the withers (see p. 148). If the quarters are to move from right to left round the forehand the legs act to send the horse forward and then block the movement on the right side by the rein acting behind the withers in a line with the left hip, which will cause the quarters to move to the left.

The response to the action of the single leg in shifting the quarters can be further improved by riding a zig-zag figure down the school and the forehand turn itself improved by riding the turn from a reversed half-volte i.e. leaving the track and returning to it from the opposite direction by making an about turn from a small circle.

Strike-offs at canter

Before the end of this stage it is necessary to obtain strike-offs at canter on a chosen leg and this is most easily accomplished from a corner. The conventional aids are the predominant use of the inside leg in a forward motion on the girth, preceded by the outside leg sliding back both to control any outward swing of the quarters and to associate in the horse's mind the action of the inward leg with a strike-off made by the horse's corresponding foreleg.

Finally, the horse must be confirmed in his forward response to the action of the legs, going forward without hesitation whenever they are applied.

The horse at this stage should be very well-prepared for the work in the following 18 months. Because of the great importance of this introductory period, it has been considered in some detail. It will be sufficient, however, to cover the remaining training stages by defining the principal objects in each stage and indicating the methods used to achieve them. It must be understood that progressive training in the school figures, concentrating on the correctness of the movement and the increasing purity of the paces, continues throughout.

The third phase – months seven to nine

The build-up of the horse's musculature is, from the outset, of great importance, since it will be impossible for the horse to perform the work that is wanted unless he has acquired sufficient physical strength.

There are six objectives in this phase. An increased engagement of the quarters must be achieved. In short, the hindquarters must be made to work harder, so that a greater propulsive effort is made by the hindlegs and, particularly, from the all-important hocks. It

Below left: Strike-off at canter is one of the first simple exercises which must be taught as the foundation of more difficult movements. It is most easily achieved, as shown, from a corner. **Below right:** One of the aims in the third stage of training – months seven to nine – is to increase lateral suppleness, and this can be brought about by riding circles and curves, with the horse's body bent correctly to the arc of the movement. This diagram shows two useful exercises, the figure-of-eight and the serpentine, and others are illustrated on page 85.

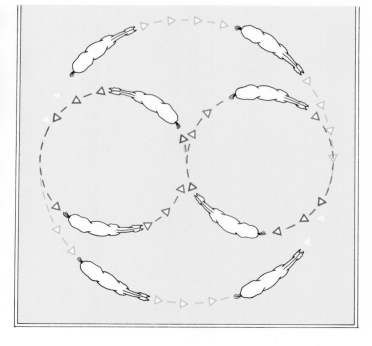

involves restraining with the hand any tendency to increase the speed so as to allow, as it were, the quarters to get closer to the forehand. In short, the aim is to achieve a shortening of the outline and of the horse's base. So long as the muscles of the loin and back have been well developed, the horse will present a more rounded top line and carry a greater proportion of his weight on the quarters, thus lightening the forehand.

The second objective is to put the horse to the bit, progressively but quite definitely. What has to be done is to create a frame within which the horse moves. This has to be achieved by increased impulsion which drives the horse into the hand which, though never moving forwards, is now holding and governing the thrust from the quarters. Unless, however, the horse is sufficiently developed, the weight of the rider on his back will cause him to evade by hollowing his back and raising his head and mouth above the hand. Similarly, unless the rider is sufficiently competent and, in particular, sufficiently supple in the back to sit with the horse in the periods of sitting trot which are involved, there is no hope of working the horse within the desired frame.

Increase in longitudinal and lataral suppleness is the third aim, attempting to have a horse resembling a spiral spring, which can be compressed and which will also bend equally and easily to either side. Longitudinal suppleness is assisted by work involving upwards and downwards transitions in the three paces and by shortening and lengthening the stride in each individual pace. Lateral suppleness is brought about by riding circles and curves, the horse's body from poll to tail being bent to the arc of the movement. At this point it should be possible for the horse to move, if only for short periods, with a vertical head carriage – the 'hindquarters advancing to the head'.

To lighten the forehand and to oblige the quarters to be engaged so as to carry a greater proportion of the weight, the half-halt is practised in trot and, most particularly, in canter. The half-halt, in fact, is no more than the preparatory aids discussed on p. 146 applied in a firmer manner, the legs sending the horse into a closing hand, this compelling a shortening of the base and a lightening of the forehand. It is a momentary check, reminding the horse of the desirable posture and effecting a re-imposition of balance.

Objective number five is to improve the canter, by short periods of work in this pace, often on a long rein, so that it becomes something of a relaxation for the horse after periods during which the rider sits to the trot.

Placing the horse on the bit for short periods of time within the schooling sessions will involve the horse flexing at the poll, the head in vertical carriage and the hocks engaged. So demanding a frame cannot at this stage be maintained for more than short periods but it should be sought for, say, five to ten minutes

Above: Improving the canter is a worthwhile end in itself but horses will also find short periods at this pace relaxing and exhilarating.

and followed by five minutes on a long rein before being asked for again.

Leg-yielding in response to pressure from either of the rider's legs is a preparation for further lateral work and is the final objective of this phase. The horse has to move diagonally (see p. 82) while remaining straight from croup to poll, although a slight flexion away from the direction of the movement is permissible. Leg-yielding, the lead-in to half-pass and much less demanding of the horse, is obtained by the use of the rein of opposition behind the withers and the leg on the corresponding side. Leg-yielding can be practised whilst hacking out along lanes or tracks and from the centre line of the manège, moving out to the boards, but it is advisable to ensure that it never becomes a parody of shoulder-in, which is a movement essential to the next phase and for which leg-yielding is again only a preparation.

The fourth phase

Months 10 to 12 take the lateral work further by teaching the best-known of the suppling exercises. Guérinière's shoulder-in is the objective in this phase. Further advantages of the shoulder-in lie in the greatly increased control obtained by the rider once both he and the horse are proficient in the work. This enhanced control allows the rider to position his horse far more accurately than previously and is, indeed, at the root of all the more difficult movements. Finally, shoulder-in is the most valuable method of straightening the horse.

SHOULDER-IN

Shoulder in is a movement in which the horse moves forward diagonally with the head away from the direction of the movement and the forelegs crossing. It is executed from a circle, the horse being prepared for the movement by the bend in the body corresponding to the arc of the circle. The classical shoulder-in is held to be on three tracks but a four-track movement is acceptable. A three-track movement would be expected where the bend is that required for a 10-metre circle and four tracks where a 6-metre circle is employed (6-metre circles, however, are beyond all but advanced category horses). It is important that the quarters remain straight, the two hip bones remaining virtually at right angles to the wall. The aids employed to obtain the movement are applied once the correct bend is obtained. The rider weights the inside seat-bone by stretching the leg down whilst the leg acts firmly on the girth. The result of weighting the inside seat bone is to push the horse towards the convex side. The outside leg remains quietly in support behind the girth and is ready to prevent the quarters swinging outwards. The inside rein acts behind the withers in the direction of the opposite hip and the outside rein supports its action after initially helping the movement to begin by leading the horse with a slight opening action. It is very important that the rider's shoulders remain in line with those of the horse whilst his hips remain square with the horse's hips. In no movement is the correct application of the aids more important.

The young horse will not, of course, be able to perform a 10-metre circle, far less the 6-metre one He should, however, be able to execute a 15-metre circle without difficulty but it is quite permissible to begin the shoulder-in from a larger circle. The movement is first carried out at walk and only when the horse can obtain shoulder-in easily in both directions is it executed in trot.

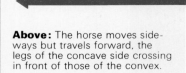

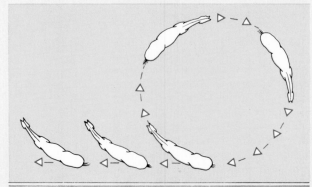

Above: The horse moves sideways but travels forward, the legs of the concave side crossing in front of those of the convex.

Right: A preliminary circle places the horse in the correct position, bent from poll to tail with head away from direction of movement.

The rein-back is also taught at this stage. It is certainly not a walk backwards but a two-time movement with the legs moving in diagonal pairs and is more difficult to execute correctly than is realised. In fact, it is unwise to attempt it until the horse is on the bit and there is no chance of his throwing up his head to evade the aids. If asked for too soon there is a danger of the horse hollowing the back as a resistance with, in consequence, the head coming upwards and off the bit. There is of course no reason why the horse should not have practised a few steps unmounted with the trainer prehaps tapping the forelegs to obtain the backward step.

It is possible to obtain the rein-back using the reins alternately but it is probably easier to understand if both reins are used simultaneously. At no time, however, is there any question of the reins being used to pull the horse backwards.

To obtain the rein-back the horse is halted square and on the bit. The legs are applied as in the aid to walk from halt. At the moment the horse inclines forward the hands close firmly to prevent the forward movement but they do not pull. The legs continue to act until the horse takes one or two backward strides. Initially, it may be necessary to ask two or three times before obtaining a result and before the horse is clear as to what is wanted.

Walk to canter is the third movement to be attempted. Shoulder-in, because of the use made by the rider's inside leg, facilitates greatly the strike-off into canter from walk. The optimum moment for the application of the aids is, in cater left, as the off hind comes to the ground in walk, and the opposite will apply for the right lead. The leg aids can be accompanied by a slight raising of the inside hand which will help produce the little jump from the hind feet which is necessary for the horse in making the strike-off from a four-beat pace.

Execution of serpentines in trot and canter is the final objective at this stage. Initially these must be large and the curves over-ridden. Serpentines in canter cannot begin until the changes of leg through walk can be made without difficulty. Changes can, however, begin from trot on straight lines and then on very big curves.

The second year

The fifth phase, which begins the second year of training comprises a three-month period as previously. From its outset the rider has to become concerned with collecting his horse. Up to this point the concern has been with the horse going freely and rhythmically forward. The collection will be obtained from the back to the front, the rider asking for increased engagement of the quarters and more activity and impulsion, whilst containing the force created with the hands. The hocks will, in time, flex sufficiently to allow them to be brought further under the body mass. Then a lowering of the croup will be possible and the horse will become significantly lighter in his forehand. Much will depend, however, on the muscular movement, the state of which will govern the degree of collection obtainable. Great attention has therefore to be given to the gymnastic exercises which will produce the necessary musculature.

The medium trot has to be established as a preliminary to extension and has to be obtained by a lengthening of the stride, not by an increase in tempo (the rate of the stride).

The transitions from one pace to another and in particular the correct use of the half-halt in all paces are essential movements in the advance towards the goal of collection, and the half-halts are also an aid to increased impulsion. A proportion of every lesson is therefore devoted to their practice.

Travers (also called 'head to the wall' or 'quarters-in'), the turn on the haunches and the transition from canter to walk also have to be introduced in this phase. *Travers* is the movement following shoulder-in in lateral work. It is a movement dependent on the circle from which it is made. Contrary to shoulder-in it is the forehand which is now required to move parallel to the wall instead of the quarters, the head being in line with the direction taken. The quarters are held inside the forehand (quarters-in) and the hind legs move on a track parallel with that of the forefeet. The horse is therefore bent in the direction of the movement, which, of course, is to

Below: The rein back is not as simple as many people imagine. It should not be attempted mounted until the fourth stage of training (months 10–12). Note the horse's legs moving in diagonal pairs.

Left: Whereas the turn on the forehand (see page 83) involves the horse pivoting round the inside foreleg, in the turn on the haunches the forehand moves round the pivot of the hindlegs. Apart from a frightened horse very occasionally turning on his quarters, neither of these movements would be performed naturally by a horse left to his own devices.

operate the horse in the opposite fashion to that required in shoulder-in. Initially the movement may be on three tracks but the ultimate aim will be to have it performed on four. The movement begins as the forehand reaches the track, the rider employing the inside leg on the girth whilst positioning the quarters by the use of the outside leg held flat and with toe pointing forward some four to five inches behind the girth. The hands are carried a shade to the inside, the outside hand predominating and acting in conjunction with the inside leg. Both legs maintain impulsion.

Just as the turn on the forehand gave lightness and mobility to the quarters, the turn on the haunches similarly lightens the forehand. The turn (half-pirouette in walk) involves the forehand moving round the pivot of the hind legs, the latter maintaining the march pace without gaining ground.

The horse is prepared at walk by the half-halt. In moving the forehand to the right an opening right rein is used supported by the left rein held on the neck, both hands being moved slightly to the right. The left, outside, leg prevents the quarters swinging to the left, whilst the right leg, with a little help from its partner, maintains the impulsion.

So long as the canter is well-balanced and the half-halts very well confirmed the transition from canter to walk, though difficult, should be possible if sufficient practice is done in the movement. It is a necessary preliminary to the flying change.

Phase six

Phase six – 16–18 months – introduces half-pass, *renvers* and changes of leg. Half-pass involves the horse moving diagonally to the original line of advance whilst the body remains parallel to the original line. If he moves in half-pass to the right the head is inclined slightly in the direction of the movement whilst the left fore and left hind cross over and in front of the right fore and hind legs.

Leg-yielding and shoulder-in are the exercises which prepared the horse for this movement, since both teach the horse to move away from an applied leg. The movement can, in fact, be taught from shoulder-in. If it is shoulder-in to the right the rider, after a few strides, places his weight centrally, releases the inside leg and acts inwards with the whole of the outside leg (left leg). The inside rein now leads the horse instead of being in opposition

TURNOUT FOR HORSE AND RIDER

Left: Richard Meade and Jacob Jones, at the 1976 Olympic Games, present shining examples of the high standard of turnout required in the dressage arena. Top hat, swallow tail coat and spurs are correct dress for this level of competition. The horse wears a double bridle and a well-fitting dressage saddle. It goes without saying that he is spotlessly clean and polished; he has also had his mane braided and a diamond pattern applied to his hindquarters with a dampened water brush.

Braiding the mane

Braiding the tail

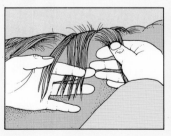

Brush the mane thoroughly so there are no knots or tangles, dampen the hair with a water brush and divide into sections.

Begin to braid so that the top of the braid is tight against the roots of the hair, encouraging any wispy pieces into the braid.

Secure the bottom end with a needle and thread, passing it through the braid and winding it round tightly several times.

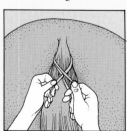

Start at the top and take the side hairs in strands towards the centre to braid them together.

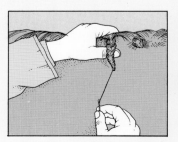

Take the loose ends of hair at the bottom of the braid and turn them underneath so that they will not stick out at random.

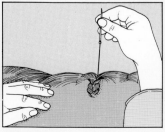

Fold the braid under so that the end of the braid comes half way up on the inside. Stitch the end firmly in position.

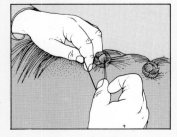

The final stage is to roll up the folded over braid, as tightly as possible, so that it forms a knob close to the poll.

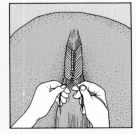

Continue to the end of the dock, then braid centre hairs to the end of the tail, turning this braid up and stitching.

SOME TOP CLASS HORSES AND RIDERS

Top left: Trisha Gardiner on Manifesto at Goodwood in 1980. **Bottom far left:** The American Gwen Stockebrand riding Bao. **Bottom left:** Princess Anne and Goodwill were members of the British team at the 1976 Olympic Games in Montreal. **Above, top left:** Christine Stückelberger, a familiar figure at top class dressage events. **Top right:** A competitor makes his bow at the start of a test. **Above:** Success in the individual event at the 1976 Olympics: Christine Stückelberger wins for Switzerland, with Boldt and Kimbe of Germany coming second and third. **Right:** Rotterdam 1980: Dr R. Klimke on Ahlerich.

HALF PASS

Left: The movement may be approached by turning down the centre line of the school, thus ensuring that the horse is well positioned before starting. The head should lead the movement, not the hindquarters, there should be no twisting in the head and neck and the horse should be bent in his longitudinal axis. **Right:** Practise making the half pass in either direction by starting at the centre line of the school, working towards the side in a left-hand half pass, taking a few ordinary strides and working back to the centre again in a right-hand half pass. This is a preliminary to a movement called counter change of hand, where no intermediate steps are allowed.

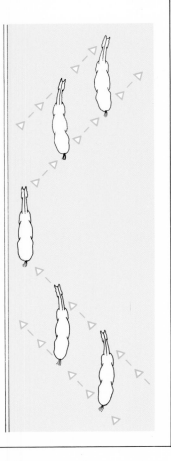

whilst the outside rein reduces the bend allowed and may oppose a little to help the outside leg move the quarters on a separate track. Half-pass is commenced at walk, then carried out at trot and finally at canter.

Renvers is the opposite to *travers*, the forehand being bought inwards whilst the quarters remain parallel to the track. It improves the co-ordination of aids and completes the suppling exercises represented by *travers*.

Simple changes of leg, making the change through a few steps at walk (ideally two or three) have to be perfected by practice and they require considerable impulsion.

Counter-canter can be introduced at this point as a test of discipline. It is not difficult if begun on large curves and if the simple changes have been established.

The final stages

In the last six months (phases 7 and 8), extension, improvement of the leg responses, the half-pass at canter and the working on 10-metre circles will occupy the first phase; in the final phase the extended canter has to be taught and the flying changes. The latter require considerable skill on the part of the rider, and whilst there are a number of approaches to the movement, the flying change made off a circle is probably as easy as any. If a large circle is ridden in counter-canter on the horses's softer side, he will be encouraged to change to the

more comfortable lead. The whole execution of the change, which involves a reversal of the aids and body weight, is concerned with the hind legs, and it is with these that the rider must be concerned. The aid has to be applied immediately prior to the moment of suspension between the last beat of one canter stride and the first beat of the next. It is usually necessary in the beginning to exaggerate the use of the outside leg, and the inside hand must be prepared to give a little. Within these final stages the horse should be accustomed to wearing a double bridle.

Haute-Ecole

To arrive at Grand Prix standard will take at least another full two years of training in which the collection will reach a point from which the ultimate *passage* and *piaffe* can be taught; the flying change will be perfected up to the one-time changes and there will be increased precision in the execution of the school figures.

To bring a horse to this standard requires great experience and whilst with the training up to Medium standard it is possible for a competent rider (who has, nonetheless, a background of proper training) to manage with occasional help, perhaps taking himself and his horse to a professional trainar two or three times a year, the advanced work is considerably more demanding and would involve a great deal more professional help.

THE DRESSAGE HORSE'S YEAR

As the majority of affiliated dressage shows are held out of doors, the principal dressage season necessarily runs through the spring and summer. That the shows are held in outdoor arenas is a simple matter of practicality; the number of classes held at any one show in one day could not all be staged in one indoor school and few establishments have access to more than one manège. There are, however, a number of small dressage shows — most of them un-affiliated — held in indoor schools through the winter.

If you and your horse are entering in affiliated dressage shows, you will be graded novice, elementary, medium or advanced according to the number of points you have accrued from your wins and placings. Once out of a certain grade, you can no longer compete in classes of that standard, but you may compete in classes of a higher standard, than your current grade. For example, if you were graded elementary, you could compete in elementary, medium and advanced classes, but not in novice.

How quickly a horse progresses up the grading scale depends almost as much on his natural talent and athletic ability as on how you ride and train him. If you feel you are progressing too quickly and look, for example, as if you are going to be out of elementary classes before you feel you really have the necessary experience, you will have to enter a few shows 'hors concours' (not competing). Alternatively, you could look for unaffiliated shows to enter.

The annual programme outlined here is for a horse in elementary grade, who is primarily, therefore, competing in elementary and medium dressage classes. Throughout the season you can aim to enter approximately one show every ten days — two in a three-week period. Remember that your horse must be in top fit condition for this, and that does not mean just physically fit; he must also be mentally prepared. Certainly dressage requires extreme physical fitness, for these classes are very demanding on a horse's physique, but he must be in the right frame of mind too. This means including other work in his routine as well as dressage; any horse that is asked to perform dressage exclusively is likely very quickly to become a nervous — and quite possibly also a physical — wreck. You will find, too, that as you progress to more advanced work in this discipline your horse is likely to become even more agitated, unless he is provided with some variation and relaxation in his weekly routine. It is a

Above: Jennie Loriston-Clarke and Dutch Courage.

good idea, therefore, to enter some small show-jumping classes at local shows and to incorporate some gymnastic jumping exercises into your routine work. Besides providing variety, these will help to get the horse's back working and generally call for more overall exercise. Another show class you could enter is the working hunter class. Many dressage horses do well in this as their dressage training makes them an obedient and pleasant ride which will instantly endear them to the judge! It is not a good idea to enter cross-country jumping competitions or to take your horse hunting, for he can so easily blemish or strain his legs in these pursuits, and if he is asked to struggle through thick mud or heavy going too frequently it can spoil his action.

The twelve-month programme below is only an outline. Adapt it to suit you and your particular horse.

Early-mid autumn: Turn horse out to grass, but do not remove shoes. As the grass is beginning to lose its goodness now, give a feed each day. This has the advantage of not letting the horse lose condition completely, so he does not become fat and flabby. To aid this still further, you could go for a gentle hack, perhaps once a week, which will also give him a change of scenery.

Mid-late autumn: Bring back into the stable and clip out after a week. Begin work with steady exercise on roads and tracks and continue this for a good three weeks before beginning dressage training again.

Winter-early spring: Steady work and gradual increase of feed to get horse fit and back in training. Incorporate dressage schooling into daily routine and gymnastic jumping into weekly programme now. Enter a few indoor

jumping shows providing the courses are not too demanding and also keep an eye out for any unaffiliated dressage shows. (The only problem with the latter is that they tend to be staged at preliminary and novice levels and if your horse has progressed beyond these grades, he may find it quite hard to perform at a lower level again. However, at this stage, the discipline is good for him.) Throughout this period, aim to have a lesson from a qualified instructor experienced in dressage at least once a week. It is essential in this sport to have some help from someone on the ground; from your position on the horse's back, it is not always possible to know for certain whether you are performing certain movements correctly.

Spring and summer: Competition season. As mentioned above, you should try to enter about two shows in three weeks, but intersperse these with occasional show-jumping or working hunter classes. Do not enter more than three classes in any one day; it is essential to work your horse for a good 30 minutes before each class, which will probably then last for about 10 minutes. Thus three classes a day means the horse has about 2 hours hard work, which is quite enough.

At the end of the show season, let the horse down gradually for a couple of weeks before turning him out. Drop the daily dressage training, but go for gentle hacks. Start reducing the feed and turn him out for longer periods each day, but still bring him in at night.

The dressage horse's week: Below is a possible weekly routine for a dressage horse during the season, assuming that the horse has competed on a Saturday. It will have to be adapted according to the days on which you have entered events.

Sunday: Turn the horse out with reduced feed.

Monday: Easy work such as a steady hack for one hour, followed by two hours turned out in the paddock (make sure the grass is not too lush).

Tuesday-Friday: Thirty minutes of dressage training each day. Much more than this is inclined to make the horse unsettled mentally, and this can lead to the development of such stable vices as wind-sucking. Follow the training with a good 30 minutes of road and track work. This gives him a change of scenery and stretches his legs. After this, turn your horse out in the paddock for two hours, whatever the weather; he needs this freedom to relax and unwind.

CHAPTER SEVEN

LONG DISTANCE

THE ART OF long distance riding is an exacting one; it involves the riding of a carefully-trained and conditioned horse over a long distance – long meaning anything from about 32km–40km (20 miles–25 miles) up to 160km (100 miles). Such rides may or may not be ridden competitively. As with so many other equestrian sports, its origins can be attributed to the mounted armies of the world, who often had to ride over very long distances in order to reach the place where they were to do battle. In more recent times, many cavalries have conducted 'endurance rides' of considerable distances over highly inhospitable terrain to test calibre and stamina.

The greatest following for the sport is in the USA, though its popularity is growing in other countries, such as Britain. In the USA, the sport is known collectively as trail riding. Under this general heading come various categories – pleasure trail, competitive trail and endurance rides.

Types of ride

Pleasure trail rides need little explanation. They embrace anything from a lone rider taking his mount for a gentle hack across familiar country to a group of riders setting off for a few days with maps, compasses and overnight equipment to explore new territory on horseback. Route, distance and speed are up to the riders themselves. Competitive trail rides, on the other hand, are held across designated, marked trails and those participating in them must complete that course within a maximum and minimum time limit. The rides may be held over one, two or three days and by and large they are judged against a standard – that is, horses that complete the course within the set average speed and additionally have no penalty points marked against them at the various veterinary examinations qualify for the top awards. Others who fall below this average speed, but still have no veterinary penalty points qualify for a slightly lesser award and so on. This eliminates any actual racing element, for it means that it is not the fastest time over the course that wins. The most important factors in the judging of competitive trail rides are the overall soundness and condition of the horse at the end of the ride.

Left: Riders competing for the Tevis Cup, which takes place in California each year over a distance of 100 miles and is considered to be one of the most demanding long distance rides in the world. **Above:** The French Cavalry on manoeuvres in 1898. Swimming across rivers is still a requirement in many long distance events.

Endurance rides are also held over designated, marked trails, but are generally either 80km (50 miles) or 160km (100 miles) long – a distance which must be completed in 12 or 24 hours respectively. Only a minimum time restriction is imposed in endurance rides, so the winner is the person who completes the race in the fastest time with his or her horse in good condition as judged by a panel of vets.

That the various types of long distance riding outlined above are so popular in the USA is shown by the number of Trail Ride Associations that are in existence. The most famous US ride is the Tevis Cup – a 160-km (100-mile) one-day ride. It has been held each year since 1955, usually towards the end of July/beginning of August, the trail running from Tahoe City across extremely harsh and testing country to Auburn in California.

Australia and South Africa are currently the two other countries with the greatest number of long distance riders, although many European countries – France, Germany and Italy in particular – also have growing interest in the sport. Australia is famous for the 160-km (100-mile) Quilty ride, which is held across the steep, rough terrain of the Blue Mountains in New South Wales. South Africa's principal ride is the National Endurance Ride, which is longer than the two rides so far mentioned by some 48km (30 miles). It is held over three days.

In Britain, the best-known long distance ride is the Golden Horseshoe Ride, which is now organized by the British Horse Society. It is held over two days and covers a distance of 120km (75 miles) across Exmoor, in the southwest. To enter for this, riders must either have completed one affiliated 80-km (50-mile) ride during the previous two years, or two of the official qualifying rides. The latter cover a distance of 64km (40 miles) and are held in various places throughout the country during March and April. The Golden Horseshoe is generally held early in May.

Attractions and dangers

To the uninitiated, long distance riding may not seem to have the instant appeal of the other equestrian sports. It does not appear to embrace the thrills and spills connected with, say, hunting or mounted games; there is no test of jumping ability or dressage skill; no prize money; no exhilarating flat-out gallop, pitting the speed of your horse against others; even the competitive element seems somewhat muted in that in the majority of rides there is no outright winner. So what is there in this sport to appeal to the ever-growing number of riders who participate in it?

First and foremost, those who have gained success in long distance riding have by no means always been mounted on expensive, well-bred horses. Preparation of the horse for the sport is more important than the type of

horse and therein lies its other major attraction. Those who participate regularly in long distance riding find immense pleasure and satisfaction in the challenge of getting a horse into the proper condition for a long ride. Preparing a horse for long distance riding requires extreme dedication, combined with considerable skill and expertize.

Another often-held misconception about long distance riding is that it is a sport for the more timid, less competitively-motivated riders; those perhaps who find no thrill in hunting, or have not got the 'nerve' to gallop round a cross-country event course. However, there is nothing 'soft' about long distance riding—in fact the reverse is the case. It is an extremely tough sport that demands similar toughness from its participators.

The dangers of long distance riding can be found equally among its attractions. Because it does not necessarily require an expensive horse or a high degree of skill as in such fields

Top: Gold and silver belt buckle depicting a Pony Express rider presented to every competitor who completes the Tevis Cup ride in under 24 hours. **Above:** Tevis Cup sunrise – Squaw Valley below, Lake Tahoe in the distance.

Above: A steep climb up Cougar Rock during the Tevis Cup. The rider leans well forward in the saddle in order to take as much weight as possible off the horse's quarters. She is wearing leather or suede chaps over her jeans and a broad brimmed hat as protection from the sun.

as dressage or jumping, the unwary could be wooed into participating in long distance riding without making the proper preparation. Probably because this has proved a problem in the past, strict rules surround participation in official rides, imposed to protect both horses and riders. Participants have benefitted too from the considerable interest shown in the sport by numbers of vets, and as a result of their studies, new information is continually coming to light relating to the reactions of a horse under stress.

Horses entering competitive long distance rides have to undergo veterinary inspections before the rides, during it (the length of the ride will determine the number of checks) and after it. Temperature, dehydration, pulse and respiration are the chief factors that the vet uses to judge the horse's condition, so a rider must be familiar with these aspects (see p. 168). In addition, the vet will be looking for any signs of lameness, injuries—particularly those

caused by badly-fitting saddlery or the horse brushing or over-reaching—and at the condition of the feet and shoes. Horses entered in long distance rides are allowed no medication or drugs of any type (including the controversial pain-killer butazolodine).

Riders therefore must be well-acquainted with the long list of rules before entering any ride. They cover such topics as qualification for entry, saddlery and tack inspections, ancillary equipment (e.g. some ride organizers ban the use of any leg bandages or boots), shoeing, age and height of horse, riders' dress, helpers, speed restrictions and allowances and so on. Currently, these rules vary from ride to ride (according to the organizing body) and from country to country. However, there are plans for some degree of standardization, as the *Federation Equestre Internationale* (International Equestrian Federation) have recently taken an interest in the sport and have now drawn up a list of guide lines.

The long distance horse

Most horses should be able to tackle the shorter competitive rides, providing they are sound in limb and wind and that they have undergone a suitable training programme to ensure that they are sufficiently fit. If, however, you are looking for a horse specifically for long distance riding, you should keep the following points firmly in mind.

Good conformation is more important than pretty looks and probably the most important aspect are the legs and feet. Look at the feet first; they should be a good and uniform shape. The horn should show no sign of splits or cracks; the sole should be slightly concave and tough so that it does not bruise easily. The heels should be fairly wide apart and the frog well-formed, tough and very resilient. The

frog's continued ability to act as a shock-absorber over the varied terrain of a long ride is of paramount importance, so examine it carefully.

Experienced long distance riders will take great note of the angle of the pastern and the shoulders, looking for a good 'slope' in both cases. Look too, for a longish forearm and a short cannon bone with a large flat knee. The hocks should be well-formed, fairly big and 'well let-down'—meaning, again, that the cannon bones are short.

Viewed from the front, check that the chest is a good width. If it is too narrow, the legs will be too close together, increasing the likelihood of the horse brushing one leg against another; if it is too wide, the legs are likely to swing out awkwardly in movement. Avoid toes or hocks that turn in or out.

Above: A first-class example of a long distance horse. Witezarif, an Arabian gelding, and his rider Donna Fitzgerald, have won the Tevis Cup four times.
Right: An example of an extremely thin chest. Not only is there insufficient room for the respiratory organs to develop to full capacity, but the legs are set so close together they may well brush or knock against one another in movement. In a long distance riding horse, this will soon lead to unsoundness. **Far right:** This horse is far better proportioned. Beware, however, too broad a chest. If the legs are set far apart the movement could be equally cumbersome and uncomfortable as that of a thin-chested horse.

CONFORMATION FAULTS

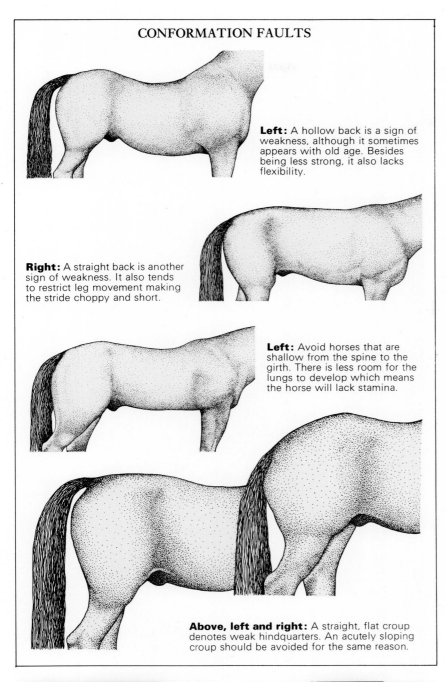

Left: A hollow back is a sign of weakness, although it sometimes appears with old age. Besides being less strong, it also lacks flexibility.

Right: A straight back is another sign of weakness. It also tends to restrict leg movement making the stride choppy and short.

Left: Avoid horses that are shallow from the spine to the girth. There is less room for the lungs to develop which means the horse will lack stamina.

Above, left and right: A straight, flat croup denotes weak hindquarters. An acutely sloping croup should be avoided for the same reason.

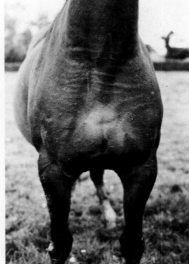

The ideal horse should be short-coupled—that is fairly short in the back. As always, the quarters are extremely important, for they house the animal's driving power. They should be strong, well-rounded and muscular. There should be a good depth of body from the back down to the girth to give lots of room for the heart and lungs. The area over the ribs should be well-rounded rather than flat.

The withers and saddle-carrying area are extremely important. The withers must be well-defined; if poorly-defined, they will not hold the saddle in the correct position. The back should dip slightly behind the withers so the saddle fits snugly and, again, the ribs should be well-sprung (rounded) so the saddle will not slip backwards. The elbows should be well forward of the girth area; if they are tucked into the animal's sides, this could lead to the girth pinching and causing sores. Check all round the saddle area—under the chest as well – to make sure there are no blemishes or evidence of old sores. Any tiny little spot will magnify one-hundredfold when work begins in earnest. Excessively thin-skinned horses should be avoided, as wearing tack for long periods could cause them problems.

The head, neck and forehand should give the appearance of lightness. The neck should not be short and heavily-muscled, as this tends to make the horse heavy on its forehand and also prone to pulling. A longer neck gives better balancing ability; but it must not be too long proportionally, as, again, this can make a horse heavy on the forehand. The head should be the right size for the rest of the body and the area under the throatlatch should be wide, so that the passage of air to and from the lungs is in no way restricted. Similarly, a horse with large nostrils has a respiratory advantage. Avoid a horse with heavy, 'rounded' bones, giving him an overall coarse appearance. Horses that are very wide or appear to have heavy muscles do not move as easily as those that are lighter in build.

How a horse moves is extremely important. Watch him walking towards you and away from you and reject any horse that shows even the slightest tendency to brush against any part of one leg with the other, or to over-reach. In long distance riding, this tendency will become more apparent as the horse gets tired, so that towards the end of a ride, a serious, open sore will have developed.

A long-striding horse that moves with relaxed, well-balanced, comfortable paces is the ideal. The more ground he covers with each step he takes, the less quickly he will tire. Look particularly at the walk: does he walk easily and freely or is he constantly wanting to break into a jog? Reject him if he does and reject him, too, if you have to keep kicking him to keep him up to the mark. As much of a long distance ride will be taken at a trot, make sure this pace is easy and relaxed and comfortable for you to ride. Ideally, the horse should feel equally

comfortable when ridden on either diagonal, although this could be something that you will have to achieve with patient training. Try, if possible, to assess the horse's natural cruising speed at a walk and a trot. For most long distance rides you want a horse that can travel 13km (8 miles) per hour, without coming under stress. Time him for some distance at his natural walk and trot (without pushing him) and work out an average from this, allowing for some cantering, too.

Many horses experience difficulty in going downhill, taking laboured, braking steps, rather than stepping out freely. Obviously this will be a great disadvantage to the long distance horse, as such a movement will become more overt the more tired he gets. When you are trying a horse, therefore, jog him down a slope to see if it is an effort for him. If each step of the hind legs is a braking step—that is, taken in such a way as to prevent him going faster—he will quickly tire the muscles in the hindquarters and this can result in extreme stiffening or 'tying-up' of the croup muscles. A vet will eliminate a horse from a ride if it shows such symptoms.

By the same token, you want a horse that is sure-footed and shows no signs of stumbling under any circumstances. A long distance riding horse should be able to pick his way easily across all types of rough ground. He should have a natural instinct for safety, which, in this instance, manifests itself by not taking risks in tricky conditions.

Temperament and attitude are vital factors. You want an animal that appears always willing to take one step more. On the other hand, he should have a relaxed, calm temperament, as ability to relax, particularly in a strange environment, is extremely important. Make sure the horse you choose is a good traveller, too.

An ability to get on with other horses, to ride along with them at the usual steady pace and not to get upset when they surge or fall behind is also essential. A long distance horse must be able to travel alone or in company with equal equanimity. Equally, he must be relaxed with strangers, accepting, say, the vet at the various examinations without fuss.

As always, have any horse you are considering buying thoroughly examined by a vet; try to find one that understands the stresses imposed on long distance riding horses. He should take blood tests as well as check the horse's teeth, soundness and the condition of the heart and lungs.

Training the long distance horse

Training a horse to participate in long distance rides means getting him fit, or conditioning him, so that his muscles are as hard and well-developed as they can be and his heart and lungs—and therefore wind—are in perfect working order. His feet and legs must also be in prime condition—that is, hard and strong—

and he must be able to wear a saddle and bridle, and carry a rider, for hours on end. In addition, he must be mentally attuned to the rigours of long distance riding, able to relax whenever he is given the opportunity, but ready to respond to his rider's requests, however tired he may be.

Such conditioning comes from following a carefully prepared schedule of regular riding, combined with an equally rigorous and regular stable management routine. Long distance riding can produce immense stress and distress in a horse if he has not been properly prepared, all riders should learn to recognize the signs of such stress and know how to deal with them. The chief problem areas to be considered are muscular distress, cardiovascular distress and metabolic stress.

Muscular distress will manifest itself by the horse beginning to flag and stumble, even when travelling on the flat. He may also be suffering clearly visible muscle tremors around the flanks and thighs. Such signs mean he is not fit enough to take the demands you are making on him and the only remedy is to ease up. If you push him at this point, he is likely to develop cardio-vascular distress as well. This you can detect by checking his pulse and respiration rate.

Opposite: The loneliness of the long distance rider. You must be sure that you are able to ride for hours on end on your own without becoming bored or losing any concentration. It is vital for your horse that you concentrate all the time; this way you can help him to pick the best route as well as assisting by riding correctly. **Above:** Competitions will sometimes ride together, at least for some of the way. Here one rider lets her horse drink while another waits. Note how the riders have to pick their own route over this stony ground as there is no prepared track. Practice over such ground is vital in order to prepare and harden the feet and legs.

At rest, a horse's pulse (heartbeat) rate varies from around 32 to 40 beats per minute, while his respiration rate should be around 12 to 18 per minute. After exertion, the pulse will rise to anywhere between 64 to 90 (even higher if the exertion was very great) and the respiration will rise to 24 to 36. From this, it can be seen that the ratio of pulse to respiration is somewhere between 2:1 and 3:1. If the horse is suffering extreme cardiovascular distress, the respiration rate may exceed that of the pulse, or they may be exactly the same – a condition known as the 'thumps'. Either of these are extremely dangerous conditions and the horse must be rested immediately. A vet will given an injection of calcium salts which brings almost instant relief, but the horse should not be asked to continue work.

Dehydration is a sign of metabolic stress in a horse. If he is clearly very hot but is experiencing difficulty in sweating – that is, the sweat is very thick and does not evaporate easily – he may well be suffering from dehydration.

Another test is to pinch a fold of skin on the neck; under normal conditions, it would snap back into position instantly, but, in a dehydrated horse, it takes longer to do so. Again, the horse must not be allowed to continue and steps must be taken to cool him down and re-hydrate him. Bathing in cold water will help to cool him, but keep this away from his loins, flanks and the area over his heart. Let him drink, but only a few mouthfuls at a time, at intervals of about 10 minutes. Extra salt given with his regular feed can help to avoid dehydration, but do not give too much or he will retain too much fluid.

Your conditioning routine will depend on whether you want to enter for the longer rides or only the short ones. A horse that is hunting fit (see chapter 2) should be able to enter for a short ride – those of no more than 32km (20 miles) – without suffering any ill effects. An extra four months should be added to the normal programme for a horse entering a 120-km (75-mile) or 160-km (100-mile) ride.

A long distance riding horse must be in the peak of good health if he is to perform to the best of his ability. Arrange for regular visits from your vet (try to find one who understands the rigours of the sport) to make routine checks on blood, internal parasites and teeth. **Above left:** A vet examines the lining of the eye during a ride. If it is dark red instead of the normal healthy salmon-pink, it denotes fatigue. **Above right:** Checking a horse's pulse. Place a stethoscope a hand's breadth above the left elbow in the girth region. Count the beats for 15 seconds and multiply by four to give you the correct reading for one minute. **Below:** If you have not got a stethoscope you can check the pulse by putting your hand on the pulse under the jaw and counting the beats for 15 seconds. Then multiply this by four. Check the respiration rate by counting the breaths the animal takes in a 15-second period, and again multiplying by four.

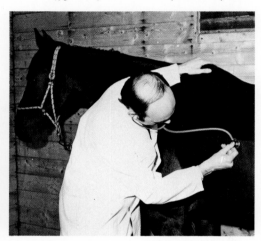

The chief difference between conditioning for a long distance ride and getting a horse fit for, say, hunting, is that all work should ideally be conducted only at a walk and trot for the first two months. Cantering or galloping, which helps to develop the wind, can be introduced into the routine when a certain amount of stamina and muscle strength has been developed. If you have brought a horse up from grass, walk it for two months beginning with an hour a day and gradually building up to three (four if you have the time). If you can divide these into two sessions instead of one, so much the better. Ride over as varied terrain as possible, including steep hills, which should be taken in both directions. Do not neglect downhill work; it places stress on an entirely different set of muscles than those used going uphill or on the flat.

Make your horse work under you when he is walking. If his walk tends to be rather slow and short-striding, work on it now, asking him to really lengthen his stride and step out. If he breaks into a jog when you ask him to walk faster, correct him instantly, bringing him back to a walk. Once established, jogging is a hard habit to break and it will prove very tiring for both horse and rider. Time his walk; the very least you want to average at this pace is 6.5km (4 miles) an hour; ideally, you want to increase this to 8km (5 miles) an hour. Try to get him into the habit, too, of picking his own way along a track or across a field at this stage. Continual guidance from you will tire both of you and it will not teach a horse to look where he is going.

Having taught your horse to walk out well, remember that this is also the pace at which he will be 'resting' during a ride so it is very important that he learns how to relax. He must never get flustered at a walk; it may need endless patience from you during the training to calm him down and teach him to rest. Your aim is a long, free-striding walk that you can ride on a loose rein.

Similarly, ask for a long-striding, easy trot

Below: Riding along the kind of tracks through the sort of country you may encounter during a long distance ride is a vital part of the conditioning programme. Working with others at the initial walking stage may help to keep your horse more alert and can perhaps help to relieve some of the tedium of these slow early sessions.

when you introduce trotting into the programme. A good trot should average about 16km (10 miles) an hour. Include some gentle trotting on roads; this will help to harden the horse's legs and prepare him for when you ask him to trot along a road on a competitive ride. By the third month introduce some bouts of steady cantering, keeping these short at first. Cantering is probably the pace least used in a long distance ride, although it is useful, when ground conditions are conducive, for making up a little lost time. It is important to include it in the training routine, however, as it is primarily cantering and galloping that develops a horse's wind capacity.

As your horse gets fitter, ride him for two hours one day and three the next, working him for six days of the week. Now he needs two different types of work: the first is to cover a reasonable distance – say about 40km (25 miles) in a day at a speed of 14km to 16km (9 to 10 miles) an hour. By and large, you should not ask the horse to go faster than this, except for the occasional gallop to act as a 'pipe opener.' The second type of work is to ride for longer distances than those outlined above at a slower speed – say 7km to 11km (5 to 7 miles) an hour. This helps to harden the muscles and leg tendons, and the steady, rhythmic pace helps to prepare a horse psychologically.

Always end a ride with a long period of walking. When you arrive home, the horse should not be sweating excessively, although the amount a horse sweats varies considerably

Above: As with all horses in hard work, long distance riding horses need some periods of freedom – if only to let off steam. If you know your horse to be particularly high-spirited make sure he is in a paddock with safe fencing where he is unlikely to hurt himself. If the weather is at all cold, protect him with a New Zealand rug.

from animal to animal. Some sweat much more easily than others, however fit they are. If he is sweating, it should be a wet sweat, rather than a lathery one. On his rest day turn him out in a paddock if possible, or lead him out in hand for a couple of hours.

The above outline is necessarily not highly detailed, as the conditioning and preparation of a horse for long distance riding will vary with every horse. This is not a sport where one person can prepare a horse and another ride it, for knowing your horse intimately is more than half the battle in long distance riding. The horse and rider that are a true team are the most likely to succeed. You must know when he is still going because he still has more to give, or whether it is his willing nature responding to your demands. By the same token, horses need differing amounts of work to get them fit; this is where checking the pulse and respiration can help you to assess your horse's fitness during the training programme. The procedure for this is outlined below; remember to record the readings you take, together with the dates, for the information is primarily of value when compared with other readings.

Pulse and respiration rates

First of all, establish your horse's normal pulse and respiration rates. Now choose a hill, or place where you generally pull up after a fairly long bout of work and take the pulse and respiration rates when you have reached the top or end of this. At the start, you will be walking; later you will be taking it at a trot. Having recorded the P and R rates, wait 10 minutes and take them again. Initially do this, say, every three days and compare the readings. As you get further into the routine, take the readings each week on the same day. When the first readings start to get lower, and the second ones indicate a drop back to almost normal within the 10-minute rest period, your horse is getting fitter and is ready for more sustained, harder work. As a guide, he is ready for harder work when his pulse begins to register less than 80 beats per minute after a bout of work. Ask him to continue when it has dropped back to about 60. Besides recording the P and R rates, make a note, too, of how fast you were travelling, how long it took to cover the distance, and the climate on each day (the exertion will take a greater toll on the horse on a hot day). In this way you can make true comparisons.

On a competitive long distance ride, the examining vets will check the P and R rates at the start of the ride, at given points along it and again at the end. They will be looking for the readings to have dropped back to near normal at the end of a half-hour period during the early checks in the ride. Recovery will take longer towards the end of a ride, when a horse is getting tired, and the vets will take this into account. In many rides they will not let a horse

SURVIVAL OF THE FITTEST

Above: Robinson Flats, one of the many veterinary checkpoints along the Tevis Cup route. These compulsory stopping places provide a rest for the riders as well as for the horses and it really is essential to have a helper to meet you so that you have a chance to recover for the next stage of the ride. **Left:** If your horse does not pass the veterinary tests, he will not be allowed to continue. **Below:** Minette Rice-Edwards receiving the Haggin Cup at the celebration banquet following the Tevis Cup ride in 1973. She came 9th overall, completing the 100 mile course in 12 hours 51 minutes, and received the cup in recognition of the fact that her horse, Bright Hope, was in better condition than any other at the end of the ride.

Above: Riders on Britain's Golden Horseshoe Ride give their horses a breather in a shallow stream. Allowing a horse frequent opportunities to have a short drink during a ride is infinitely more.beneficial than giving him a long drink at the compulsory halts.

continue until his pulse is below 70 again.

Pulse and respiration rates should not be your only guide to your horse's fitness. Judge this too by his willingness and alertness, and his general attitude to work, as well as by his appearance (is he losing weight? are his muscles hard, not flabby?) and appetite.

There are one or two factors to bear in mind, relating directly to the exercise routine. When riding these kind of distances out on exercise every day, it is sometimes not too easy to vary the route, yet this is absolutely essential. If a horse travels the same country every day, he will soon get to know it; he will anticipate the changes in pace, when he is nearing home for instance, and his actions will become mechanical. He will become bored and stale. In addition, it is imperative to ride him over as much varied ground as possible. Alternatively, to make a change from riding out on exercise and to keep your horse alert, you can exercise him by lungeing, making sure he really works on the lunge rein. If you lunge correctly, it can be an ideal exercise to include in the training of a long distance riding horse and can do much to establish good rhythm of pace.

Final stages

Make sure the various circumstances you will encounter are incorporated into your daily rides. Stop at streams, and encourage him to drink; make sure he will wade across, or even swim rivers. Make certain he does not spook or get upset when asked to cross a narrow bridge, or jump forward if you take off your anorak while on his back. Get him used to trotting freely downhill on good ground. Few horses will trot downhill naturally, yet, if they can be taught to do so, they will find it less tiring than walking. This means time can be gained going downhill with less expenditure of energy, and it is just such opportunities you should be looking for. Trotting downhill also teaches a horse to balance well, and can make him more surefooted. Teach your horse to trot by using gentle slopes to begin with, and on no account let him break into a canter. Choose the hills carefully; do not ask him to trot out if the going is very hard or soft, slippery, uneven or littered with stones.

Probably the most important thing to train your horse in is to maintain a steady, easy

pace throughout a ride, unlike in general hacking, where you are likely to be asking for constant changes in speed and tempo. A fit horse in the fourth or fifth month of his training should be able to trot steadily for two hours (providing the terrain is not very hilly) without breaking the rhythm of the pace and without being unduly tired at the end of it. A long period taken at a steady, rhythmic pace will tire a horse much less than if he is constantly being asked to alter his stride. It will also encourage him to breathe deeply and rhythmically, thus helping to develop his lung capacity. You must be sure he trots evenly and willingly on both diagonals and that he will canter equally with either leg leading. Obviously it is important that he is moving with his hocks well engaged beneath him, not hammering along on his forehand, which will soon tire him, as well as putting too much strain on his front legs. If you find he is heavy on his forehand, intersperse rides with some schooling work.

Towards the end of the training, include some longer rides in the weekly routine. Aim to do one ride of 48km. (30 miles), once a week,

and make sure you have done at least one of 64km (40 miles) before entering a 120-km (75-mile) ride. It will prepare your horse for such a distance and give you a taste of what it is like to spend six or seven hours in the saddle. Plan such long rides to include a number of streams or rivers, or other sources of water, so that the horse can drink along the route. Follow these rides with a day or two of lighter work.

If there are competitive long distance rides of a suitable length being held during your training programme, you can use these as part of the conditioning routine and to see how your horse reacts.

A long ride will give you an idea of how your horse's back will stand up to being saddled for an extensive period. An important point to bear in mind is not to remove the saddle the moment you dismount. Instead, walk the horse round for 20 minutes, then loosen the girth a little and walk him again for the same period. Then remove the saddle. If you remove the saddle immediately, the sudden rush of blood to this compressed area can cause pressure bumps to erupt.

Above: In some long distance rides, horses have to wade through fairly deep water — in fact it is not unknown for swimming to be necessary. Make sure you have accustomed your horse to this beforehand or you may well have a problem when you face him with a wide, fast-flowing stream. Let him stand in water coming half-way up his legs as the rider is doing here. She and her horse are both obviously thoroughly enjoying the experience.

Above: Correctly fitting tack that is comfortable for horse and rider is of prime importance in long distance riding. Note how this rider has placed a saddle blanket under the sheepskin numnah. A sheepskin numnah used on its own is very difficult to keep clean and tends to get lumpy after continued use. Choose a saddle pad carefully, however; it must be highly absorbent or else it will retain the heat on the back and cause heat bumps. It also must not slip on the horse's back or else it will begin to wrinkle, which will soon cause pinching. The pad as well as the numnah should be pulled well up into the arch of the saddle; if it is drawn tightly across the withers it will put pressure on the spine. This rider has also chosen to use a form of breastplate to help prevent the saddle from slipping backwards, which can easily happen on long uphill stretches of a ride.

The fit rider

The fitness and condition of the rider is just as important as that of the horse. Six or seven hours at a stretch in the saddle is extremely tiring so, particularly if the ride is to continue over the next one or two days, it is essential that a rider should be properly prepared. A tired rider becomes a real hindrance to a horse, especially since the tiredness will usually occur at a time when the animal needs all the help he can get. Tiredness in a rider generally means he or she begins to displace weight unevenly and incorrectly over the horse's back and rides out of rhythm with the pace. In addition, slouching in the saddle and a loss of concentration induces similar reactions in a horse. These are perfect conditions for a bad stumble and fall.

A daily exercise routine – including such activities as swimming, cycling, and jogging, as well as riding – should be built up gradually. Combine this with a sensible, high-protein diet that will provide you with the energy you need.

As much of your riding will be at a trot, you should learn to use the minimum of energy at this pace. Rise to the trot as effortlessly as possible; a high, exaggerated rise will tire you quickly. Sitting to the trot is very tiring and before long you will be bouncing rather than sitting, which will soon give your horse a sore back.

Tack

Considerable attention should be paid to the tack for long distance riding. A saddle whose fit is slightly suspect may be adequate for light, ordinary hacking, but if worn on a long distance ride it could cause a large, bleeding sore on the horse's back.

Correct fit is therefore the prime consideration. The pressure should be distributed evenly over the horse's fleshy sides; none should come on the spine. It is worthwhile having a saddler look at the saddle on the horse, so he can judge whether the padding is properly proportioned. Remember though, that as your horse becomes fitter and better muscled, he will change shape, so that the saddle that fitted him at the beginning of training will not do so at the end. It will be necessary, therefore, for the saddler to come and look at it again and possibly to re-stuff it.

It is important that the saddle is comfortable for you as well as the horse, so that it allows you to sit correctly, with your weight properly distributed over the horse's back. If you become saddle-sore, you will begin to shift about in the saddle and sit awkwardly to try to relieve the soreness.

Many types of saddle are available, and the type you choose will be personal preference as well as what fits you and your horse the best. Use the saddle you mean to use in competitive rides throughout the training, so that you can be sure it produces no problems. Switch to a new saddle, and you will immediately be introducing a new set of pressure points.

You may find that it is necessary to use a breastplate and/or a crupper to help keep the saddle in position. However well-fitting a saddle may be it can still slip forwards or backwards when travelling up or down very steep gradients. Most riders find string girths more satisfactory than leather or nylon.

The same applies to a bridle; make sure it fits comfortably and that none of the straps cause even slight rubbing. Choose the simplest bit you can (some riders use a hackamore); a thick bit is generally more comfortable and less likely to cause sores at the corners of the mouth than a very thin one.

Try to choose tack that is light and simple. Then keep it scrupulously clean and supple and subject it to regular, rigorous checks. Really tug at the stitching on stirrup leathers, for example; they must be able to withstand considerable pressure. Have any suspect stitching re-worked straight away; a long distance ride is no time to trust to luck.

HORSE EQUIPMENT

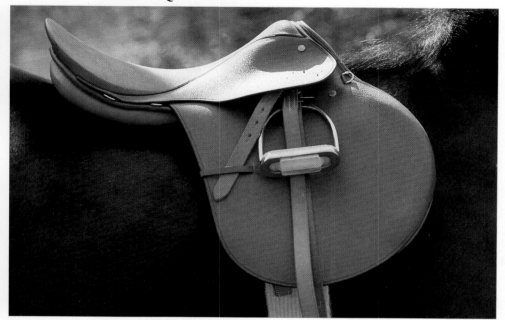

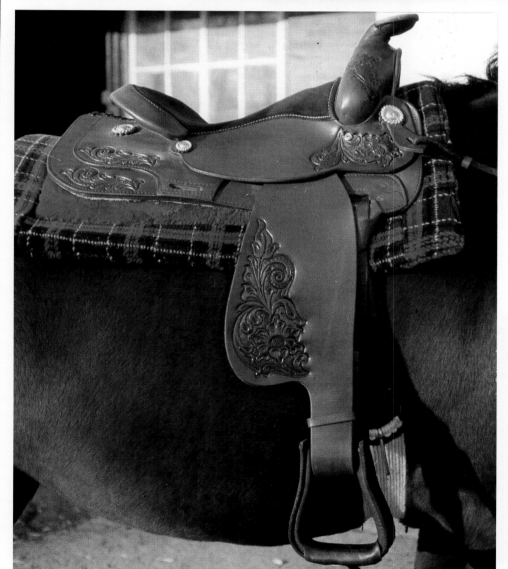

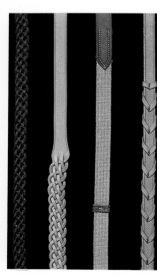

Top left: There should be a clear line down the centre of the saddle, so that no part rests on the spine itself. **Above left:** The numnah should be pushed well up into the front arch, and there should be space between this and the withers. **Above:** Riders may perhaps opt for this type of general purpose saddle. So long as it fits the horse perfectly and is comfortable for the rider, the design is not of prime importance. **Left:** Many riders prefer to use a western saddle, which was originally designed with the cowboys' long hours spent in the saddle in mind. **Below:** The type of rein will again be a matter of preference, but choose reins that will not slip through your hands in wet conditions. The plaiting or thonging of these reins help to prevent slipping.

Meticulous stable management is essential for success in long distance riding. **Top left:** Rubbing with methylated spirit helps to harden the skin under the saddle. **Top right:** Sores such as these are just what a rider hopes to avoid. White hairs on the back are a sign of previous bad sores, a result of bad management. **Centre left:** Picking out the feet is part of the daily routine for all horse owners. **Above left:** A leather pad fitted across the shoe can help to protect the sole from bruising caused by uneven ground and sharp stones. However, small stones can work their way underneath on a long ride, causing acute discomfort. **Above right:** Studs should be used with great caution as over a long distance they can lead to tendon trouble caused by the horse throwing his weight forward. They are also not suitable for all the many different types of going you could encounter on a ride. **Opposite:** A good farrier is of vital importance to the long distance rider.

Stable management

Any serious long distance rider must spend a fair amount of time each day on the general care and attention of his or her horse. Grooming, for example, is extremely important; he should have a thorough strapping every day. Besides cleaning the horse's coat, this supples the skin, improves the blood circulation to the skin and tones up a horse's muscles. All of these are vitally important to the long distance riding horse, the last in particular. Because of this, pay extra attention to wisping, as this really massages the muscles. Pay particular attention to highly muscular areas such as the sides of the neck and the hindquarters. Do not wisp the loin area though – this is very tender.

Make sure areas that come under the tack – the saddle and girth area, under the breast-plate and the head – are kept scrupulously clean. Any tiny particles of dried mud here could cause larger sores through rubbing. If the skin seems at all soft in these areas, rub them with surgical or methylated spirit to help harden them.

If your horse has an excessively long coat, he will be far better off if he is clipped, whatever time of year. Not only is it much easier to keep him clean, but he will also sweat far less and it will be easier to keep flesh on him. Leave the hair on his lower legs and around the saddle and girth area for protection, though.

Examine the legs daily to make sure there are no puffy swellings or splints beginning to form. Examine the feet regularly, too. Here, it is vital to have a farrier. Try to find a farrier who does hot-shoeing, as this ensures a much better-fitting shoe. Take note of the number of holes used for the nails; if new ones are made each time, the wall of the hoof becomes weaker. A good farrier will often be able to use the old holes twice. Similarly, he should not rasp the outer surface of the hoof to make it fit the shoe, nor cut the heels too low to the ground. Always have your horse shod with new shoes a few days before a competitive ride, just in case any troubles should develop.

The other important person as far as you and your horse are concerned is your vet; try to find one that understands the stresses suffered by long distance riding horses. Have him make regular checks on the horse's blood and teeth and advise you on a worming routine. It is essential that the horse be kept free from internal parasites; he cannot possibly give of his best if he is sharing his food with a multitude of worms.

The feeding programme

Your vet may also advise you of a suitable feeding programme for your horse, based on the result of the tests he conducts. Otherwise the normal rules apply – the hard feed must be increased and the bulk feed, such as hay, decreased as the horse becomes fitter and is asked to work harder. A horse in peak condition should have almost as much corn as he will eat (unless you know him to be a very greedy eater), but try and vary this hard feed as much as possible. You may find he begins to go off his food the fitter he gets, so tempt him with succulent carrots and tasty molasses and make sure that you feed him the highest-quality food you can purchase. If you feed commercially prepared nuts or other foodstuffs, follow the manufacturer's directions and do not mix different makes. The exception to this rule is when you want to change from one make to another; then mix the two together for a few feeds, so that the changeover is gradual.

As mentioned previously, salt is a vital part of the diet of a long distance riding horse. Just providing a salt lick is not enough; mix about 28g (1oz) of common salt with the feeds daily or give him salted water. Divide the day's food rations into at least three feeds; four would be ideal when you are giving top rations.

On a horse's rest day, cut down the corn

Above: On a long ride, a helper to meet you at the compulsory stops is essential. Giving your horse required attention would soon put an extra strain on you, making you very tired, and a tired rider puts an extra burden on her mount. Here a helper washes excess mud off the rider's stirrup iron. If allowed to remain it could either cause the foot to slip or, if hardened, would provide an uneven foot rest. Over long distances, such seemingly small points assume a far greater importance and can make a tremendous difference to the quality of riding.

ration by half. When not working, his digestion takes a rest, too, so, by decreasing the grain, you can ensure his whole system has a break. Try to let him graze on his rest day. The night before is an ideal time to give a warm mash; rather more bran than usual will have a laxative effect, which may be beneficial.

Make sure your horse always has access to clean water when he is in the stable or in the field, so that he can drink as and when he likes. In cold weather, it is extremely advantageous to give him slightly warmed water. If he drinks cold water in cold conditions, he will use energy in warming it up – energy which should be used for improving his condition. Note that on many official rides, though, you are not allowed to give artificially warmed water. On a hot day, take the chill off water by leaving a couple of buckets in the sun.

Preparing for the ride

By and large, the preparations immediately before a long distance ride will be the same, whatever distance is to be covered. The example given here is of a 120-km (75-mile) ride over two days – 80km (50 miles) the first day and 40km (25 miles) the second. Adapt the procedure for rides of different lengths.

Before deciding to enter any ride, you should thoroughly acquaint yourself with the rules and try to go over at least part of the route (either by riding, driving or walking) to make sure that it is suitable for your horse.

The organizers of most rides send competitors a map with the route marked. Make sure you really study this, both to memorize the route and so that you know where the steep hills, woodland, watering places and so on, are located. Try to find landmarks – a particular church or small copse – to act as markers, so that you know how far you have travelled when you get to them. Then, knowing the maximum time allowance for the ride, you can plan the approximate time it should take you to reach these points.

Your arrival time at the given points will depend on the average time you want to achieve over the whole ride and this, in turn, will depend on what you know to be your horse's capability at that particular time. A long distance rider's aim should always be to finish the ride with no veterinary penalty points, rather than to do it in a faster time but be penalized because the horse was found to be in a bad condition at the checks.

Riding over part of the route is of great value to you and the horse. An ideal section to choose would be those paths that will mark the end of each day's ride, as your horse may then recognize them and realize he is nearing home, which will make him perk up and stride out more willingly.

Make a list of the equipment you are going to need. It should include a comprehensive first aid kit (for you and the horse), full grooming kit, rugs and stable bandages, feed and feed buckets – a haynet included – a spare set of shoes for the horse, towels (for rubbing him dry), tack and a complete set of spares, together with tack-cleaning equipment and a change of riding clothes for you. If you have someone who is going to assist you during the ride (some organizations insist on this), make sure he or she knows exactly what must be done at all times, where to meet you on the ride with a drink for the horse, and so on.

Settle your horse into his new surroundings in the way that you know suits him; that is, does he like to be led around to see where he is or would he rather be left quietly in the box, knowing you are close by? Make sure he is well-groomed and ready for the official inspection, which generally takes place the night before the ride proper.

The morning of the ride, give the horse his feed and make sure he has a good supply of water three hours before you are due to start. Leave him in peace to eat and digest his food, but leave yourself adequate time to groom and saddle him so that you arrive at the start, mounted, at the correct time without either of you being flustered. There is no need to ride him round to settle him down before the start; he needs every bit of his energy for the ride ahead, so use the first half an hour or so of the ride to settle him.

Although your helper will be meeting you with such things as sponges to wash out the horse's nostrils, riders should carry a few

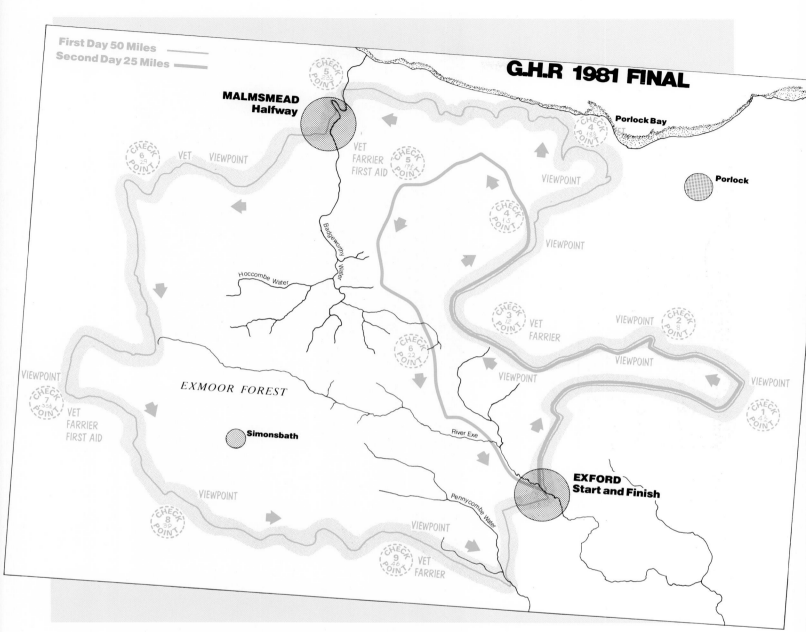

First Day 50 Miles
Second Day 25 Miles

G.H.R 1981 FINAL

MALMSMEAD
Halfway

CHECK POINT 5

Porlock Bay

CHECK POINT 4

Porlock

VET
FARRIER
FIRST AID

CHECK POINT 5

VIEWPOINT

VET VIEWPOINT

CHECK POINT 6

CHECK POINT 4

VIEWPOINT

Badgeworthy Water

VIEWPOINT

Hoccombe Water

CHECK POINT 3

VET
FARRIER

VIEWPOINT

CHECK POINT 2

VIEWPOINT

CHECK POINT 6

EXMOOR FOREST

VIEWPOINT

VIEWPOINT

VIEWPOINT

River Exe

Simonsbath

VIEWPOINT

CHECK POINT 7

VET
FARRIER
FIRST AID

CHECK POINT 1

VIEWPOINT

EXFORD
Start and Finish

Pennycombe Water

CHECK POINT 8

VIEWPOINT

VIEWPOINT

CHECK POINT 9

VET
FARRIER

emergency items with them. Principal among these are a hoof pick, a clean handkerchief and a bandage – the two latter items in case the horse should cut himself badly en route.

On the ride

Make sure your watch is synchronized with that of the starter. In most cases you will be given a maximum and minimum ride time, so many riders like to set their watch at twelve o'clock. Then they know throughout the ride how much time they have in hand.

If you have chosen to start with others, make sure their pace will suit you. Thereafter ride your own ride, following the plan you have made, but being flexible enough to change it – if, for example, you find you are falling behind time. Generally speaking, you will find your concentration is better when you are riding alone. Remember your horse needs the highest possible degree of concentra-

tion from you to control his pace and help him pick the best route. If you ride up behind others on the way and want to overtake them, warn them, asking which side they would like you to pass. Do not rush by at a fast canter which could easily upset their horses and only pass other riders when you really want to, not at a point when you mean to slow down. Do not go past and then settle at a pace exactly the same as their's, directly in front of them. Only pass, too, when you are sure it is safe for all of you.

Recognize when you should guide the horse and when it is better to let him pick his own way. On uneven ground, for example, he is usually best left alone, although this does not mean you should not keep alert and watch where he is going. If there is a choice between a hard road and a grass verge, be absolutely sure that the grass verge presents better going for him before guiding him on to it. It may be very soft, or rutted and stony, which will make

Above: Map showing the route for the final of the 1981 Golden Horseshoe Ride. This is a two-day ride, covering a total distance of 75 miles, with the longer distance scheduled for the first day. It takes riders through coastal and moorland scenery, providing plenty of viewpoints worthy of a halt in addition to the compulsory veterinary checkpoints.

SCENES FROM A LONG DISTANCE RIDE

Left: Riders and horses who meet the required standard in the Golden Horseshoe ride will receive one of these coveted rosettes. **Right:** A member of the British Horse Society's Long Distance Riding team kitted up for travelling. The team has competed in France. **Below left:** A rider splashes confidently through a ford during a ride. **Below right:** Competitors soon become accomplished at using a stethoscope. It is an essential item of equipment for long distance riders. **Bottom left:** A vet examines a horse's mouth during one of the veterinary checks. Pressing the gums is one way of checking a horse for dehydration; if it takes a long time for the capillaries to refill, dehydration is indicated. **Bottom right:** A general scene during a halt in a ride. Officials and helpers attend to horses and riders. **Opposite top:** Riders follow one another uphill. Leaning forward will help to relieve the strain on the horse's hindquarters. **Opposite bottom left:** An anti-sweat rug is thrown over a horse's back at the end of a ride, but note how the saddle has not yet been removed. If it is taken off straight away the rush of blood to the area could cause heat bumps to form. **Opposite bottom right:** Long distance riding can be a companionable sport at times!

it harder work. Always adjust the pace to suit the terrain, and never let him rush up and down hills, however much he may appear to want to. Going fast uphill will take a great deal out of him; going fast down them could put a great strain on the back muscles and jar the front legs.

Always be aware of your riding; you should always sit in the centre of the saddle, not leaning to one side or slouching over the withers, for example. If you dismount and run beside your horse at any stage, mount and dismount on the uphill side. It is not so far from the ground into the saddle, which means less energy expenditure, and less likelihood of shifting the saddle as you mount.

Providing it is not a very hot day, allow your horse to drink as much as he likes whenever the opportunity arises (this may mean by pre-arrangement with your helper, who will meet you at certain spots en route). If the day, and therefore the horse, is very hot, restrict this to about six to eight swallows, rest him for 10 minutes and then let him drink again if he is still thirsty. Never canter or gallop immediately after a drink, but ask your horse to walk briskly. This both helps to warm the water he has just drunk and also avoids any possibility of his muscles seizing up. Do not ignore watering stops; if you ask your horse to go the distance without a drink he will be severely dehydrated.

Aim to come into the half-way stop (where there will be a veterinary check) at a walk, having ridden at a slower pace for the last five or ten minutes. This will help the horse to dry off a little and his pulse and respiration rates will fall slightly, too. It will also mean that being asked to stand still will not be such a shock and it may help him to relax during the half-hour stop. Make his walk-in active, though; it gives a better impression if you arrive on a horse that looks alert, rather than one that is dragging his feet listlessly.

The examining vets will take the horse's P and R rates when he arrives and then again after 20 to 25 minutes. They will only allow him to continue if they are satisfied with the recovery rate. It is at this stage that your helper's job is essential. He or she should remove the bridle and slacken off the girth. A sponge-down with a damp sponge over the horse's head, neck and legs (particularly between them) will help to cool him, but keep the water well away from the loins and flanks. Rub the legs dry with a towel and inspect them for injury. If you are sure your saddle really fits well, so that your horse does not suffer from pressure bumps, then it can also be removed and the area underneath washed and dried and inspected for any signs of saddle sores. Put a rug on the horse, particularly on chilly days and examine his mouth to make sure the bit has not started to rub. Pick out his feet and examine the shoes. Let him have a few pickings of grass to help him to relax. Some horses cool down and benefit from being walked

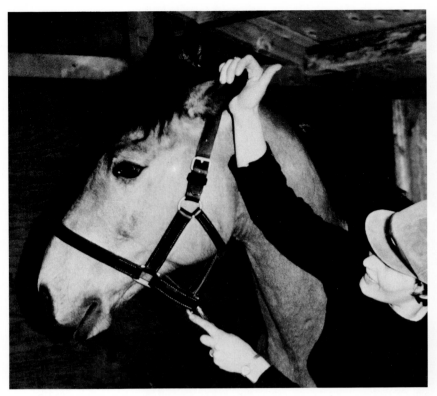

Above: At the end of a long, hard ride, you may find the horse becomes cold after he has been in the stable for some time. Like tired people, tired horses feel the cold more acutely. If he is trembling or hunched up, put an extra blanket on him and rub his ears vigorously; this helps to get the circulation working more efficiently. Remember that even if a horse breaks out in a cold sweat, it is important to get him warm before worrying about drying him off.

around gently; others will rest better if kept quiet and allowed to graze.

The bit should be washed over and changed, if necessary. The reins and the underside of the saddle (if removed) should also be washed if they have become very sweaty. Before you are due to start again, the horse can have a fairly long drink, to which you can add a good measure of salt, providing he is used to drinking salted water. As the rider, you should also take the opportunity during this half an hour to have a breather and recover your resources – which is why it is important to have a reliable helper. Make sure to have something to drink yourself.

The remainder of the day's ride follows the same pattern, though you must make allowance for the fact that both you and your horse will be getting more tired all the time. Thus, the better the time you can achieve in the morning – without over-doing it – the more relaxed you can be in the afternoon. Again, finish the ride at a walk.

After the ride

At the end of the day, the procedure is similar to that at the half-way halt, but it needs to be considerably more thorough. It is very important, since it can make a great difference to the horse's condition and therefore his ability and attitude to continue the following morning. The bridle can be changed for a headcollar, but now it is wise not to loosen the girth for about 15 minutes after dismounting, and to remove the saddle only about another 15 to 30 minutes after that. During this time, the horse should be walked around gently to allow his

muscles to unwind gradually; if he were to be put straight in the stable, he would undoubtedly stiffen up. Put a sweat rug, or the equivalent, on him as soon as you dismount at the end of the ride. Offer him a drink of water – no more than half a bucketful – and let him have a few mouthfuls of grass if he wants them, while he is being walked around. The examining vets will be checking his P and R rates again.

The horse should be walked around for about an hour, being offered smallish drinks of water at, say, quarter-hour intervals, before he is put in his box. Brush the mud off his legs, if it is dried; sponge it off otherwise. Then rub the legs dry with straw and put on some warm stable bandages to help reduce any strain. Look him over for any cuts or lacerations and treat them accordingly (observing the ride regulations on medications). Give him a small feed – ideally a warm mash which is easily digested – and a small hay net. His digestion will not be up to a big feed yet; give him his normal feed later in the evening after he has had several hours' rest.

Before the evening feed, groom him thoroughly in preparation for the next morning. Rug him up, putting on as many rugs as necessary to keep him warm. Return to the stable after he has finished his last feed to make sure he is comfortable. If you have any worries, consult the ride vet.

The procedure before the start of the ride the next morning is the same as the day before; the most important point is to ensure he has his feed three hours before he is due to start. Ride with the same care and consideration as yesterday and you should arrive at the finish, tired, but pleased with your horse's performance.

Remember that your horse will be extremely tired at the end of the ride, so, even if the event is over by lunchtime, you should not expect him to travel home until the following day. A very hard ride, followed by a long box journey the same day, is asking too much of any horse.

As with all sports which demand long months of training and preparation to reach a high level of fitness, the horse needs careful attention in the weeks, and even months, that follow. If you aim to compete in more rides before giving your horse a complete rest, make sure he has adequate time to recover between them. It will be a good month before he can compete in another long ride of 120km to 160km (75 miles to 100 miles). During this period, he should be led out in hand for the first few days and thereafter carefully ridden to maintain his level of fitness and to keep him alert and interested, without tiring him. When you have ridden your last ride for the season, you must let the horse down gradually, giving him ever-decreasing periods of exercise and corn each day. You will be able to see when the muscle begins to turn to fat and you should know him well enough to realize he is ready to be turned out for a complete break.

THE LONG DISTANCE HORSE'S YEAR

The usual season for long distance rides is from spring to early autumn. Your season could consist of two 160km (100-mile) rides and, if your horse is in prime condition and fitness, another two 80km (50-mile) rides at the maximum. Obviously such a decision will be based on personal preference and what you consider to be your horse's capabilities. The schedule below allows for a horse to enter one 160km and one 80km ride, giving him two months' complete rest in the year.

Mid-winter: Bring horse in from grass. Start six-day week exercise routine, consisting only of walking and trotting.

Late winter: Introduce cantering into exercise routine and begin going for longer rides.

Early spring: Go for longer, slower-paced rides and shorter, faster rides for two-month period. Enter two qualifying rides and perhaps a short pleasure ride.

Late spring: Cut down the length of rides, but keep horse alert and interested and maintain his condition.

Early summer: First 120km (75-mile) ride over two days. Following this, reduce exercise and feeding rations gradually and then turn out for complete rest for three weeks.

Midsummer: Bring up and begin conditioning programme again.

Early autumn: Enter competitive 80km (50-mile) ride.

End autumn-mid-winter: Gradually decrease work and feed; complete rest for your horse at grass.

CHAPTER EIGHT

POLO

POLO IS A tough, high-spirited, highly skilled and extremely fast sport – in fact, it is the fastest team game in the world. Just when and where it was first played is not wholly certain; we know that a version of the game was being played in ancient Persia some 2,500 years ago, but how closely this resembled the modern game is open to conjecture.

Polo as it is known today was first introduced to the western world from India by cavalry officers in the middle of the nineteenth century. These officers had seen versions of the game played on tough little native Indian ponies, with the local village streets acting as the playing grounds. Such rules as there were varied from place to place, as did the number of players – this, it seems, largely depending on how many people wanted to join in. Nevertheless, the officers realized the potential value of the game, both as a relaxation from their duties and as a valuable means of training horses and young officers. Hence, they began to play it among themselves, bringing it back to Britain around the end of the 1860s.

From there the game quickly spread to the Continent and across the Atlantic to the USA, where today it has an impressive following. Gradually the rules became ordered and standardized internationally. In the first matches, the rules stated that the game should be played on ponies standing no higher than 13.3hh (although those used were often considerably smaller). Soon a new height limit of 14.2hh was imposed, until it was realized that even this was impractical and the restriction was abolished altogether. Nowadays most people ride 'ponies' of about 15hh–15.2hh and this is generally thought to be the ideal height.

Polo is now played world-wide from Australia, New Zealand, Hong Kong, Singapore and Malaysia to India, Pakistan, South Africa, Nigeria, Malta and Cyprus, the USA, Argentina, Jamaica and Barbados. It has a following, too, in France and Germany, as well as in Britain. The game most common to all these countries is regulation or standard polo, but there are other recognized modifications of the game, of which paddock and arena polo are probably among the most widely played. These versions have only three players

Left: Four polo players gallop beside each other in perfect formation, but they have clearly overtaken the action! A polo player has to be a 'natural' horseman, able to ride without thinking about it so that he can concentrate all his attention on the game.
Above: A 17th-century version of polo played in provincial Mughal. It was not until the 19th century that the game was discovered by the western world.

Above: Polo is among the oldest of equestrian sports, and India was one of its early strongholds. This print, dating from 1889, shows natives of North Kashmir, taking on an army team. Note the old-fashioned shape of the sticks.
Right: Another print dating from the late 19th century shows a fiercely contested game in India. Even then, the players realized the necessity of bandaging their ponies' legs. **Below:** A polo game against a romantic setting at the White Grass Ranch in Jackson, USA. The game crossed the Atlantic to America towards the end of the 19th century and today it is the home of many of the sport's top players.

per team (as opposed to four in regulation polo) and are played in a considerably smaller area. Arena polo is often played in an indoor stadium or school and is popular in the USA.

Such modifications of polo are generally ridden at a rather less furious pace and often serve as an introduction to regulation polo for many riders. Another way in which young riders are finding their way into the sport is through the Pony Club. Many branches intersperse games of paddock polo with rallies and other events, and there is also a recognized game of Pony Club polo. The rules for paddock and Pony Club polo are based on the official rules.

The game

The game of polo varies very slightly depending on whether you are concerned with paddock or arena polo (which may be played indoors or out), Pony Club polo or regulation outdoor (standard) polo. Furthermore, different countries have their own regional modifications in rules and play. Having said this, however, all the variations are very slight and by and large, general principles are similar whatever game you are playing.

In paddock or arena polo, as mentioned, there are only three players a side; in other polo games there are four. Numbers one and two are the attacking players or the forwards; number three – the half-back – is described as the pivot of the team in that he is both attacking and defensive, while number four, known generally as the back, is the principal defensive player. (When there are only three players, numbers one and two are combined.) Each player holds a specially designed mallet or stick, with which he hits the ball. It has a long cane shaft and a cigar-shaped head. The ball in standard polo is made of willow or bamboo root and is about 8cm (3¼in) in diameter. In paddock and arena polo, the ball is a little larger and softer, being made either of leather (inflated like a football) or plastic. The size of the playing area varies from 279m (300yds) long by 146m (160yds) for standard polo, to an area about a third of this size for arena polo. For standard polo the width is increased to 183m (200yds) if there are no marking boards bounding the area.

In all kinds of polo, the object of the game is to score goals and the winning team will be the one with the greatest number of goals to their credit at the end of the match. Goals are scored by players hitting the ball through the goal posts, which are situated at either end of the playing area in the centre of the short sides of the pitch. A match is divided into periods of play known as chukkas. The number and length of chukkas depends on the type of polo and the importance of the match. As examples, tournaments of topclass standard polo are usually divided into six chukkas of 10 or seven-and-a-half minutes each, while paddock or Pony Club polo may comprise only two chukkas of six minutes each. Chukkas are separated by intervals of three to five minutes.

(The actual time of a chukka may be longer than that specified for the match, as the clock is stopped each time a foul is committed until play resumes.) Play is divided into these comparatively short spells because of the extremely fast pace at which polo is conducted. It would be inhuman to ask a horse to continue for longer without a break – in big matches a player will ride two or three ponies, alternating them between chukkas.

Players line up in formation at the start of a game and the referee or umpire throws the ball in between the lines. The play is mainly conducted up and down the field (between the goal posts) and the players mark each other whilst always attempting to move the ball in the direction of their scoring goal. Player number one will generally aim to be nearest to the goal posts through which his team will score, with the other players spread down the field so that number four stays closest to the end he is defending. Number one therefore plays opposite the other team's number four, number two against their number three and so on.

The ball is passed between players towards the opposing goal, while the other team tries constantly to intercept it. When a goal is scored, the teams change ends and play begins again. If a ball goes over the side lines, the teams line up as for the opening of play 4.5m (5yds) from the side and the umpire throws it between them again. If the attacking side hit the ball across the back line without scoring a goal, the defending side hit it back into play from that position. If the defending side hit the ball across the back line, the attacking side are given a free hit from a prescribed distance away from their goal. If the ball is still in play at the end of a chukka, it is thrown in to the teams who still line up in the usual way, but the ball is thrown towards the side where it had been when play stopped.

Riding-off and right of way

Players attempt to intercept the line of the ball or stop a member of the opposition getting it by riding-off their opponents, leaning against them and by knocking or hooking sticks. Riding-off means riding alongside an opponent, using your pony to push his off the line of the ball, whilst hooking an opponent's stick is done by blocking the line of his swing as he nears the lowest point, thus catching his stick before it reaches the ball. A string of regulations surround these and other manoeuvres, all designed to safeguard the players and their

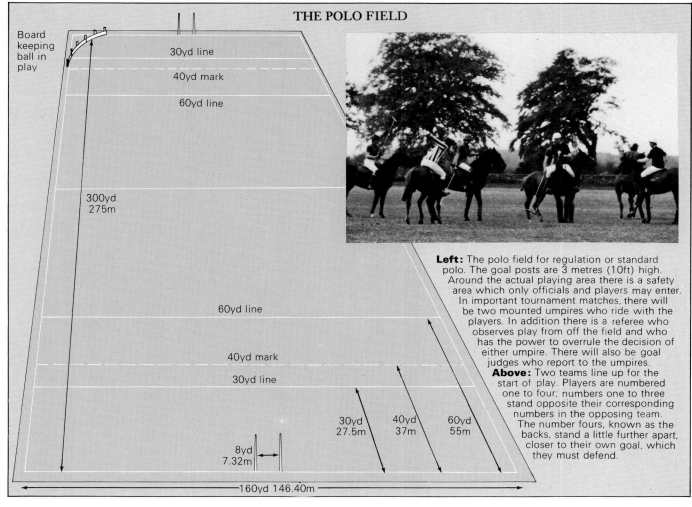

THE POLO FIELD

Board keeping ball in play

30yd line
40yd mark
60yd line

300yd 275m

60yd line

40yd mark

30yd line

30yd 27.5m 40yd 37m 60yd 55m

8yd 7.32m

160yd 146.40m

Left: The polo field for regulation or standard polo. The goal posts are 3 metres (10ft) high. Around the actual playing area there is a safety area which only officials and players may enter. In important tournament matches, there will be two mounted umpires who ride with the players. In addition there is a referee who observes play from off the field and who has the power to overrule the decision of either umpire. There will also be goal judges who report to the umpires.

Above: Two teams line up for the start of play. Players are numbered one to four; numbers one to three stand opposite their corresponding numbers in the opposing team. The number fours, known as the backs, stand a little further apart, closer to their own goal, which they must defend.

mounts. Any infringement will lead to a foul being declared against and a penalty awarded to the opposition. Penalties generally take the form of a free hit at goal taken from a designated place down the field, the distance depending on the severity of the foul.

The rules surrounding right of way are the most important to understand fully, for infringement of these generally accounts for the greatest number of fouls in a match. The official rules go into the various possibilities in some detail, but, in essence, the player who is following the exact line of the ball – that is, the direction in which it is travelling – so it will be on his off-side, or is at the smallest angle to that line, has the right of way. No other players may cross this line if by so doing there would be a risk of collision, unless the player with the right of way were to check his speed, although they can attempt to ride off that player. There are exceptions – for instance, when two players coming from directly opposite directions will have equal right of way – so players must go deeper into this aspect before entering the game.

Probably the most important overall point to remember about playing polo – whatever the type – is that it is a team game, in which players must continually support one another and play in co-ordination. Experienced players will have team tactics and strategies worked out; less experienced players do better to adopt a policy of always backing up other team members, so that if someone misses the ball, there is a member of his or her team not far behind to take over play.

Before you begin

Before you start to play polo, you must know the procedure and rules of the game, you must have a suitable mount and you must have at least a rudimentary skill in the various strokes used to hit the ball. In addition, you should attend several games of polo before playing yourself, and watch these closely, preferably in the company of an expert who can explain what is happening as the game progresses.

There are four basic strokes used in polo – the off-side forehander, the off-side backhander, the near-side forehander and the near-side backhander. A beginner need only concern himself with these initially, although, as he becomes more experienced, he will learn a number of variations and refinements, which will obviously enhance his skill. A player must learn how to make these strokes – that is the correct basic swing of the stick in each case – before he attempts them from horseback. If he does not, the chances of him avoiding hitting and injuring his mount are minimal.

The strokes can be learnt and practised sitting astride a wooden horse with a saddle strapped to it; ideally this should be approximately the same height from the ground as the back of the horse you intend to ride. If you belong to a club, you may be able to use their 'polo pit'. This consists of a wooden horse with a saddle attached, situated in a recessed place with sloping floors leading down to it. Thus the ball rolls back after you have hit it.

You will learn the basic swings before you attempt to hit a ball, but even before this, you must learn how to hold the stick, the rest position (in which you hold the stick when not actually striking the ball during play) and the 'brace', which is the position you must adopt in the saddle when aiming to hit the ball. Note that there are two recognized grips of the stick – 'normal' for the off-side forehander and the near-side backhander and 'reverse' for the near-side forehander and the off-side backhander. In both cases, the thong is looped around the thumb and then taken across the back of the hand. Note, too, that the stick should be held in the right hand. Left-handed players should make every effort to play polo right-handed or they will be at odds with all the other players.

Although, as mentioned above, you will learn the basics of each swing before attempting to hit the ball, bear in mind that it is the centre of the stick head that strikes the ball, not the end. This means you must turn your wrist outwards as you make the swing. Players generally begin by learning the off-side forehander; not only is it the easiest stroke to master, it accounts for about three-quarters of the strokes in most polo games. All strokes at the practice stage should be started from the rest position, but tighten your grip before beginning the stroke.

Once you feel reasonably confident about being able to swing the stick correctly in a smooth, even arc in all the strokes, you can try hitting the ball. The ball must be positioned in relation to your pony for all the strokes. Your shoulder, arm and stick should be in a straight line as you hit the ball and you should be leaning out from your pony's side so that you come directly above it.

As in all stick or racquet and ball games, the essence of making a good hit is to keep your eye fixed on the ball. This you can do only by keeping your head well down. There is often a temptation, too, to try to hit the ball very hard. This will only have the effect of wearing you out and quite possibly straining your muscles, too. It is an even, well-timed swing that will carry the ball well forward, not a clumsy attempt to give it a good, hard whack.

Start practising the strokes and hitting the ball from horseback only when you are really confident of your ability – that is, sure that you will not hit your mount. As a novice player, you should also try to make your first strokes mounted from astride an experienced polo pony. If this is not possible and the two of you are learning together, follow the procedure outlined on page 197 for getting a pony used to the stick before trying to hit a ball.

For all strokes, adopt the brace position in the saddle (see page 193). Move the left hand slightly forward as you make each stroke to avoid jerking your pony in the mouth. **Top to bottom:. The off-side backhander 1.** Shift the grip to reverse (see page 190). **2.** Move your right arm forward so the stick lies almost parallel with the pony's back over your left shoulder. **3.** Swing the stick in a backwards arc, rotating your shoulders from front to back. Keep watching the ball. **4.** Continue to rotate your shoulders after hitting the ball, until they are almost in line with the pony's spine.

The off-side forehander 1. Swing the stick backwards, by turning your right shoulder back so that it points towards the pony's tail. **2.** Turn your wrist outwards and pause for a moment at the top of the swing to help you time the stroke correctly. Your left shoulder should be pointing forwards and you should be leaning to the right. **3.** Keep your head still, looking down at the ball, and bring your right shoulder forwards, keeping your arm straight as you hit the ball. **4.** Let the stick swing forward to follow the stroke through.

The near-side backhander 1. Tighten your grip on the stick and raise your hand to the right. **2.** Begin to turn your body to the left, bringing the stick forward. **3.** Swing the stick in a backward arc by rotating your shoulders. Keep looking at the ball and lean to the left. **4.** Follow through by continuing to rotate your shoulders and bringing your hand up level with your shoulder.

The near-side forehander 1. Shift your grip to reverse and begin to take your stick to the left side. **2.** Take your arm right back, turning your body from the hips. **3.** Swing the stick in a forward arc, keeping your hips still. **4.** Allow the stick to follow through, so that you end up leaning well forward in the saddle.

THE FOUR BASIC STROKES

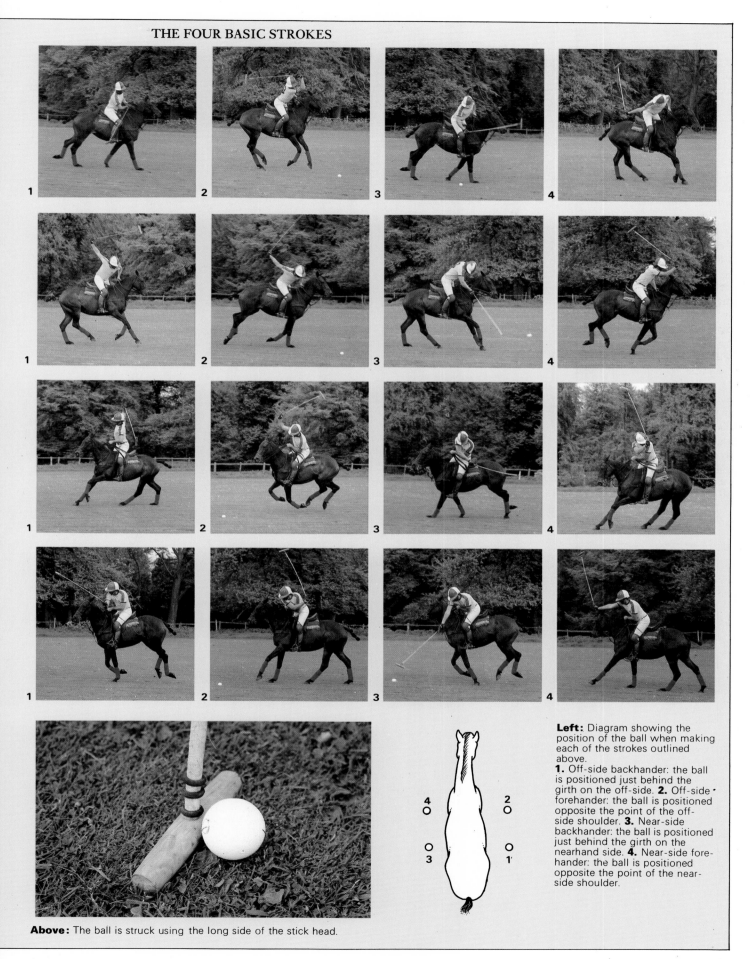

Left: Diagram showing the position of the ball when making each of the strokes outlined above.
1. Off-side backhander: the ball is positioned just behind the girth on the off-side. **2.** Off-side forehander: the ball is positioned opposite the point of the off-side shoulder. **3.** Near-side backhander: the ball is positioned just behind the girth on the nearhand side. **4.** Near-side forehander: the ball is positioned opposite the point of the near-side shoulder.

Above: The ball is struck using the long side of the stick head.

HOW TO HOLD THE STICK

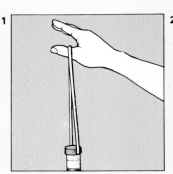

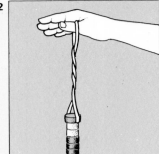

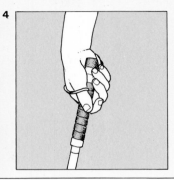

Normal grip
1. Slip your thumb through the sling.
2. Rotate the stick so that the sling twists.
3. Pass the sling over the back of the hand.
4. Grip the handle of the stick by wrapping your fingers around it. The end of the handle should rest against the fleshy part of the hand.

The **reverse grip** is used for the near-side forehand shot and the off-side backhand shot. Move your hand slightly round the handle of the stick in an anti-clockwise direction, so that your thumb points down the handle.

The picture on the **right** clearly shows how the sling is looped over the back of the hand, not passed through it. If the sling encircles your wrist it is extremely difficult to disentangle your hand from the stick in the event of a fall and this can be very dangerous.

The polo pony

The polo mount is always known as a pony, even though in many instances he will stand higher than 14.2hh. The term pony stems from the time when the official rules imposed a height restriction of no more than 14.2hh for all horses to be ridden in polo matches.

The type and size of mount you will be looking for will depend very largely on the type or class of polo you intend to follow and also, up to a point, in which country you are going to play. Most polo-playing countries produce a 'polo pony' of some sort and, by and large, for an average-standard game (i.e. not high-level tournament play) this is usually the best to buy, as it is likely to be best suited to the prevailing conditions.

If your involvement with polo is to be playing Pony Club polo with other Pony Club members, an ordinary pony – preferably one that excels at mounted games – is ideal. His participation in the latter will have developed his agility and his ability to stop and start quickly and turn tightly. In addition, he is attentive to you so that he responds quickly to your commands. All he will need, therefore, is a little additional training to get him used to the stick swinging by his side and to make him familiar with the most common techniques.

It may be, however, that you want to look for a pony just for polo. Although there are certain guidelines you can follow, your choice will again largely be governed by the type of polo and your experience and standard as a player, as well as by how much you can afford. If you are a complete beginner, it is best to start playing on an experienced polo pony – one who can teach you a thing or two about the

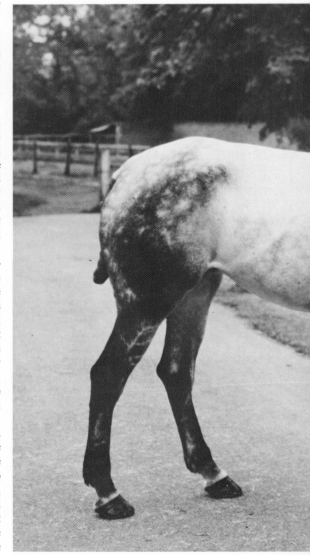

game. Ask the advice of an experienced polo player and a good judge of horseflesh before making your choice. A trained polo pony will be at least six years old (his training could not have been completed before this time), ideally between 15hh and 15.2hh. He should be fast, with a smooth, low-galloping action, able to stop instantly from a gallop on command, willing to move off into a fast canter from a halt and with the ability to turn very tightly whilst moving fast. In addition he should be familiar with the 'riding-off' technique and leaning against other horses whilst moving at a gallop, as well as being able to hold a straight line to the ball at whatever pace he is moving. A polo pony will be at his prime between eight and 10 years old and a good one of this age will be extremely expensive. One that is a little older, perhaps 12, would still have a good few years' playing in him (particularly in slower matches), would be more reasonably priced and could still teach you a great deal about the game.

If you have some experience of the game, you may prefer to buy a pony that appears to have the potential to become a good polo mount and train it yourself. For top-class polo,

it is generally considered almost essential to ride a Thoroughbred, as this is the breed that possesses the necessary turn of speed. Many people look for ex-racehorses – those that have been consistently beaten on the race track by faster horses, not those that have been rejected from racing because of persistent leg trouble. Providing a racehorse is sound (have him very carefully checked by a vet), not too big and has not been ruined during his racing career by having too much asked of him, he could be made into a superb polo pony by someone who knew how. And as a reject from one sport, he may be comparatively inexpensive.

As mentioned above, the ideal height for a polo pony is about 15hh to 15.2hh. A taller pony than this will not be so agile and will not maintain the desirable pony characteristics, such as a smooth but not too long galloping stride. The higher he is, too, the harder you will find it to hit the ball as you will have further to lean down. If you are planning to train your own pony, you could look for a horse of about five years old; below this age he will not yet be physically mature enough to be subjected to the rigours of training for polo.

Below: Three pictures of polo ponies. To the untutored eye these ponies may appear rather thin, but they are just so fit that there is not a bit of extra flesh on them. Another factor about polo ponies well demonstrated here is that they often appear to be rather ewe-necked. This is because of the way they are ridden and the fact that they are not asked to flex as much as horses schooled in other disciplines. All the ponies have been well posed for the camera with the legs furthest away held 'inside' so that all legs can be clearly seen. The grey pony is from Argentina; home of the most famous polo ponies in the world.

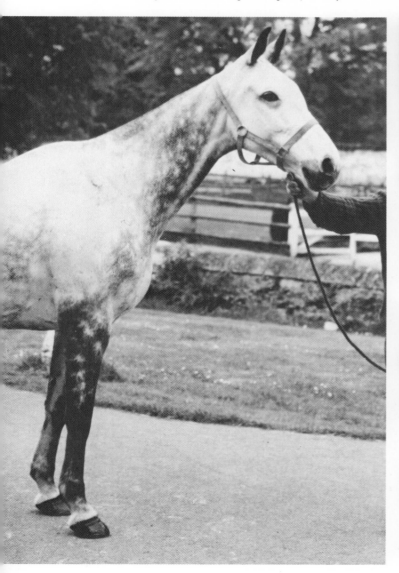

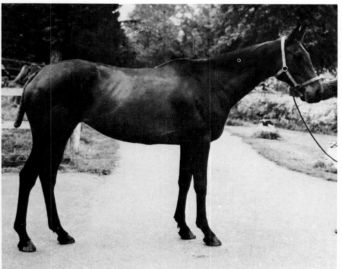

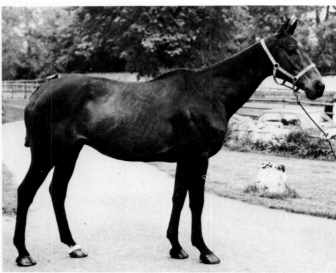

The conformation you would look for in a good, or potentially promising, polo pony is similar to that of an eventer – that is, an athletic appearance; not too long in the back; rounded, muscular hindquarters; well-rounded ribs; good depth of girth; sloping shoulders; shortish, well-proportioned neck; pleasing head with a kind eye; clean legs with a long, upright humerus (top part of the foreleg), a low-down stifle; well-formed hocks; short cannon bones and sloping pasterns. The feet must be well and evenly shaped – the right size for the horse. He should look well able to carry your weight, but not too clumsy or cumbersome.

Soundness is of paramount importance, but if you are buying an experienced polo pony, you will be very lucky to find one with perfectly clean legs. Take professional advice to ensure that any blemishes you see or feel on the legs will not affect the pony's action or performance.

Temperamentally, you want an animal that is intelligent, eager and bold, but calm in character and ever-willing. Above all, he must be obedient.

Argentinian ponies are almost universally considered to be the best polo ponies in the world. Polo was first played in Argentina as a means of relaxation and friendly rivalry among the cowboys and ranch hands. So well-suited to the game did the handy little cow ponies prove to be, that astute players began to breed the ponies more selectively, by crossing them with imported Thoroughbreds. The offspring were then trained in the techniques of polo-playing, and they are now widely exported to the polo-playing countries of the world. Their popularity can be judged by the fact that international players are prepared to pay extremely high prices to procure them.

Training the polo pony

Training a pony to participate in top-class tournament polo is a highly skilled and exacting task. Generally, it is a role reserved for an expert trainer, who is himself an experienced polo player. Most riders, however, are content to achieve a somewhat lesser standard, at least until they themselves are more knowledgeable about the game. With this aim, it is quite possible to train your pony to such a level that the pair of you can participate in a friendly polo match and acquit yourselves with honour.

Before any specialized training in the techniques required during a polo match can take place, you should give your pony some elementary dressage training. He should move forward freely at all paces, with his hindlegs well beneath him, lengthening and shortening strides as you give him the appropriate aids. He should be instantly obedient to your leg aids, moving away from your leg (as in leg yielding) when you ask him to and he should be well-balanced and supple throughout all his movements. You should have practised

some two-track or lateral work and be confident that your pony can strike off on either leg – according to the aids you give – at a canter, so that he can also execute a smooth counter canter. He should also be able to rein back correctly in two-time. In other words, he should be a thoroughly pleasant ride – well-mannered, well-balanced and obedient, never fighting you for his head or resisting your requests.

The most important skills a polo pony must learn are to stop abruptly from any pace, turn very tightly, accelerate quickly (the greatest extreme of this being to move into a gallop from a halt) and to decelerate with equal ease and quickness, to hold a straight line to the ball, to effect flying changes of leg at the canter and to 'ride-off' opponents. In addition, he must be thoroughly used to a polo stick being swung by his side, so that this neither makes him alter his stride or change his course of direction.

All the techniques outlined above have to be carried out during a game by the rider holding both reins in one hand – the left. It is wise, however, to teach the pony the manoeuvres with the reins in both hands, changing to hold them in just one hand only when you are completely satisfied that he understands what it is you are asking of him, and that you are sufficiently competent to guide him. It is very important that you pay constant attention to the way you are riding, particularly to your rein hand. If the pony starts to associate swings taken at the ball with a jerk in the mouth, he will soon shy away from the ball as you ride him towards it. Similarly, if a tight turn or an abrupt stop mean a sharp bang on the teeth, he will quickly become unwilling to co-operate.

Try to get into the habit of riding your pony during training sessions on a light contact with the mouth, for this is how you should

Below: The rider must adopt the brace position before he makes a stroke at the ball. It gives him a firm basis in the saddle; if you attempted to hit the ball from an ordinary riding position your body would give you no support and as a result your stroke would be less forceful. To adopt the brace position, stand up in your stirrup irons and grip the sides of the saddle with your knees and thighs. Practise turning to the left and right from your hips, in preparation for the strokes.

Opposite below: HRH Prince Charles is an avid supporter of the game of polo and a highly proficient player. Here he is seen preparing his mount for a quick about turn to the left. Notice how the pony's back legs appear to be immobilized; the pony will pivot round on the near hind, making a 180° turn.

STOPPING AND TURNING

Left, above: Stopping quickly from a gallop is an important part of a polo pony's technique, but it is extremely difficult — considerably more so than stopping from a canter. A pony can be trained to stop in one stride from a canter, but few can achieve this from a gallop. Although the abrupt halt pictured here would be frowned upon in a dressage arena, the pony does stop with his hocks well beneath him, ready to obey his rider's next command. **Left:** Turning quickly at a moment's notice is another important movement in the polo pony's repertoire. In this quick turn to the left, note how the pony's head is inclined to the right; his weight is thus thrown on to his left shoulder and in order to maintain his balance he must move to the left. As you can see he virtually pivots on his inside hind leg and is ready to move off at a gallop as soon as he has made the turn.

control him in a game. At the same time, you do not want him to come off the bit so that he starts to lean on the forehead and no longer engages his hindlegs beneath him. Practise cantering circles, gradually lightening your contact and enlarging the circle but still maintaining the rhythm and evenness of the pace.

Teaching a pony to stop abruptly from any pace begins by teaching him to stop instantly and correctly at a walk. As it will help if your pony responds to changes of your body weight too, rather than just to your hand and leg aids, put a neckstrap round his neck and pull on this, shifting your weight backward slightly. At the same time, use your legs to drive him up to the bit and your other hand to resist the forward movement. Get into the habit, too, of always saying 'Whoa' when you ask for a halt. A pony will quickly learn to respond to his rider's voice and will react to this as much as to the other aids.

When you are satisfied that your pony is stopping abruptly, but smoothly, from a walk, with his hindlegs well beneath him, ask him to do the same from a gentle, controlled trot. Urge him forward with your legs, then resist with the reins, pull gently on the neck strap and shift your weight slightly back in the saddle. Remember that the halt should be absolutely smooth — no throwing about of the head in discomfort or anxiety. Having achieved this, do the same from a gentle canter; your ultimate aim is to get him to stop instantly from a gallop, but this stage of training should not be rushed. Take it steadily, praising him when he stops correctly, and never asking him to halt from a faster pace until you are sure he is confident — and correct — at the slower paces.

THE FLYING CHANGE OF LEG

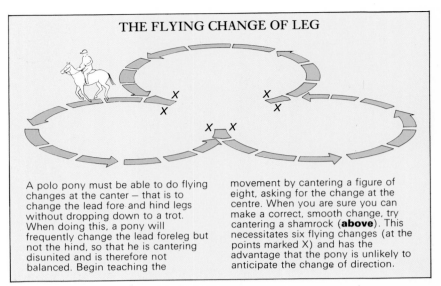

A polo pony must be able to do flying changes at the canter — that is to change the lead fore and hind legs without dropping down to a trot. When doing this, a pony will frequently change the lead foreleg but not the hind, so that he is cantering disunited and is therefore not balanced. Begin teaching the movement by cantering a figure of eight, asking for the change at the centre. When you are sure you can make a correct, smooth change, try cantering a shamrock (**above**). This necessitates six flying changes (at the points marked X) and has the advantage that the pony is unlikely to anticipate the change of direction.

strongly with your legs and then resist gently once or twice with your hands. To make the turn, use your outside leg very strongly behind the girth, and support this with your inside leg at the girth. Lean inward very slightly, in the direction of the turn.

When asking your pony to turn quickly at a canter, he should always come out of the turn with the inside leg leading. Thus if you are cantering with the off-fore leading and want to do a tight turn to the left, the pony must first do a flying change of leg (see left). If he comes out of the turn with the off-fore leading (or with the near-fore leading but cantering disunited) he will be thrown off balance.

Neck-reining

Although you will train your pony to do tight turns using both hands on the reins, in a polo game, as already mentioned, you must hold the reins in your left hand only. For this reason, you must teach your pony to respond to an indirect rein aid, that is to turn left or right when you apply pressure to the opposite side of his neck. This is known as neck-reining.

Teach your pony to neck rein whilst holding the reins in both hands. To turn to the left, move the right hand slightly forward and brush the rein against the pony's neck, just in front of the withers. At the same time, apply strong pressure evenly with your legs at the girth, and very slightly move your weight over his left shoulder. This helps to throw the pony's weight in the direction of the turn. At this stage, support the action with your left rein, so as to guide him round the bend. Practise turning to the left and right with these aids at all paces using both hands before progressing to holding the reins in your left hand only. When you are holding the reins in your left hand, ask for a left turn by bringing your hand slightly backwards and to the left (that is towards your left thigh). The pressure exerted

Tight turns

The training for teaching a mounted games pony to execute tight turns (see p. 18) can be used to some extent in the training of a polo pony. Practising cantering fairly tight figures-of-eight will help to educate your pony in turning tightly, too. It is generally desirable that the pony should turn on his haunches, that is by pivoting on one or other hind leg. Start by doing this at a halt and turning through 90 degrees, then 180 degrees, practising to left and right. The pony should not take a step backwards or throw his quarters out to the opposite side during the turn. Gradually you can begin to ask him to make such a turn from a walk and then a gentle canter.

In order to ensure that the turn is made on the haunches rather than on the forehand, it is very important to collect your pony together before asking him to make the turn. Thus his hindlegs will be well beneath him and his body will be compressed. Sit well down and slightly back in the saddle, push forward

Right: This rider is demonstrating how to hold the reins in just one hand — something all polo players must be able to do. He is using double reins and separates them in their pairs. The top reins are held between the thumb and forefinger and the bottom pair between the fore and middle fingers.

on the mouth in this way helps to ensure that the pony is back on his hocks, so that he can pivot round his inside hind leg. To turn to the right, take your left hand backwards and to the right.

Change of paces

Quick acceleration and deceleration is generally quite easy to bring about in a pony that has been taught to lengthen and shorten his stride and is obedient to his rider's leg aids. Begin by asking for an active trot from a walk, then ask for a canter from a walk. Next ask for a canter from a halt; you may find it helps if you take a few steps backwards first, as, correctly done, this helps to bring the hocks right underneath the pony, thereby putting him in the best position for forward propulsion. Remember that these upward transitions should be completely smooth – that the pony should strike off into a balanced and even canter without throwing his head up in the air or flattening his back. The back should be gently arched and rounded, not hollow or flat. You will only achieve a prompt, smooth response if the pony is totally alert and listening to you. Gradually increase the speed of the pace from the halt, so he can strike off into a fast canter or gallop.

Practise smooth and prompt deceleration, first by coming from a gallop down to a slow canter and then straight to a walk. Again, there should be no noticeable jerkiness in the pony's bearing or stride. Remember that it is more important always to achieve a smooth result, than a very prompt one. It is easier to work on sharpening the response once the principle has been instilled.

Get into the habit of shifting your weight slightly in the saddle to indicate acceleration (lean forward) and deceleration (sit down deep in the saddle and lean very slightly backwards). Your pony will soon learn the implications of your movement and will be more prepared to respond to the specific aid when you give it.

Working with the ball

To train your pony to hold a straight line to the ball, place some balls at random spots around the field and ride at each one with the intention of passing close by one or other (designated) side. Do so at a fast canter, with the reins in your left hand only. This exercise will also help you in placing your pony correctly for you to hit the ball. As you ride past the ball, try standing up in the brace position and leaning over slightly to the left or right, according to which side of the ball you have elected to ride. Many polo ponies become so adept at this movement that they will often spot the ball before their riders do and will immediately gallop towards it, taking the rider unawares. Remember that if you fall off in a game, play does not have to stop to allow you to remount.

A polo pony must be taught to neck-rein – that is to turn to the left or right when pressure is brought to bear on his neck, rather than by direct pressure from the bit on that side of his mouth. **Top left:** The rider is turning to the right. He takes his rein hand to the right, and uses his left leg strongly against the pony's side. His right leg is more passive resting on the girth. He puts slightly more pressure on his right seat bone so as to bring the pony's weight back on to his hocks and to encourage him to pivot on his off-side hind leg. **Top right:** Neck-reining to the left, reversing the aids for the right-hand neck-rein. **Above:** Riders group together round the goal posts during a match. **Left:** When not in use the stick is held in the 'rest' position. These riders are moving at speed; at a slower pace they would hold the stick upright, letting their hands rest easily on their knees.

A flying change of leg at the canter means that the horse changes both the front and hind lead legs whilst maintaining the rhythm of the pace – that is without dropping back to a trot to make the change. It is very important that he changes both legs; it is not an uncommon sight to see an inexperienced horse (or a horse with an inexperienced rider on board) change just the lead foreleg when asked to do a flying change, resulting in a disunited canter.

A rider asks a horse to change legs at the canter by applying the aids for the new lead sharply and precisely. The aids are the same as those you would normally apply when asking your pony to strike off into a canter (from a trot) on a given lead. As he will make the change at the end of a complete stride (i.e. after the third beat of the canter, it being a pace in three-time), it will help if you give him the aid just before this. This should be just after he has touched down with the diagonal. As you see the lead shoulder come forward, therefore, prepare to give the aid, and then give it immediately after the next step, which will be that taken by the diagonal.

Progress towards executing flying changes by beginning with a simple change (i.e. trotting for a few strides before striking off on the opposite leg) asked for in the centre of a figure-of-eight. Keep decreasing the number of trotting strides, until you are trotting for no more than two paces. Then ask for a change without dropping back to a trot. Another way is to canter in a straight line on one lead, bring the pony back to a walk from the canter and strike off on the other leg after a few strides. Again, gradually reduce the number of steps taken at a walk until you are asking for a flying change.

Include regular practice in flying changes in your schooling sessions, but vary the way you introduce it so that your pony does not always anticipate the movement. If, for example, you always practise flying changes by cantering a figure-of-eight, he will soon get to realize this and do a change at the cross-over point automatically. Not only will he not be responding to your aids when you give them; he may well become disunited as a result. Instead ask for flying changes when riding in straight lines and circles as well as during figures-of-eight. Effecting flying changes whilst cantering in a circle will greatly improve both the pony's balance and the fluency of his stride. A useful exercise which entails six changes of leg, is to canter a 'shamrock'.

Learning to ride-off

Training a horse to ride-off entails the aid of a mounted helper. Begin by walking and then cantering your pony alongside your helper and his mount, keeping the ponies close together on a straight course. Then, from a walk and then a canter, apply pressure with the leg furthest away from your helper, so that by

answering your leg aid and moving away from it, your pony begins to push against the other one. In the early stages of this training, your helper should give way easily to help increase your pony's confidence. If you canter a circle with the helper on the inside (both of you leading with the inside leg), it will be very easy for your pony to push the other one in towards the centre of the circle. In doing this successfully, he will quickly get the idea of what is required and you will find it is a manoeuvre that he will greatly enjoy.

The secret of successful riding-off is to get

Top and above: The art of 'Riding-off' is an important part of polo-playing technique. The idea is to ride up alongside an opponent and push him out of position – either off line to the ball, or so he cannot attack another player. The trick is to get your pony's shoulder in front of that of your opponent's pony. You can also lean over and push him yourself as demonstrated here. When practising riding-off, remember to try the manoeuvre on both sides.

the point of impact – that is when your pony actually starts pushing against the other – as sharp as possible, for it is the shock of your pony's weight against the other's side that will throw him off course initially. Practise this by riding the two ponies in opposite circles and bringing them together with a bump.

Obviously, you must also learn how to deal with getting ridden-off yourself by an opponent. Make sure your pony is cantering with the leg next to your opponent leading, then urge him forward so that you can get in front of your attacker and ride him off instead.

Stick and ball

Getting your pony used to the stick and ball can be started quite early in the training if you so wish, thereby running concurrently with the various manoeuvres you are teaching. You must, however, be perfectly competent at guiding and controlling your pony with your reins in your left hand only before starting any stick work.

Be prepared to exercise great patience in getting your pony used to the stick. Providing you take it gently, step-by-step, you should not find this difficult and it will take surprisingly little time before you can practise strokes from his back. However, if the process is rushed or tackled insensitively, you may end up with a pony who always has a fear and mistrust of the stick; and such a pony will never make a good polo pony.

Begin by standing at his head, talking to him gently while you show him the stick. Then gently brush it along his neck and shoulders, still holding his head and talking to him quietly. Then lead him along at a walk and at the same time gently swing the stick by your side. Do not attempt to do long, follow-through swings at this stage, just swing it so that it moves slowly by you. When he is completely used to this, you can begin to swing it very gently while you sit on his back. It is a good idea to take the stick with you when you go out for a hack and just swing it gently beside your pony every now and then.

Let it go well forward, so that he can see it out of the corner of his eye and let it brush very lightly against his shoulders and hindquarters too. Do this at a walk, trot and canter, gradually swinging the stick further and in a fuller arc.

Only when your pony is completely relaxed with the stick swinging all around him should you start hitting a ball. Again, if he shows marked anxiety, begin by hitting the ball while you stand at his side, using a soft rubber or tennis ball, rather than the harder polo ball, which will make more noise. Do no more than just dribble the ball forward – certainly do not attempt to hit proper strokes yet. Hit the ball from the near and off-side; if your pony shows any anxiety when you swing the stick over his head to do near-side strokes, try

Above: A rider demonstrates the early stages of getting a pony accustomed to the stick. He is standing up in his stirrup irons and swinging the stick past the pony's eye whilst keeping him standing still. Although the ball is on the ground, the rider makes no attempt at all to hit it.
When the pony shows no fear of the stick swinging by his side at a halt, you can repeat the exercise on the move. Do not attempt to hit the ball until he is perfectly happy and relaxed.

your pony's shoulder just in front of that of your opponent's pony. When you are confident about riding-off your opponent when starting alongside him, try coming up from behind, bringing your pony alongside and then getting just in front before asking him to move over and start pushing against the other pony. At the same time, you can lean a little out of the saddle and push the point of your shoulder into your opponent's side. Do not do this, though, until your pony is confident about riding-off another one, or you may find yourself on the ground. It also helps if you can make

tapping the ball holding the stick in your left hand until he gets used to it swinging on this side, too. Always work at a walk and easy trot before trying strokes at a canter.

Once you start taking proper strokes at the ball, it is wise to protect your pony's legs with special polo boots or bandages. Official polo rules insist that boots are worn during play, for even experienced players sometimes catch their pony's legs with their swinging stick. In the early days of practice, your pony is very likely to suffer a few knocks, either through your inexperience or because he may suddenly shy off course, thereby interfering with the timing of your stroke.

Should you miss the ball at any time, ride on past it; never pull up your pony abruptly to turn him back to the ball. Instead, bring him round in a large circle and have another shot at the ball. Lining your pony up well in advance to ride to the ball, and getting into the habit of keeping your eye fixed on it, should help you not to miss it. Because ponies are so frequently asked to turn sharply immediately after their riders have hit a backhanded shot, they sometimes get into the habit of wheeling round each time. Discourage this by practising hitting backhanded strokes, and then riding forward in a straight line.

Hitting the ball from a canter is quite an advance from hitting it at a walk or a trot, mainly because the pony is more likely to become excitable at this faster pace and may,

perhaps, change legs just as he reaches the ball, so upsetting your stroke. Practise riding at the ball at a steady, easy canter on as long a rein as you can, taking gentle swings at the ball. When you can be sure your pony will always keep on course and remain calm, you can start swinging the stick more vigorously and also asking him to accelerate slightly, just before you begin your stroke. This makes it easier for him to hold the straight line and also gives your hit more impetus.

Training in company

Whenever possible, do your training in the company of other polo players, for ponies must get used to doing all the things described instantly on command, while others are galloping hither and thither around them. Begin by schooling in the same paddock or field as your friends, but each follow your own training routine. Then allocate some time to working together – perhaps hitting the ball to one another (stand quite close to one another initially for this).

You should also practise riding straight at one another, for there are frequent occasions in a game when two players will approach the ball from directly opposite sides. Begin by riding towards another mounted person, both of you holding your stick in the rest position. Pass close to one another – off-side to off-side – at a walk, then at a trot, canter and finally at a

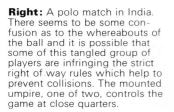

Right: A polo match in India. There seems to be some confusion as to the whereabouts of the ball and it is possible that some of this tangled group of players are infringing the strict right of way rules which help to prevent collisions. The mounted umpire, one of two, controls the game at close quarters.

gallop. If your pony tries to shy away as he passes your colleague, try to practise in an indoor school, or one with a fence round the outside. Keep to the outer track yourself, and have your colleague ride towards you on an inside track. The boundaries of the school will prevent your pony from veering off the track, away from the oncoming pony.

Practise 'hooking sticks' with an opponent. This is a manoeuvre designed to interfere with an opponent and thus prevent him from hitting the ball. The technique is to place your stick in front of his, just behind the ball, as he is making his stroke. Your stick then hooks with his as he approaches the lowest point of his swing. This is important; you should not swing your stick at his, taking wild, indiscriminate swipes. Besides finding yourself accused of foul play, you could also break your stick. Hooking sticks may only be done on the side the opponent is making his stroke, and from directly behind. On no account may you reach over (or under) your opponent's pony to get his stick.

Mock games

Before long, you can try playing a mock game. Three-a-side is the best number to begin with and if there is an extra mounted person who can act as an umpire, so much the better. Play for periods of about five minutes a time, with rests of between five and 10 minutes

between them. Change the position you play in different games, so that you can find out where you play best. Do not dominate the ball; pass it as quickly and frequently as possible, so that you get as much hitting and passing practice as you can. Remember too, that it is possible to be of tremendous value to your team even if you do not hit the ball through an entire game by simply preventing the opposition getting hold of it. Do not expect these games to be ordered or structured, and do not be surprised if you simply do not know what is going on or where the ball is for a good percentage of the time. The more games you play, the more you will be able to follow what is happening and the greater will be your knowledge and understanding of the sport.

It is impossible to give a definite timing for how long it would take to train a polo pony, for it will depend on what standard you are wanting to attain, the pony's natural aptitude and whether the training and riding it has already received have prepared it in any way. Also, your ability and experience as a trainer and polo player will have a strong bearing on the results. Most ponies that are reasonably fit should be able to participate in friendly matches of paddock polo or Pony Club polo after two or three months of fairly regular training. To train a pony from scratch to take part in top-class tournament polo would take at least 12 months and this should not be attempted in one straight-off period.

HOOKING STICKS

Hooking an opponent's stick is a manoeuvre that interferes with his swing and thus makes him miss the ball. The defending player rides up behind his opponent and places his stick so that it will break the line of the opponent's swing, as shown in the sequence of three pictures above. The rules say that a player can only hook an opponent's stick from directly behind and on the side he is making the stroke. Also, hooking can be attempted only when an opponent is trying to hit the ball and not, for example, as a delaying tactic as he is galloping down the field towards the ball. If a player tries to hook your stick, take an early swing at the ball in the hope that he will catch you at this less important moment, giving you time to take another swing when he is unprepared (**right**).

HORSE AND RIDER EQUIPMENT

Above centre: A polo player kitted out for a game. He wears a strong protective hat kept in place by a wide chin strap. Note the guard over his face for added protection. The other items of special equipment are his knee guards, thick leather pads which help to prevent injury. He has chosen to wear one glove only, on the hand that holds his stick, so that he can keep a good, natural grip on the reins.
Top left: Many people prefer to use a bit that offers stronger control than an ordinary snaffle, and a Pelham is one answer, but make sure you can handle two pairs of reins in one hand.
Above left: Polo sticks should be hung by the slings — not the heads — when not in use.
Top right: All polo ponies need to wear some leg protection during a game, particularly on their front legs.
Centre right: Overreaching is quite common amongst polo ponies as a result of continual galloping and quick turning. Boots help prevent injury.
Above right: The amount of turning and stopping in a game of polo makes studs almost essential for extra grip.

Fitness is certainly a consideration in playing polo. A pony wanted for regular matches throughout the season must be very fit indeed, and you would need more than one pony. A tournament polo pony needs to be every bit as fit as a horse wanted for point-to-pointing, for example. Consider the pace at which a game of polo is conducted and you will understand why this level of fitness is required. However fit a pony is, he is not really capable of playing more than two chukkas in one day's game of top-class match polo and he could play no more than five or six chukkas a week.

Tack and equipment

The only special item of equipment a polo pony needs when playing polo is polo boots. These are designed to protect the legs from possible injury should he be hit by a stick. Various types are available; all are designed to protect the fetlock joint as well as the lower leg, without interfering with the action of the knee or hock joints. They are generally made of felt with a covering of elastic or leather. Leather ones are the most expensive, but will last a long time and give the best protection.

In fast games of match or tournament polo, it is best that all four legs are protected with proper polo boots. In slower, more informal games, however, protection can usually be adequately given by bandaging the legs with an ordinary elasticated bandage over a thick piece of gamgee. Remember that the fetlock joint must be covered (but its movement not impeded) on both the front and hind legs.

Special polo saddles are made, although these are in no way essential, particularly if the pony is to be ridden in other equestrian pursuits as well and has only one saddle for all of them. A polo saddle is similar in design to a hunting saddle; the flaps are cut fairly forward, but not too far. A jumping saddle, for example, is not really suitable for polo, as the forward cut panels are designed for riding with short stirrup leathers and a polo player must ride with quite long leathers so that he can stand up and adopt the brace position.

Many people find that even if they use an ordinary snaffle bit on their mounts for hacking, or even hunting, they have to change to a slightly more severe bit to give them the control necessary in polo. The excitement of the game with its fast galloping, twisting and turning, frequently encourages a pony to take a stronger hold of the bit than usual. If you find this to be the case, try a simple pelham or kimblewick bit and see if this improves your control. Many experienced players like to ride in a double bridle, but you should be sure of your horsemanship before attempting to use this, particularly as you will be holding two pairs of reins in one hand. If you do have to use a more severe bit for polo, revert to your usual milder one for exercise and hacking.

If you find that you need a standing martingale to help your control, make sure it is properly adjusted. Do not be tempted to fit it so tightly that the pony is forced to keep his head well down.

In a fast game of polo, it is wise to bandage up your pony's tail, using an ordinary tail bandage. If you do not do this, the stick may well be caught in the swishing hairs, thereby interfering with your stroke.

It is generally necessary to fit some kind of studs to the pony's shoes to help his footing as he turns. Special polo studs are available. If the ground conditions are good – that is, not too slippery, shoes fitted with calkins should be sufficient.

Preparing for the game

Having trained your pony, you prepare him, getting ready for a match in much the same way as you would prepare a horse for any other equestrian sport. The stable routine, for instance, is similar to those outlined in other chapters. Make sure your pony has the high protein diet that is necessary if he is to work hard and perform well. He should be groomed thoroughly daily and given sufficient exercise to get him to the level of fitness you require. In the days before a match (particularly a high-level one), exercise him gently to maintain his condition and keep him alert and interested in life. It is a good idea, incidentally, to make a daily habit of running your hands down your pony's legs, so you know how they feel under normal circumstances. The legs will often puff up in places after a fast match, or they may have suffered some knock which results in that area being hotter than usual. If you know exactly how the legs feel normally, it will be easier to recognize any abnormality.

Below: A beautiful picture of a polo player taken at a game in Abadan, Iran. The somewhat less formal attire of the rider and the less complicated bridle worn by his pony show that polo is not just for the sophisticated sportsman.

Above: As with top class tennis players, it seems that one polo stick is not enough! Polo is an extremely exhausting game, and this rider looks as though he will be glad of a rest.

paring to hit it, backing-up a team member, riding-off or preparing to hook sticks with an opponent, or generally hindering and interfering with the other team (within the limits of the rules, of course) to prevent them getting to the ball. If you find yourself standing around doing nothing, you are certainly not playing the game correctly.

At the Game

Ponies generally travel to the match on the day it is to be held. After tacking-up, a short ride around to loosen them up, stretch their muscles and calm them down may be necessary, but do not overdo this; if the play is to be fast, a pony will need all the energy he possesses.

Presuming that you are going to ride your pony in two chukkas during the match, he will need some attention in between play. Slip off the bridle and wash out his mouth with a spongeful of clean water. Then, using a different sponge, wash around his ears and either side of his neck, where he will be sweaty. If it is a warm day, remove the saddle and wash the saddle area, including under the girth. Remove the excess water with a scraper, then rub him dry with a stable rubber or towel. If it is a cold day, do not sponge him down; just rub the areas mentioned with a rubber or towel.

Replace the saddle and bridle, buckling the girths loosely and throw a rug over the pony's back, so there is no risk of him catching a chill. Use a summer sheet, sweat rug or a special cooler for this.

After the game

At the end of the day, he can be given similar treatment to that given between chukkas, but it should be more thorough. He should be walked around calmly until he is quite cool and then taken home, especially if there are no stabling facilities at the match ground. It is unfair to ask a tired horse to stand for a long time in the usually fairly cramped conditions of a horse box or trailer.

The nature of the game means that polo ponies do sometimes suffer mouth injuries, even with the most careful riders. It is very important, therefore, to check the mouth most carefully after every game. If a serious injury has been sustained, seek veterinary advice immediately. Obviously the pony may not be ridden until there has been a substantial improvement. Mild injuries should be washed with salt and water and a mild, thick rubber bit used until the soreness has completely healed.

At home, examine the pony thoroughly – his legs in particular – for any sign of injury, and put on stable bandages overnight to help reduce any strain. As usual, give him plenty of time to recover before giving him his evening feed.

Perhaps the most important pre-match preparation concerns you and your fellow teammates. You should have practised together as a team and will have a good idea of the sort of strategy you want to adopt. The captain will generally run through this with his team shortly before a match; listen to what he says and stick to it as far as you can. Playing as a team, with proper team spirit, is the essence of polo, but there are a few points to bear in mind as individuals. Always hit the ball purposefully – that is to another member of your team or a sensible aim at goal. Just whacking it hard in the general direction of your goal is senseless. Hit it as quickly as you can when you have an opportunity, trying to pass it to another member of your team. Do not always hit it just ahead of you and then chase after it to hit it again. Should you miss the ball, ride on; another member of your team should be behind you to back you up and will be able to hit it instead. Remember that you should act as a back-up in this way whenever necessary.

In a match, a polo player should always be doing something – riding after the ball, pre-

THE POLO PONY'S YEAR

The outline procedure given here for a polo pony applies to ponies used only for standard match polo. Some people may feel that, if the season has been a particularly hard and fast one, they should stop playing a little earlier so their ponies can have a slightly longer rest. Bear in mind that the polo-playing season varies from country to country; three months, however, would be the minimum time to allow for getting a pony fit for playing polo and, even with this amount of time behind him, a sensitive player would probably give his mount an easy time for the first month of play.

Mid to end winter: Bring up from grass and put through regular exercise routine to get the pony fit. Include some training to refresh the animal's memory and prepare him for the game.

Spring to late summer: Polo-playing season. If matches are fast, ponies should play in no more than about six chukkas a week (i.e. three days' matches). Allow one day of rest when pony is walked around for half-an-hour and turned out in the paddock for a couple of hours or so. On days between matches, exercise sensibly to keep the pony alert and on his toes, and include practice in any technique of the game that needs it.

End of season: Let the pony down quite quickly, giving it perhaps an hour's exercise a day and turning it out in the paddock for longer periods over a month.

Early autumn-mid-winter: Complete rest at grass with shoes off for two months.